HOW TO SURVIVE

MIDDLE SCHOOL

ENGLISH

See page 514 for text credits.

Visit us on the Web! rhcbooks.com
Educators and librarians, for a variety of teaching tools, visit us at RHTeachersLibrarians.com
Library of Congress Cataloging-in-Publication Data is available upon request.
ISBN 978-0-525-57142-1 (trade)
ISBN 978-0-525-57147-6 (ebook)
Printed in the United States of America
10 9 8 7 6 5 4 3 2 1
First Edition

Writer: Nina Ciatto
Curriculum Consultant: Charles Logan
Equity Consultant: Sonja Cherry-Paul
Sideshow Media Editorial Team: Dan Tucker, Julia DeVarti
Penguin Random House Publishing Team: Tom Russell, Alison Stoltzfus, Brett Wright, Emily Harburg, Eugenia Lo, Katy Miller

Produced by Sideshow Media LLC
Illustration and Design by Carpenter Collective

HOW TO SURVIVE MIDDLE SCHOOL

A DO-IT-YOURSELF STUDY GUIDE

ENGLISH

Nina Ciatto

Random House, New York

TABLE OF CONTENTS

CHAPTER 3 127

THE REAL TRUTH ABOUT NONFICTION

CHAPTER 4 165

PICTURES FROM WORDS: READING POETRY

CHAPTER 5 201

USING THE PRACTICES OF EXPERT WRITERS

GROWING A LOVE FOR ENGLISH

Middle school is a special age. You enter your teens at this time, get some new privileges, and gain independence. Sure, it comes with some bonus features, such as sudden growth spurts and pimples. But don't let these nuisances get in the way of the great stuff happening for you. Your brain is growing super-fast and is capable of new things every day. These changes set you up to do amazing things as a reader and writer. You are going to see stories in exciting new ways. Middle school and adolescence are going to come together to create a whole new literary you!

Let's get you ready. You need to take care of your middle school self so you're in a position to make the most of all that middle school English has to offer.

FORMING GOOD HABITS

What do you need? A few good habits will help you to be your strongest.

COMPONENTS OF HEALTHY MIDDLE SCHOOL LIVING	
Healthy eating	Without proper nutrition, our bodies become unhappy. Use your increased independence wisely. Remember, both your brain and body are working overtime as they grow. They need fuel for that. So, fuel them well by eating healthy.
Great sleep habits	Rest up for this great journey into middle school. More than ever, you need sleep. Adolescents should typically spend at least 33% of a 24-hour period sleeping. Yes, you're older and wiser, but without at least eight hours of sleep per night (nine is better), you are less equipped to manage the stress of a middle school day.
Healthy relationships	In making the most of middle school years, don't forget the importance of relationships. They help you feel ready for what's ahead. Middle school can be a tricky social arena. Just remember, you are not alone. Everyone your age is feeling awkward and insecure. They just show it in different ways. Take time to evaluate your friendships. Things will go much better if you choose your friends with care. You deserve wonderful, compassionate friends.

Stress management	All of the changes that happen during middle school can result in some feelings of stress. Luckily, there are some options that you can use to manage stress both in school and at home. • Keep a journal or diary. Write down what is going on and how you feel. • Get a coloring book. These used to be just for kids, but now people of all ages, including both teenagers and grown-ups, have rediscovered how relaxing they can be. • Try a breathing or mindfulness activity. There are lots of great suggestions for these online. • If the stress is too much, *always* seek out an adult to talk to. You may need to talk to more than one adult to find someone who can provide help.

Taking care of your body and relationships gives you a foundation upon which you can manage your days.

One of the big shifts in middle school and high school is that you are more independent. Woo hoo! However, independence can be a double-edged sword. This means that independence has two sides. It is great. You're on your own. People have faith in you. You have privileges you haven't had before. But as school becomes more your responsibility, it, well, becomes more *your* responsibility. The icing on this cake is that you are old enough and wise enough to manage this well.

ORGANIZING FOR RESPONSIBILITY

When middle school hits, you must be armed with a calendar or planner! Choose one you like, and follow these tips for keeping yourself organized and prepared for all that is to come.

PLANNER TIPS:

- Write in your planner every day. Have it close at hand so you can easily jot down homework and reminders at the end of each period. Record homework and due dates as soon as you hear of them.
- Check your planner when you get home from school every day. Use it to set priorities about your homework time.
- Before you go to sleep, check your planner to make sure your backpack is organized and ready for the following day.
- Keep information such as teachers' email addresses, office hours, and homework help options right inside your planner.

FIND YOUR STUDY SPOT

Now that you know what assignments are coming up and when things are due, how can you best get it done? Consider *where* you can do homework.

Your **workspace** is where all the ELA magic happens at home!

Set up a good workspace. It should be quiet. It might be a desk in your room or the kitchen table. If you are using a shared space, you can organize your supplies into a box that you pull out at homework time. Make sure your workspace is comfortable—a place you can spend some time in.

Consider what tools you will need. For ELA, you will need a dictionary and thesaurus, which can either be old-fashioned paper books or online versions. Paper and pens, online access, and a good computer are helpful.

The most important thing about this space is that it works for you. Some questions to ask yourself:

- Do you work best when others are around?
- Do you need a space with no distractions?
- Does music help you, or do you find yourself spending too much time trying to figure out what song you are going to listen to?

You know yourself. Create a space that looks, feels, and sounds good for you.

GIVE YOURSELF *TIME*.

You've created a beautiful space, you've pulled tools together, and you've got that handy planner. Now you just need to put them all to work. Scheduling in homework time helps.

Think about the rhythms of your family and home. For example, if you have highly active younger twin siblings, you might want to plan on working when they are off at martial arts class. Also, don't forget about your extracurriculars. Be realistic.

Let's look at the schedule below and see if we can make some suggestions.

SUNDAY	
10–2	Family time
MONDAY	
8–3	School
4-5	Cello
TUESDAY	
8–3	School
3:15–4	Math HW help
WEDNESDAY	
8–3	School
3:30–5:30	Soccer practice
THURSDAY	
8–3	School
FRIDAY	
8–3	School
3:30–5:30	Soccer Practice
SATURDAY	
9-12	Soccer

This schedule looks pretty full. But this person also needs to eat, spend some time with friends, and travel between activities. They should find time to read for 60 minutes every day and homework time five to seven days per week. Plus, they should allow themselves free time to spend alone, with friends, or with family.

A more detailed schedule may look like this:

SUNDAY	
10–2	Family time
2–4	Free time!
4–6	Homework and reading (use this time to work on bigger projects and essays)
MONDAY	
8–3	School
4-5	Cello
5–6:30	Homework
8–9	Reading
TUESDAY	
8–3	School
3:15–4	Math HW help
4:30–6:30	Homework Read at HW time if there isn't much or before bed
WEDNESDAY	
8–3	School
3:30–5:30	Soccer practice
5:45–6:30	Homework
Before Bed	Read
THURSDAY	
8–3	School
3:30–5:00	Free time
5–6:30	Homework Read at HW time if there isn't much or before bed
FRIDAY	
8–3	School
3:30–5:30	Soccer Practice
5:45–6:30	Homework
Before Bed	Read
SATURDAY	
9–12	Soccer
1–5	Free time
5–6:30	Homework and reading

This person now has about twelve hours for homework and reading. Just as important, there are about eight hours of scheduled free time.

BE FLEXIBLE!

You have probably realized that life does not always go as planned. Sometimes, all of your teachers may assign big projects at once, and that happens to be the same week you are performing in the school musical. Or, you just used a bit of that scheduled homework time as free time for a couple of weeks, and now you have found yourself with due dates and not enough time in your schedule. Yikes. What do you do?

First: take a breath or use a stress-management activity mentioned on page 3.

Second: plan to talk with your teachers. A few tips:

1. Find out a time that is good—before or after class, if they have office hours, or even arrange something by email.
2. Take responsibility where you need to, and be clear about what you need. Use statements such as:

   "I did not realize how much time this project would take."

   "I am sorry."

   "I need some help."

3. Follow through with the plan you create.
4. Express gratitude for the time and help. A short email or a sticky note is likely to make your teacher very happy!

And you're off to middle school. Enjoy it. You are ready.

PACKING UP (OR . . . HOW TO USE THIS BOOK):

But wait! Before you go, we have some tools that you might want to take on your journey.

When you read a book for the first (or second!) time, you are the one who has to understand it, right? No one else can understand it for you. Sure, maybe in elementary school you could sit back and listen to your teacher read a story aloud, but middle school is all about learning to be independent! Of course, being independent doesn't mean never asking for help. Just the opposite actually—independence means using ALL the resources available to you to succeed. These tools will help you stop and think critically about what you're reading and how to make sense of it all. Using them will help you absorb more information and develop learning strategies that will benefit you later on. And if there's ever something that doesn't make sense, dog-ear or put a sticky note on the page and return to it later!

We are not only giving you the tools below, we will remind you to use them! In the pages ahead, you'll see the tools pop up, along with some questions and ways to think about what you're reading. Check them out:

You'll find definitions for important **vocabulary terms** in yellow boxes like this one near the first time a term is used. They're also listed for you again at the end of each chapter.

YOUR MIDDLE SCHOOL SURVIVAL TOOLS

SYMBOL/ TOOL	WHAT IT IS	HOW TO USE IT WHILE YOU READ
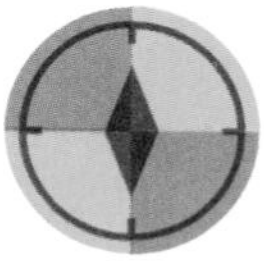	People use a GPS so they don't get lost. It helps them get the lay of the land. You can use a GPS to figure out where you are, get directions, or explore a new area.	When you see the GPS, stop and get yourself oriented. Ask yourself some general questions before you start your journey... • Think about what genre you are reading or writing and what the purpose of the piece is. • What is this text mostly about? • Who is telling this story?
	Boots give hikers sure footing, even on rocky paths. All serious hikers pull on their boots before setting out. Your boots travel with you, and can tell the story of where you've been and what you learned.	Think of boots as knowledge you already have that supports new knowledge. When you see the boots, it's time to activate your prior knowledge and ask... • What do I already know about this? • What does this remind me of? • Can I compare this to anything I am familiar with?
	A pickaxe is a tool for digging deeper. You can use the sharp point to explore small cracks and uncover what is under the surface!	Your pickaxe will help you analyze your reading or writing for meaning. Take it out when you need to... • Find evidence and important details to support a claim or argument. • Pull apart the text to think deeper about tone, word choice, and other literary devices.

	People use binoculars to see things that are far away. But depending on where you are looking from, your view might be very different from someone else's!	Binoculars will help you to consider point of view in a text. You will need to think about things like... • Who is the narrator for a story, what point of view are they using? • Whose story is NOT told? What perspectives might you be missing? • Is your narrator or source reliable? Is it biased? Is it trying to convince you of something?
	People use a magnifying glass to examine something up close. Only after looking closely at all the details can you really see the big picture!	When you see the magnifying glass, stop and consider how your observations and evidence contribute to the big picture. You can magnify your understanding by asking... • What's the big idea here? • How would you summarize this text if you had to share it with someone else? • How do the details of a text contribute to my overall understanding of it?
	A field journal is a tool that allows you to record observations in the wild. When you review your notes, you can bring your experience home with you and learn from it.	The field journal will give you an opportunity to reflect on your experiences while reading and writing. You can use it to respond to questions like... • What notes will help you understand this later on? • What do you want to remember for your future reading and writing? • What parts were easier for you, and which were more challenging?

And here's the thing. . . it's up to you to use the tools. Teachers and researchers have figured out that these learning strategies really work. So when you see a question or a strategy prompt, stop and try it. See if it helps keep you interested, clarify things, or go deeper into the idea or topic. As you get better at learning and thinking, you'll be set for middle school—and you'll kill it in high school, too. You've got this. Onward!

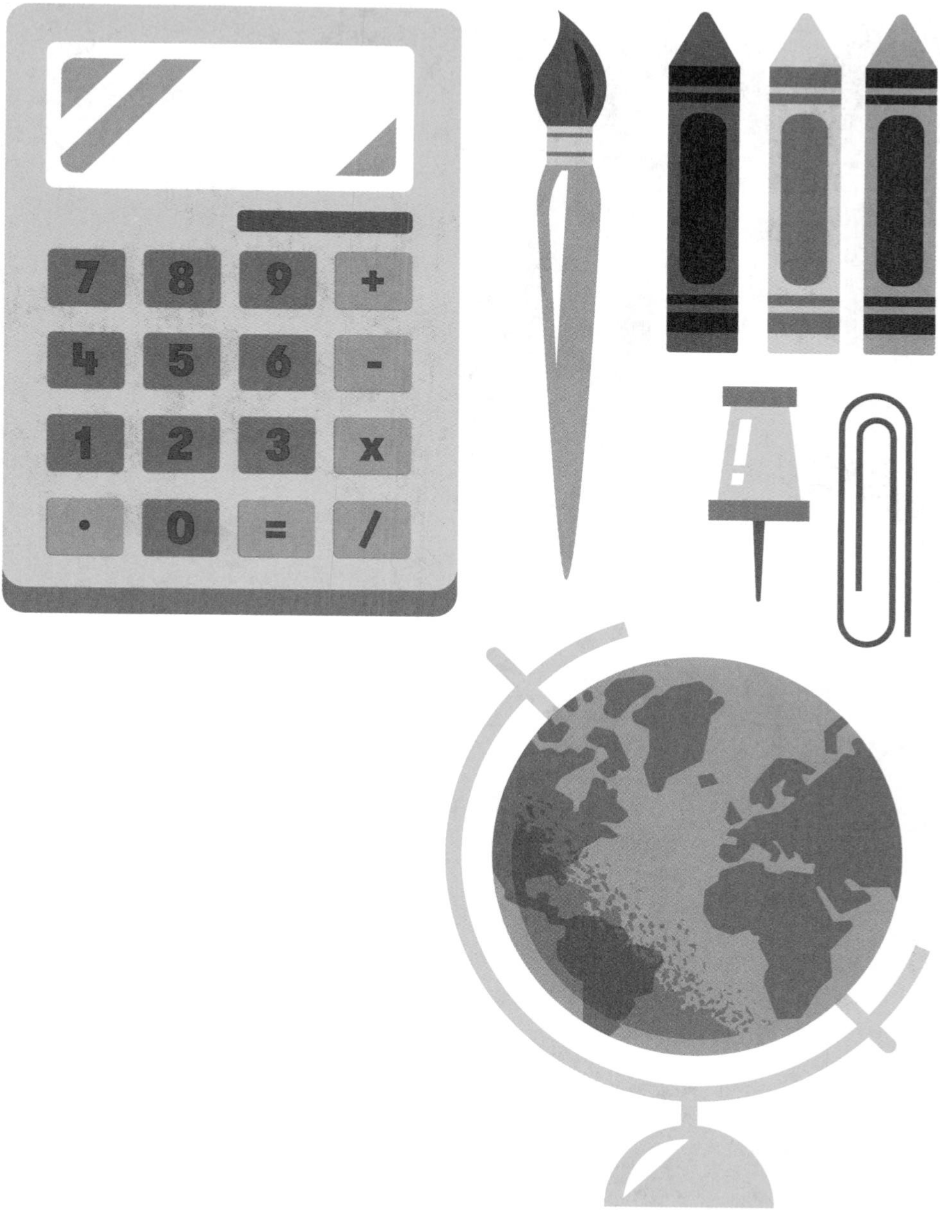

1 USING THE PRACTICES OF EXPERT READERS

Let's discuss one of the best things the world has to offer tweens and early teens: books. Walk into any library or bookstore and look at the covers of books written for you. Writers of these books get you. They write books that illuminate your experiences. Also, they write books that allow you to "live" experiences very different from your own. Reading opens up a world filled with space travel, mythological figures, magic, arguments, dreams, and school lockers. Let's explore the worlds that reading will open up for you!

CHAPTER CONTENTS

READING POWERFULLY

Reading is a superpower. *Your* superpower. It will carry you to other worlds and across time. It will make your heart race. It will calm you. It will inform you. And most important, it will make you wonder.

The world of literature has gotten much bigger since you were a little kid. The texts you read are more complicated. But guess what? Your brain is bigger and more ready than ever to tackle the twists and turns of the literary world. In this chapter, we are going to explore reading practices that you can use with all sorts of texts.

READING ATHLETICISM

Every great athlete puts in hours of practice. That practice builds **stamina** and skill. *Stamina* is essential when you want to do anything for extended periods of time. And middle school books are so delicious you will want to spend hours and hours devouring them!

stamina: the ability to keep up a physical or mental effort for a long period of time

SOME EXAMPLES OF GREAT BOOKS

PIECING ME TOGETHER
by Renée Watson

INTERNMENT
by Samira Ahmed

GHOST
by Jason Reynolds

SPEAK
by Laurie Halse Anderson

THE CROSSOVER
by Kwame Alexander

I AM MALALA:
HOW ONE GIRL STOOD UP FOR EDUCATION AND CHANGED THE WORLD
by Malala Yousafzai
with Patricia McCormick

CORALINE
by Neil Gaiman

DRAMA
by Raina Telgemeier

READY PLAYER ONE
by Ernest Cline

THE WITCH BOY
by Molly Knox Ostertag

EL DEAFO
by Cece Bell

You may find yourself asking, "How do I build reading stamina? It's not like I break a sweat when I sit down to read."

While cozying up in a comfy chair with a book may not make you sweat, it does work out that reading muscle, also known as your brain. Perhaps you have noticed that the more time you spend practicing your jump shot, or that pirouette, the better you get at it. The more time you spend reading, the better at reading you become.

BUILD YOUR READING STAMINA!

Here are some tips to keep you on track:

- **Keep track of how much time you spend reading each day.** Read for at least 45 minutes every day. As you start out, it's OK to break this time into smaller chunks.
- **Keep track of your reading rate.** How many pages do you read in that 45 minutes?
- **Dedicate time and space for reading.** Some people like to read before they go to sleep, while others go to the library after school. Planning ahead is key.
- **Find books you love.** This is super important as you get started. You can introduce challenges later on, once you've found your reading groove.

Reading benefits all of you—your heart, your soul, and your way of interacting with the world. Choose your books deliberately, thinking about how they can help you learn about yourself as well as others.

ACHIEVABLE READING GOALS FOR YOU

Pull this all together into some achievable goals using these guidelines:

	MINUTES PER DAY	BOOKS PER WEEK
Your current average		
Recommended goals for the end of eighth grade	sixty +	one +
Your plan for the next month		

Now that you've got your time set, a spot picked out, and an interesting selection of books at hand, read. Without a doubt, you will find yourself not wanting to put your book down. You will probably feel sadness as you finish books and excitement over the next book on your list.

As your reading muscle grows, you naturally become a stronger reader. A great basketball player, however, doesn't just have muscle. They have skills, and they turn basketball into an art form. Expert readers use certain strategies. (A *strategy* is a plan or a way to get something done.) These strategies will help you navigate all sorts of texts with precision, and you will use them throughout your reading adventures. Throughout this book, you will discover many strategies that will help you refine your reading.

WHAT WE READ

Almost as important as *how* we read is *what* we read. We don't just read to get better at reading—we read because books can teach us about our world, and the worlds of other people too! Some people like particular genres, or particular authors, but it's up to you to find the stories that matter to you. Books work in all sorts of ways to show us so many different worlds.

MIRRORS, WINDOWS, AND SLIDING DOORS

A wise teacher once described books as windows, mirrors, and sliding doors.

- Mirrors show us ourselves or tell stories of people like us.
- Windows give us a chance to see the reality of others' lives.
- Sliding glass doors allow us to both see the reality of others' lives, and to step into their worlds and experience them as though we're there.

The mirror/window/sliding glass door framework encourages us to think about *who* we read about. You'll want to read plenty of books that mirror your life. Your life has many parts to it, so make sure you are reading stories of characters who represent different elements of your identity. Books are also a chance to better understand how different identities and communities affect people's experiences.

To know the world better, you may choose to read books set in communities different from your own. Also, you may read stories of people whose gender, race, and ethnic identities differ from your own. And hopefully as you read books that are windows, some of those will become sliding doors, where you are able to experience more deeply—perhaps through feeling or learning of details—lives that are lived differently from yours.

This is a lot to take in! To work out some of this, let's look at a few books to figure out if they are mirrors or windows for you. We will focus on just main characters and primary settings.

EXAMPLES OF BOOKS AS MIRRORS AND WINDOWS

I LOVE YOU SO MOCHI
Sarah Kuhn

SETTING: The main character travels to Japan, the home of her grandparents, where some things are familiar, but other things are unknown.

√ *check one:* ☐ **mirror** ☐ **window** ☐ **some of each**

IDENTITY OF THE MAIN CHARACTER: Japanese American teenage girl

√ *check one:* ☐ **mirror** ☐ **window** ☐ **some of each**

THE FIRST RULE OF PUNK
Celia C. Pérez

SETTING: The main character moves from Florida to Chicago with her mother.

√ *check one:* ☐ **mirror** ☐ **window** ☐ **some of each**

IDENTITY OF THE MAIN CHARACTER: Mexican American girl, parents are divorced

√ *check one:* ☐ **mirror** ☐ **window** ☐ **some of each**

WONDER
R.J. Palacio

SETTING: New York City

√ *check one:* ☐ **mirror** ☐ **window** ☐ **some of each**

IDENTITY OF THE MAIN CHARACTER: A fifth-grade white boy with physical differences

√ *check one:* ☐ **mirror** ☐ **window** ☐ **some of each**

THE BEST AT IT
Maulik Pancholy

SETTING: Small Midwestern town

√ *check one:* ☐ **mirror** ☐ **window** ☐ **some of each**

IDENTITY OF THE MAIN CHARACTER: A gay Indian American boy

√ *check one:* ☐ **mirror** ☐ **window** ☐ **some of each**

THE WITCH BOY
Molly Knox Ostertag

SETTING: Otherworldly

√ *check one:* ☐ **mirror** ☐ **window** ☐ **some of each**

IDENTITY OF THE MAIN CHARACTER: 13-year-old white boy who does not fit perfectly into the gender expectations of his world

√ *check one:* ☐ **mirror** ☐ **window** ☐ **some of each**

DEAR MARTIN
Nic Stone

SETTING: Atlanta

√ *check one:* ☐ **mirror** ☐ **window** ☐ **some of each**

IDENTITY OF THE MAIN CHARACTER: African American teenage boy who attends an elite school on an academic scholarship

√ *check one:* ☐ **mirror** ☐ **window** ☐ **some of each**

This is a short list of books. You will want to find your own. In writing down details about your own mirrors and windows, you will be able to use those details to search for books that have characters and settings that you want to read about.

What worlds and experience would you like to better understand?

Groups you would like to see in your books (ethnicity, gender, race, socioeconomic class, family structures, and so on)	Communities you would like to see in your books (urban, rural, suburban, states, countries, planets, galaxies, universes, time periods, and so on)

How will you benefit from reading books that:

Mirror your identity?

Are windows into the identity of others?

Are sliding glass doors that allow your imagination to help you feel the experiences of others?

DISCOVER YOUR NEXT FAVORITE READ!

- ☐ Ask your friends for suggestions.
- ☐ When you have read a book you enjoyed, look for other books by that author.
- ☐ Look for a good series (Cirque du Freak, The Shadow Children, Track, Uglies)
- ☐ Browse. Take your time. Look through the stacks at your local library, use online booksellers, or search for book lists for middle school readers.
- ☐ Give new books a try—take risks.
- ☐ Don't be afraid to put down a book if it's not working for you!

READING STRATEGIES FOR DIFFICULT TERRAIN

You've chosen your book, and you're getting hooked, but then it happens—you come across a passage that leaves you stumped. What do you do? Here are some strategies.

ACTIVATING PRIOR KNOWLEDGE

There's something comforting about broken-in boots. In traveling with you, they have learned your feet, and now they fit comfortably around your ankles and toes. They have also gathered in their soles bits of dirt and grass from all the places you have been. Your brain works the same way, collecting information from all that you have learned and experienced. You know stuff. By activating your **prior knowledge**, you are harnessing those bits of information you have acquired over your lifetime and using them to help you navigate the text in front of you. It's similar to how those well-worn boots reveal the story of where you have been while they get you where you are going!

ASK AWAY!

Below are a few questions you can ask yourself to activate your prior knowledge.

- ☐ What do I already know about this?
- ☐ What does this remind me of?
- ☐ Can I compare this to anything I am familiar with?

Perhaps you open a magazine and see an article titled: "Why Save the Red-Eyed Tree Frog?"

You think: "Yikes! I know *nothing* about red-eyed tree frogs. I didn't even know such a thing existed. I have zero prior knowledge."

Guess what? If you dig a little deeper, you will find that you do have a foundation on which to build new ideas and ask some great questions as you read.

PRIOR KNOWLEDGE AT WORK!

"WHY SAVE THE RED-EYED TREE FROG?"		
QUESTIONS	**THINKING ABOUT THE QUESTIONS**	**HOW THIS MAY HELP ME**
What do I already know about this?	Frogs are slimy little creatures. I thought they live in water, not trees.	Paying close attention to the habitat of this frog—do they spend their whole lives in the trees? Where are these trees?
What does this remind me of?	Vampires and zombies that have red eyes 	Zombies and vampires are not real! I will read to figure out why these frogs have red eyes. Do they even really have red eyes?
Can I compare this to anything I am familiar with?	Saving the whales. Rescuing polar bears. Bees are dying.	Using knowledge of animal conservation will help me focus on how and why people think we should save these tree frogs.

It turns out that even when you think you know *nothing* about a text, you actually know something. And that's enough to give yourself a head start.

FIGURING OUT TRICKY WORDS

You're reading along, enjoying a great story, *feeling* that story, when *bam*! There's a bump in your reading road. Your surroundings look unfamiliar. The way forward is unclear. You have hit a tricky word. Yikes! That word can mess up your reading rhythm. But here's the truth: that tricky word will help your brain grow.

DEFINITIONS

There are some easy solutions to help you with those tricky words and, ultimately, grow your vocabulary. All of these solutions ask you to look carefully at the sentences and words surrounding that tricky word.

Sometimes writers know they are introducing a tricky word and sneak in a **definition**. Here is an example.

> In a quiet ceremony, the disgraced wizard **abnegated** his position as King Wizard. He officially gave up his position as king.

In the second sentence, the writer provides a definition for *abnegate*—to officially give up a position.

SYNONYMS

There may be a **synonym** provided for you very close to the tricky word. (*Crabby* and *grouchy* are synonyms. So are *pleasant* and *nice*.)

> There was an air of mystery surrounding the ice cream truck's appearance in the dead of winter; it was an **enigma**.

In this sentence, the writer includes a synonym of *enigma* in the first half of the sentence: mystery.

ANTONYMS

Or you may notice an opposite, or **antonym**, conveniently placed near that tricky word. (For instance, *pleasant* and *grouchy* are antonyms.)

> The **glabrous** animal contrasted with its caretaker, a person with thick, long hair.

From the idea that long, thick hair contrasts with a glabrous animal, we can infer that *glabrous* means to have little hair. (In fact, it means to be hairless, but we got pretty close using that opposite!)

EXAMPLES

Identifying **examples** is something else we can use to figure out tricky words.

> My older sister is so **haughty!** She acts as if she is the ruler of our house and knows more than everyone.

In the second sentence, the author gives examples of haughty behavior. Based on these, we can gather that *haughty* means to think you are better than others.

INFERENCE

Inference is used when the author doesn't give you the meaning. Instead, you must use the context and what you already know so you can figure out the meaning. Sometimes people refer to making an inference as "reading between the lines."

> The scent of the awful stew his mother was making **permeated** the house and could even be smelled in the yard.

What we read: the smell of the stew was awful and permeated the house and outside.

What we know: smell can travel.

What we infer: to *permeate* means to go everywhere or go around.

definition: a description of the meaning of a word

synonym: a word that has the same or similar meaning to another word

antonym: a word that has the opposite meaning of another word

example: a specific thing that demonstrates the meaning of a word or concept

inference: a conclusion based on context and prior knowledge rather than examples

Dear reader, books make us smarter in so many ways. Those tricky words are going to broaden your vocabulary. Having just the right word to express an idea is powerful.

READING DEEPLY

Just as a hiker uses GPS to figure out where they are and what is around them, an expert reader assesses their text and how they are doing with it. The goal should not just be getting to the end of the page, but really understanding what is on it. One way they can do that is by asking questions.

ASKING QUESTIONS OF THE TEXT

As you become a more sophisticated reader, you engage more with the texts you read. It's almost as if a conversation is going on in your head. You find yourself asking questions and making demands of the text in front of you. It's a little like when a parent asks you to empty the dishwasher, and words like *why?*, *when?*, and sometimes even *how?* slip out. Your parent may not appreciate these questions too much, but questions are important!

Let's shine a light on this natural tendency to ask questions because experienced readers ask questions as they read.

QUESTION #1: DOES THIS MAKE SENSE?

Strategic readers check to make sure they are understanding what they are reading. As you read, ask yourself, "Does this make sense?"

As you challenge yourself to read more complicated texts, and to read for longer periods of time, inevitably there will be a time when you discover that what you're reading doesn't make sense to you. First: congratulations for challenging yourself! Then: believe in yourself, go back a page or two, and reread the text.

Always trust yourself when you are confused. There are so many reasons that a text can suddenly stop making sense to us. There may be outside distractions, such as someone cooking bacon in the next room. Or there may be text distractions, such as a sudden change in setting.

When things don't make a lot of sense, go back and reread, looking for missed information.

QUESTION #2: WHAT IS THIS TEXT MOSTLY ABOUT?

Readers determine the **central idea** of the text they are reading. The *central idea* of a text is what it is mostly about, the main point. What is the author trying to tell you?

Let's give it a quick try. Read this article, keeping Question #2 in mind.

HOW A TEEN INVENTOR IN AFRICA USED TRASH TO REACH MIT

MIT stands for Massachusetts Institute of Technology. It's a famous university that trains people in math, science, engineering, and many other fields.

In Sierra Leone, a small West African country, the electricity comes on maybe once a week. The rest of the time, says teen inventor Kelvin Doe, people live in darkness in his hometown, a district of Freetown, the capital.

Commercial batteries are costly, so at age 13, he started making his own using basic supplies: acid, soda, metal, a tin cup, and tape. As early as age 10, Kelvin was building cool things out of stuff he salvaged from the garbage.

He made a radio station for his town and a generator (using a discarded voltage stabilizer) to power it. He found staffers for the station—their average age was 12—and played music and reported the news, using the broadcast handle DJ Focus.

"They call me DJ Focus," he said, "because I believe if you focus, you can do an invention perfectly." Kelvin said he wanted to give a voice to the youth of Sierra Leone and enable his countrymen to debate issues. What's more, his neighbors can charge their phones using his generator.

In March 2012, David Sengeh, a PhD candidate at MIT who's also from Sierra Leone, went home to start a national high school innovation challenge. Innovate Salone, as he called it, asked teens to propose solutions to problems around them. About 300 smart kids participated, but Kelvin stood out.

He stood out so much, Sengeh arranged for him to visit the World Maker Faire in New York and also MIT and Harvard, where Kelvin lectured to college students and became the youngest person ever invited to MIT's "Visiting Practitioner's Program."

Kelvin later won his nation's Presidential Medal and met the Clinton family in New York, when he spoke at the Clinton Global Initiative's closing ceremony. He even joked with Chelsea about wearing a suit.

In 2013, he signed a $100,000 contract with a Canadian WiFi company to develop a solar-panel technology for installation at 400 sites around Sierra Leone. He's also been working on a windmill, which may be done by the time you read this. And Kelvin will probably be doing some new cool thing by then too.

"Through innovation," he says, "we can build our nation Sierra Leone."

WHAT IS "HOW A TEEN INVENTOR IN AFRICA USED TRASH TO REACH MIT" MOSTLY ABOUT?

This article is mostly about a boy from Sierra Leone whose inventions helped his community and also got him noticed by the scientific community.

In answering this question, you are thinking about the details so you can figure out the main point of the text. This helps you know what you are reading. It also helps you check your understanding. In other words, you are coming up with a quick summary.

QUESTION #3: WHO IS TELLING THIS STORY?

One job of a reader is to figure out who is telling the story. This matters across all types of text. When you receive an email, you pay attention to who sent you the email. Why? It gives you **context**. No matter the genre, ask yourself, who is telling this story? (In the text you just read, a reporter or a team of reporters told the story.)

Let's give it a try with this poem by William Carlos Williams.

This Is Just To Say

I have eaten
the plums
that were in
the icebox

and which
you were probably
saving
for breakfast

Forgive me
they were delicious
so sweet
and so cold

Who is telling this story? The person who ate the plums!

The person who was saving the plums would probably tell a very different story, and the meaning behind it would not be the same.

context: the circumstances, events, and details around a situation, providing information that helps you understand that situation

Give it a try. Pretend you are the person who was saving the plums for breakfast, and rewrite this poem.

What changes when a different person tells the story?

POINT OF VIEW AND PERSPECTIVE

Point of view is the format a writer has chosen for telling the story—in other words, the way the story is narrated. For example, a story about a family could be from the point of view of a parent, a child, a neighbor, or a stranger.

Perspective is how the speaker perceives (views or understands) what is happening in the story. For instance, the story of a race from the perspective of the winner is different from the same story told from the perspective of the last-place finisher.

The perspective of our plum-eater seems to be that it was wrong to eat the plums but perhaps worth it. In re-telling this poem from the place of the plums' original owner, you are deciding on their perspective—their view of this event. Maybe the original owner is angry. Maybe they figured that someone was going to eat the plums. Maybe they are happy the other person enjoyed the plums. Those are some possible perspectives, or understandings, that that person could hold.

We will look more closely at point of view and perspective in both fiction and nonfiction later on.

This question
of
Who is telling the story?
is just to say
that you should always ask
Who is speaking?
in every type
of text.

WHAT HAVE YOU LEARNED?

THREE QUESTIONS TO ASK YOURSELF AS YOU READ	HOW YOUR ANSWERS TO THESE QUESTIONS HELP YOU
1	
2	
3	

VISUALIZING THE TEXT

When we read, we are transported into other worlds. It is magical. One thing readers do to nurture that magical experience is **visualize** the text. When a reader is visualizing a story, they are making pictures in their mind. A writer puts together lots of words for you to read. Visualizing is what your imagination is doing with those words—it's transforming them into pictures, or even movies. Your imagination is what brings the story to life.

visualize: form a mental image or images based on the text while you are reading

Here's the thing: We have to nurture this skill. However, once you start allowing your imagination to bring words to life, you won't stop!

Here's something to give it a try with—the beginning of a short story called "The Lottery" by Shirley Jackson. As you read, really tune in to what's happening in your imagination: What details do you notice, and what emotions do you feel?

> The morning of June 27th was clear and sunny, with the fresh warmth of a full-summer day; the flowers were blossoming profusely and the grass was richly green. The people of the village began to gather in the square, between the post office and the bank, around ten o'clock....

Jackson gives us plenty to work with. Give it a try below by sketching what you "see." You can either draw your best artistic stick figures or do a "word sketch" using lots of describing language to explain the place you just read about.

SKETCH	BULLETED LIST OF DETAILS
	• • • •

Let's look closely at some of her details. What did you include in your illustration or visualization?

- ☐ "The morning"—the sun is still low in the sky.
- ☐ "June 27th was clear and sunny, with the fresh warmth of a full summer day"—it's warm, no clouds, and feels like summer. But the leaves on the trees still look like late spring—maybe they're light green.
- ☐ "Flowers were blossoming profusely and the grass was richly green"—many flowers, so perhaps some yellow or pink, and grass like the green of a crayon.
- ☐ "People of the village began to gather in the square between the post office and the bank"—a few people, in a small-town square, with a post office and a bank on the edges. Maybe there are some other buildings too—maybe a place of worship or a school?

As a reader, your picture keeps changing with each new detail that you come across. You may add in a detail or two of your own, using some of your prior knowledge. Every reader sees a text differently—this may be why we are often disappointed with the movie version of a book we read.

Visualizing the text is not only a gift to your imagination. It also helps you keep track of setting, characters, and events across books. It helps you picture the worlds that writers find so dear or so terrifying. It helps you become *part* of the story.

ANALYZING AS YOU READ

You can get a lot of information by asking questions and visualizing a text. But there's another way to gather information and gain a deeper understanding about what you're reading. Expert readers **analyze** the text for clues about what the author is trying to say.

analyze: think about the details, structure and other elements of a text and draw conclusions

IDENTIFYING TONE

In the wild, a hiker needs something sharp! A tool that breaks apart dirt and digs into the ground—a pickaxe—comes in handy. Middle school literacy asks us to dig deep into texts and ideas to find hidden gems. It's what we do when we analyze a text. Your pickaxe is going to help you uncover so many elements hidden within your text—elements such as tone.

Literature is moody. Perhaps sometimes you feel as if someone is yelling at you through text messages, or you are certain that a birthday card message really is filled with love. **Tone** is the attitude of the speaker or writer as it is expressed through the text. (Maybe you have heard someone say, "I don't like your tone" or "Don't take that tone with me!" That will give you an idea of what this term means.)

Examples of tone you may come across in writing include academic, angry, joyful, serious, sad, respectful, sarcastic, and comical.

A moment before a big game in *Friday Night Lights: A Town, a Team, and a Dream* provides us with a great opportunity to identify tone.

"We're one game away from playing a state football championship game. We deserve it, because we've worked our a** off in off-season, worked hard in August, had two-a-days, came up to practice in the morning. You got to have it in your heart that you want it worse than Carter does. It is a team sport, football is a team sport, the team that wants it the worst is gonna win this football game." There was no other moment like it, and anyone who had ever played high school football could still recall it with perfect clarity, that emotional peak, that time in life when all energy was concentrated on a single point and everything was crystal clear. Whatever happened afterward, whatever success, or failure, or happiness, or horror, it could not be forgotten.

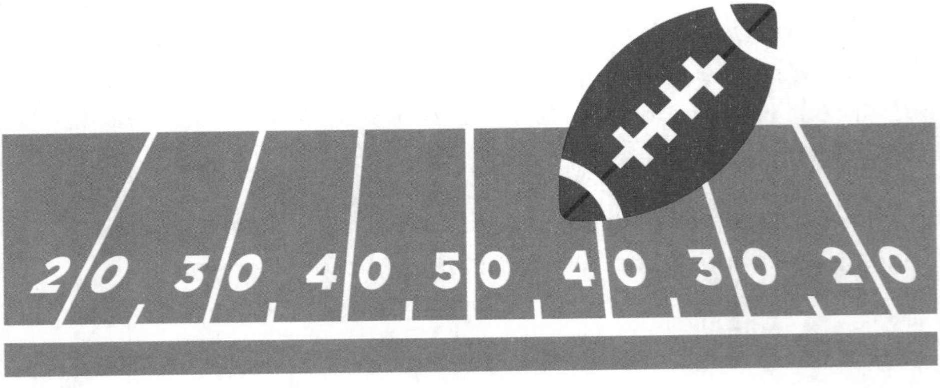

How does this speaker, Coach Gaines, feel about his team and the game?

In uncovering the tone Coach Gaines is using, we will look for how he feels about:

- The game
- This moment in time
- His audience

When we use our pickaxe to pull apart this text, looking for words that reveal emotion, his tone of voice becomes clear:

> "We're one game away from playing a state football championship game. **We deserve it**, because **we've worked** our **a** off in off-season, worked hard in August**, had two-a-days, came up to practice in the morning. You got to have it in your heart that you want it worse than Carter does. **It is a team sport, football is a team sport**, the team that wants it the worst is gonna win this football game."

Coach Gaines repeated certain words as he spoke to his team. These words and phrases work together to convey his tone: inspirational. He wants to inspire his team to win.

REPEATED TERMS:

- *Worked*
- *Team sport*

THE ABCs OF TONE

Here's a **taxonomy**, in this case an alphabetical list, of words that describe tone. There's space for you to add to the collection:

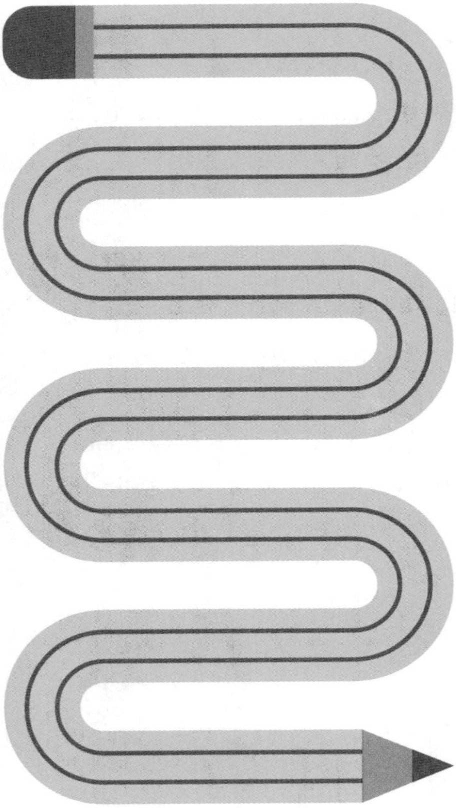

Taxonomy: a taxonomy is a system used to organize or classify information.

A
APATHETIC
AMUSED

D
DISMISSIVE
DELIGHTED

G
GRACIOUS
GREEDY

J
JUDGMENTAL

M
MEAN
MOCKING

P
PESSIMISTIC

S
SURPRISED
SARCASTIC
SUPPORTIVE

V
VINDICTIVE

Y
YEARNING

B

BRAVE
BITTER

C

CAUTIOUS
CRUEL

E

EAGER
EMPATHETIC

F

FORMAL

H

HOPEFUL
HUMBLE

I

INDIGNANT

K

KNOWLEDGEABLE
KIND

L

LOVING

N

NERVOUS

O

OPTIMISTIC

Q

QUESTIONING

R

RESENTFUL

T

TEASING
THREATENING

U

URGENT
UNCONCERNED

W

WISE
WRY

X

Z

ZEALOUS

LOOKING FOR CRAFT AND STRUCTURE

In the world of middle school literature, you will find yourself traversing landscapes as varied as your imagination. Writing is an art, and writers assemble words in all sorts of ways.

As a reader, you want to take a close look at how those words are put together. In other words, you want to look at **craft** and **structure**. To find these, look at:

- The form the writing takes—how the writer organizes ideas and how parts of the text build up or relate to each other.
- Interpret the words and phrases—look carefully at word choice and how those choices affect meaning and tone.
- Consider how perspective is developed and how it varies between characters or narrators.

We will get into the nitty gritty of this once we dive deep into fiction, nonfiction, and poetry. But until then, here are a few rules of thumb to keep in mind.

1. The structure of texts matters—in other words, how the writer formats their text and what choices they make about order of information and ideas.
2. Writers make deliberate **word choices**. Specific words and phrases can have multiple meanings.
3. The point of view is the position the story is being told from—is there only one, or does the writer use a variety of perspectives to share different insights?

craft: the author's intentional use of literary elements like word choice to create an effect on the reader

structure: the organization, formatting, and perspective the author uses to build their work

word choice: specific words and phrases used by a writer to show meaning

Let's take a quick look at an excerpt from the novel *Speak* by Laurie Halse Anderson.

> I'm in the bathroom trying to put my right contact lens back in. She's [Rachelle] smudging mascara under her eyes to look exhausted and wan. I think about running out so she can't pull the evil eye on me again, but Hairwoman, my English teacher, is patrolling the hall and I forgot to go to her class.
>
> Me: "Hi."
>
> Rachelle: "Mmm."
>
> Now what? I'm going to be completely, totally cool, like nothing has happened. Think ice. Think snow.
>
> Me: "How's it going." I try to put in my contact, and poke myself in the eye. Very cool.
>
> Rachelle: "Eehn." She gets mascara in her eye and rubs it, smearing mascara across her face.

Let's start with structure. Even though this is a novel, the author chose an interesting structure—there's formatting that looks like a play. Why would she do that? How does that change the feel of this scene? It affects the tone, making it cooler.

Speak is a book artfully crafted with deliberate word choice. Look over that excerpt. What stands out as deliberate, perhaps unexpected? The author chose these standout words and phrases to make us think or feel. Don't miss out on that opportunity!

ANALYZING WORD CHOICE

EXAMPLES OF STANDOUT WORDS AND PHRASES	SOME THOUGHTS ABOUT THEM
Hairwoman	The capital "H" shows us that rather than using this person's name, the speaker substitutes that name with a description. This one word shows us how the speaker feels about this teacher. She's a caricature, not an accessible person.
Think ice. Think snow.	There's a deliberate choice to write two sentences of only two words each. There's also a repeated idea. As a reader, ask yourself how this choice affects your sense of the character and the tone or feeling of the moment.

And lastly, let's look at point of view. From whose view are we understanding this moment? It's only one point of view, our speaker who is trying to put her contact lens back in. She shares her frustrations, but there's no insight into why the other characters are behaving as they are.

Which character do you feel like you understand best?

____

____

For which character are you feeling empathy?

____

____

In sum, the author of *Speak* used craft and structure to make us feel empathy for her narrator. Take a close look at the books you are reading. What deliberate choices are those authors making?

ZOOM IN ON CLOSE READING

Every great adventure includes a challenge, such as crossing a stream by moving from slippery rock to slippery rock or climbing a really steep hill. Accepting those challenges brings us to new heights—literally—where we enjoy spectacular views. Reading also presents fantastic challenges, which reward us with new ideas and perspectives. **Close reading** is the absolute best method to work with those challenging texts. So get out all your tools, grab a pencil, and let's climb that mountain—er, read that challenging text. As you read, annotate the text. That's a fancy way of saying, "jot down your ideas and questions." If you own the book or you're reading an electronic copy, you can highlight and add circles and notes right in the book. If you don't, use sticky notes, or take notes in a notebook.

close reading: rereading and analyzing a text to deepen your understanding of it

Close reading requires you to read a text multiple times. For this reason, use it with short texts or parts of longer texts. For example, maybe you are reading a challenging book. In that case, use close reading for the first few paragraphs. Also, use close reading for getting to the deep meaning hidden in poems or to understand the true meaning of a historical document.

Here's the magic of close reading: each time you read, you read with a different purpose!

CLOSE READING IN ACTION

	PURPOSE	QUESTIONS TO ASK YOURSELF	ANNOTATIONS
FIRST READ	**Get the gist (impression or main point) of the piece.** Don't worry about details yet.	What do I notice? What is this mostly about?	Jot down a first impression. Underline key phrases. Put a question mark next to confusing parts.
SECOND READ	**Begin interpreting the text.** Closely examine the text structure and author's craft.	What words stand out, and what do they mean? How is this text organized? What patterns do I notice? What is the point of view of this text?	Underline standout words. Jot down meanings and interpretations of words and phrases. Trace connections between words and lines. Make short summaries of small sections.
THIRD READ	**Pull it all together to develop your understanding.** Recognize the purpose of the text.	What is really going on in this text? What is the speaker's attitude toward this subject? How do I know? Who is the speaker's audience? Do I have evidence for my ideas?	Write a quick description of what this text is really about. Make notes on what the speaker is arguing and what their attitude is about their topic. Note down any evidence for your ideas.

We can give it a try with this short piece written by Sandra Cisneros. On the first read, it seems quite simple. In the second read, we see how carefully she wove together her ideas. And in the final read, the purpose of this piece becomes clear.

> ### Those Who Don't
>
> Those who don't know any better come into our **neighborhood scared.** They think we're **dangerous**. They think we will attack them with **shiny knives**. They are stupid people who are lost and got here by mistake.
>
> But we aren't **afraid**. We know the guy with the crooked eye is Davey the Baby's brother, and the tall one next to him in the straw brim, that's Rosa's Eddie V., and the big one that looks like a dumb grown man, he's Fat Boy, though he's not fat anymore nor a boy.
>
> All brown all around, we are **safe**. But watch us drive into a **neighborhood of another color** and our knees go **shakity-shake** and our car windows get rolled up tight and our eyes look straight. Yeah. That is how it goes and goes.

FIRST READ

Who are those?

It's about a neighborhood and being scared.

The people from the neighborhood are named or nicknamed.

ADD YOUR OWN FIRST IMPRESSIONS:

SECOND READ

First paragraph—about outsiders and how they view people from the speaker's neighborhood.

Words like *dangerous* and *shiny knives* are aggressive.

"Stupid people" shows how the speaker views those outsiders.

Second paragraph explains who actually lives in the neighborhood—the view from **inside**.

Third paragraph—"all brown all around" shows us that the speaker lives in a neighborhood filled with people of color.

It starts out with the view from inside, where they feel safe in their own neighborhood.

The speaker leaves her neighborhood, viewing another from the outside. Now the speaker is scared of those who are scared of her neighborhood.

"Shakity-shake" stands out. Maybe it's a lighter way of saying *shaking*?

Pattern:

1. Outside view
2. Inside view
3. Inside view
4. Outside view

"Goes and goes" makes it sound like a circle going round and round.

WHAT DO YOU THINK AFTER YOUR SECOND READ?

THIRD READD

After pulling it all together, this text seems to be about how groups of people view other groups as scary.

In mentioning skin color, it's about how people are judged based on it.

In "Those Who Don't," *those* might mean all of us when we are in places where we feel like we don't belong.

This speaker is explaining to us, the readers, how our views of other racial groups make us feel scared when we are outside our usual space. Not only is her group viewed as scary, but her group views other groups as scary. This is supported by the way the speaker includes different perspectives.

WHAT DO YOU THINK AFTER YOUR THIRD READ?

SUMMARIZE AND REFLECT

We have already looked at many practices that expert readers use. But there's one more thing before you move on! Expert readers **summarize** what they have read and **reflect** on those ideas. When you summarize a text, you distill it into its most basic idea. It's good to try to summarize in one sentence that briefly explains what the text was about. When you reflect on a text, ask yourself what you learned, or think about how what you read will or won't help you.

Let's summarize this chapter. What was this chapter about?

This chapter presented different ways readers expertly navigate all sorts of texts.

WRITE YOUR OWN REFLECTION ABOUT THIS TEXT

What two things from this chapter will you try right away, and how will those two things help you?

AT A GLANCE: PRACTICES THAT EXPERT READERS USE ACROSS ALL GENRES

PRACTICE	WHAT IT MEANS	READER NOTE (OR HOW DOES THIS HELP?)
Reading stamina	Reading daily, working to increase the amount of time reading and the number of books completed	
Access prior knowledge	Use what you already know to help you understand the text	
Define tricky words	Use clues to figure out the meanings of new words	
Ask questions	Use self-questioning to monitor your understanding of a text	
Visualize	Let the words work with your imagination to make pictures of the text in your head	
Identify tone	Recognize the attitude of the text and/or speaker	
Look for craft and structure	Notice and appreciate the organizational and artistic choices the writer made	
Close reading	Read a text repeatedly, using different lenses each time	
Summarize and reflect	Wrap up reading by condensing it into a short recap and considering what you learned	

CHAPTER 1 VOCABULARY

analyze: to think about the details, structure, and other elements of a text and draw conclusions about that text

antonym: a word that has the opposite meaning of another word

central idea: what something is mostly about; the main point

close reading: reviewing and analyzing a text to deepen your understanding of it

context: the circumstances, events, and details around a situation, providing information that helps you understand that situation

craft: the author's intentional use of literary elements, such as word choice, to create an effect on the reader

definition: a description of the meaning of a word

example: a specific thing that shows the meaning of a word or concept

inference: a conclusion based on context and prior knowledge rather than examples; people sometimes call it "reading between the lines"

perspective: how the speaker perceives what is happening in the story

point of view: who is telling or narrating a story or account; for example, a story from the first-person point of view would likely contain a lot of "I did" and "I said"

prior knowledge: what you already know or can infer (figure out) about a topic based on what you've learned and experienced

reflect: to ask yourself questions about your reading experience, such as what you learned or how it will or won't help you

stamina: the ability to keep up a physical or mental effort for a long period of time

structure: how the writer formats their text and what choices they make about order of information and ideas

summarize: to "boil down" a text into its most basic idea or ideas; a summary is shorter than the original text

synonym: a word that has the same or similar meaning to another word

taxonomy: a system used to organize or classify information

tone: the attitude of the speaker or writer as it is expressed through the text

visualize: to form a mental image or images based on the text while you are reading

word choice: specific words and phrases a writer uses to show meaning

2 LEARNING THE ROPES OF FICTION

In this chapter, we'll be making our way through the forest of fiction (you know, the made-up stuff!). There are all different kinds of fiction you'll encounter in the wild, from funny to fantastical to freaky. But they all share the same key elements. We're going to explore how those elements shape fiction and what tricks you can use to recognize them.

CHAPTER CONTENTS

THE WIDE WORLDS OF FICTION

Fiction is the telling of a story using imaginary characters and events. It usually takes the form of "regular writing," also known as **prose**. This is the kind of writing you'll typically find when you open the page of a book. In fact, you are reading prose right now! But of course, there is more than just one type of prose.

EXPLORING GENRES

The world of fiction is broken up into what we call **genres**, or categories. Here's a list of some of the genres you will find in middle school books. There's something that will appeal to everyone's literary tastes!

GENRES OF FICTION

GENRE	DESCRIPTION	EXAMPLES YOU MAY KNOW OR WILL WANT TO READ!
Diaries	The story is told through the diary or journal of a character.	*Diary of a Wimpy Kid* *The Princess Diaries* *Dork Diaries*
Realistic fiction	Conflict and emotion are central in these stories. You may see that conflict in the actions of characters, their dialogue (words that different characters speak), and even some inner thinking.	*The Fault in Our Stars* *Aristotle and Dante Discover the Secrets of the Universe* *Looking for Alaska* *The Hate U Give* *King and the Dragonflies* *A Good Kind of Trouble* *All American Boys* *Persepolis 1 and 2* *Other Words for Home*
Dystopian	The setting of the story is an imagined world where the society suffers due to oppression, cruel governments, disease, and so on.	*The Hunger Games* *The Marrow Thieves* *Uglies* *Internment*

Fantasy 	The setting is in other worlds that are often completely made up. The characters may be inhuman or have powers people don't normally have.	*Children of Blood and Bone* series *Tristan Strong Punches a Hole in the Sky* *Percy Jackson and the Olympians* series *The Witch Boy*
Historical fiction	These stories take place in the past, in a real historical setting but with made-up characters.	*Between Shades of Gray* *Chains* *Code Talker: A Novel About the Navajo Marines of World War Two* *Journey to Topaz*
Humor 	This is fun, entertaining, and makes you LOL!	*Boy Meets Boy* *Wayside School Gets a Little Stranger* *New Kid*
Mystery	There's crime, suspense, and secrets.	*Goosebumps* series *People Like Us* *One of Us Is Lying*
Science fiction 	Usually taking place in the future, these stories explore how science could change the world—from the likely to the fully imagined.	*Flowers for Algernon* *A Wrinkle in Time* *The City of Ember* *Pet*

prose: regular writing made up of sentences and paragraphs rather than poems, which are in verse

genre: categories of fiction including Dystopian, Fantasy, Mystery, Historical Fiction, and more

NARRATIVE FORMATS

These genres show up in different forms of fiction:

Short stories are, well, short. Typically, you can read one in one sitting.

Novels can be long. They usually consist of many chapters.

Novellas are somewhere between the length of a short story and a novel.

Graphic novels and **comics** tell stories using a combination of words and pictures.

Plays are written to be performed on a stage. The format includes information about how people should move across the stage and lighting as well as what each character says.

CHOOSE YOUR CHARACTER

When you are out in the woods exploring the landscape, you may notice how all the parts come together into one beautiful place. Along your path, there may be hills, streams or puddles, all sorts of plants, and even some animals. A work of fiction is similar to your favorite spot in the wild. It has lots of different parts. In fiction, the author crafts pieces of all these parts together to make rich stories.

Characters are the figures that live in stories. The main character will often be considered the **protagonist**. The **antagonist** works against the protagonist. **Secondary characters** play a supporting role in the text. Often they help us to understand the main characters without changing much themselves.

You can go back to the stories of your youth for some practice with characters! There's space for you to add your own.

WHO'S WHO?

STORY	PROTAGONIST(S)	ANTAGONIST	SECONDARY
Little Red Riding Hood	Little Red Riding Hood	Wolf	Mother
Snow White and the Seven Dwarves	Snow White	Evil queen	The seven dwarves
Superman	Superman	Lex Luthor	Lois Lane

protagonist: the character we are rooting for, typically the character who undergoes the most change

antagonist: the character who works against the protagonist to prevent them from reaching their goals

You may have noticed that the characters in the books you have been reading recently are more complicated than Little Red Riding Hood and the wolf. Sometimes, you may have a hard time naming the protagonist and the antagonist. That's a good thing! It means that you're reading books with sophisticated characters. Just like people in real life, these characters don't always seem to fit neatly in boxes.

DYNAMIC AND STATIC CHARACTERS

A **dynamic** character is one who changes over the course of the story, either for better or for worse. Protagonists, antagonists, and secondary characters can all be dynamic. **Static** characters are characters who don't change. Did you see *Black Panther*? King T'Challa begins the story sure of his position as king and protector of his people. Over time, he reflects on his position, embraces broader convictions, and even expresses regret for things of the past. King T'Challa is a *dynamic* character.

CHARACTER MOTIVATION

You may also notice that the characters in the books you are reading are experiencing multiple pressures, kind of like you. You may feel competing pressures from family, extracurricular activities, friends, and schooling. These pressures sometimes require you to make some difficult choices. And those choices can have positive impacts on some parts of your life and can cause some disappointment in other parts.

Here's a protagonist from *The Tiger Rising* managing competing pressures.

> At lunch, he [Rob] sat out on the benches in the breezeway. He did not go into the lunchroom; Norton and Billy Threemonger were there...
>
> He sat on the bench and unfolded his drawing of the tiger, and his fingers itched to start making it in wood. He was sitting like that, swinging his legs, studying the drawing, when he heard shouting and the high-pitched buzz of excitement, like crickets, that the kids made when something was happening.
>
> He stayed where he was. In a minute, the faded red double doors of the lunchroom swung open and Sistine Bailey came marching through them, her head held high. Behind her was a whole group of kids, and just when Sistine noticed Rob sitting there on the bench, one of the kids threw something at her; Rob couldn't tell what. But it hit her, whatever it was.
>
> "Run!" he wanted to yell at her. "Hurry up and run!"
>
> But he didn't say anything. He just sat and stared at Sistine with his mouth open, and she stared back at him.

Rob, a protagonist in the story, by definition should be a good guy. But did he do right by our other protagonist, Sistine? Rob is experiencing conflicting pressures: standing up for Sistine and preserving his place as someone who is (currently) not the object of bullying.

Here's a way to consider the pressures on characters and the choices they make. Try filling in the boxes below based on a book you are reading.

WHY DID THEY DO IT?

1. PRESSURES THE CHARACTER IS EXPERIENCING	2. CHOICE THEY HAVE TO MAKE
3. THE ACTION/DECISION	**4. WHAT THIS CHOICE TELLS YOU ABOUT THE CHARACTER**

EVALUATING CHARACTERS

As you grow up, your world broadens. The same will be true of the characters in the books you read. You will find characters navigating multiple places, internal pressures, and external pressures. They will encounter moral dilemmas (in other words, struggles to decide what is the right thing to do). Expert readers work to notice these patterns.

Here's a list of questions to help you really get to know the characters in your books:

- How does this character act toward others? Why are they acting this way?
- How does this character act in the different places and settings that they encounter?
- What factors are influencing this character?
- What does this character really want? Does what they want change over time? Why?
- What relationships does this character have? What are those relationships like?

Asking questions like these helps you deeply understand characters and get more out of what you read.

SETTING THE SCENE

The **setting** of the story is where and when it takes place. When reading books of different genres, you'll discover that the settings help transport you away from that cozy nook in the corner of your room and into places you have never seen before! You absolutely do not want to speed your way past these meaningful worlds.

To help you really notice setting, here are a few questions to ask yourself:

1. **When** does this story take place? Historical era, season, time of day. . .
2. **Where** does this story take place? Urban, rural, natural environment, in space. . .
3. What is the **weather** like? Stormy, dry, pleasant. . .
4. What is the **social environment** like? Segment of society, economic class, period of struggle. . .
5. What **mood** does the setting create? Somber, dramatic, cheery. . .

For many stories, the setting is almost like another character. It affects the story in really big ways. This brings us to one final question:

6. How does this **setting affect** the story?

- Is it just a backdrop, not really making an impact on the story?
- Or does it alter the course of the story? Does the story depend on the time, place, or both?

Here are clues that the setting plays an important role in the story:

- The author describes it in detail.
- The period in which the story takes place connects directly to the conflicts characters are facing.

CLOSE READING FOR SETTING

The first few paragraphs from *Pride*, a novel by Ibi Zoboi (in which she retells the story of *Pride and Prejudice*), provide an opportunity to practice looking closely at setting.

> It's a truth universally acknowledged that when rich people move into the hood, where it's a little bit broken and a little bit forgotten, the first thing they want to do is clean it up. But it's not just the junky stuff they'll get rid of. People can be thrown away too, like last night's trash left out on sidewalks or pushed to the edge of wherever all broken things go. What those rich people don't always know is that broken and forgotten neighborhoods were first built out of love.
>
> The new owners are moving into the mini-mansion across the street today. For the last few months, construction crews have been giving that abandoned house an Extreme Makeover: Bushwick Edition. They gutted and renovated the best thing on our block—that run-down, weed-infested, boarded-up house. Now it looks like something that belongs in the suburbs, with its wide double doors, sparkling windows, and tiny manicured lawn.
>
> I pull back the curtains to greet my little corner of Bushwick and Jefferson Avenues, my very own way of stretching out my arms and yawning at the morning sun. This is where I see words swim in and around my neighborhood like dust from overhead train tracks. It's all poetry. So I pull those words together and try to make sense of it all: my hood, my Brooklyn, my life, my world, and me in it.

WHAT CAN YOU LEARN ABOUT THE SETTING?

QUESTION	WHAT YOU KNOW	EVIDENCE
When does this story or scene take place?	In the morning	"I pull back the curtains to greet my little corner of Bushwick and Jefferson Avenues, my very own way of stretching out my arms and yawning at the morning sun."
Where does this story take place?	Bushwick, Brooklyn, part of New York City	"For the last few months, construction crews have been giving that abandoned house an Extreme Makeover: Bushwick Edition."
What is the **weather** like?	Sunny	"... yawning at the morning sun."
What is the **social environment** like?	City neighborhood Run-down Beloved Potential conflict: presence of both rich and others (she doesn't describe the economic status of the "not rich")	"What those rich people don't always know is that broken and forgotten neighborhoods were first built out of love." "... when rich people move into the hood, where it's a little bit broken and a little bit forgotten, the first thing they want to do is clean it up." "... gutted and renovated the best thing on our block—that run-down, weed-infested, boarded up house. Now it looks like something that belongs in the suburbs... "

continued...

What **mood** does the setting create?	Comforting Foreboding (as if something bad is going to happen)	Comforting: "... greet my little corner of Bushwick and Jefferson Avenues, my very own way of stretching out my arms and yawning at the morning sun. This is where I see words swim in and around my neighborhood like dust from overhead train tracks. It's all poetry." Foreboding: "People can be thrown away too, like last night's trash left out on sidewalks or pushed to the edge of wherever all broken things go." "They gutted and renovated the best thing on our block..."

To check what you have learned about the setting at the beginning of Pride, you can write in your field journal. Summarize the role of setting at this early stage in *Pride*.

Compare your summary to this example. Would you make changes to either yours or the example?

The setting of *Pride* is a Brooklyn neighborhood. Gentrification happens when richer people and businesses arrive and change the character of a community. Because the author spent so much time describing the setting, focusing on the change to the building across the street, it seems that the setting will matter a great deal to this story.

Reflect on what you learned about identifying the setting and its role in the novel.

NOW YOU TRY!

You can try this on your own with the first paragraphs of *Uglies*, a dystopian novel by Scott Westerfeld.

> The early summer sky was the color of cat vomit.
>
> Of course, Tally thought, you'd have to feed your cat only salmon-flavored cat food for a while to get the pinks right. The scudding clouds did look a bit fishy, rippled into scales by a high-altitude wind. As the light faded, deep blue gaps of night peered through like an upside-down ocean, bottomless and cold.
>
> Any other summer, a sunset like this would have been beautiful. But nothing had been beautiful since Peris turned pretty. Losing your best friend sucks, even if it's only for three months and two days.
>
> Tally Youngblood was waiting for darkness.
>
> She could see New Pretty Town through her open window. The party towers were already lit up, and snakes of burning torches marked flickering pathways through the pleasure gardens. A few hot-air balloons pulled at their tethers against the darkening pink sky, their passengers shooting safety fireworks at other balloons and passing parasailers. Laughter and music skipped across the water like rocks thrown with just the right spin, their edges just as sharp against Tally's nerves.

PRACTICE IDENTIFYING SETTING

QUESTION	WHAT YOU KNOW	EVIDENCE
When does this story or scene take place?		
Where does this story take place?		
What is the **weather** like?		
What is the **social environment** like?		
What **mood** does the setting create?		

To check what you've learned about the setting at the beginning of *Uglies*, you can write in your field journal. Summarize the role of setting at this early stage in *Uglies*.

Reflect on what you learned about identifying the setting and its role in the story.

THE PLOT THICKENS

The **plot** of a story is how events are organized. Think about the acts of a play . . . or maybe the levels of a video game. There's never just one challenge in a video game. Each new event builds on what came before to create layers of story, and these layers form the plot of the story.

CONFLICT

Conflict is the crux (the most important part) of the story. It's what drives the rest of the plot. It is the battle between forces that oppose each other. The conflict can present itself in two ways:

Internal conflict means that the character's struggle is within that character. This may have to do with resolving emotional issues, moral conflict, or ideas about self.

External conflict means that the struggle is with something outside of the character. There are a few varieties:

Character versus character: the character's struggle is against another character, battling for something like physical dominance or place in society.

Character versus nature: a character is facing a struggle against the outside world. This can include the forces of nature, such as a tornado, a flood, extreme cold, or a meteor.

Character versus society: a character is pushing back against society, perhaps in support of their own beliefs or sense of morality. For instance, a character might speak out against inequality or harmful laws.

We can try this out with a couple of familiar stories.

"Snow White" is the tale of a young woman who is struggling against the power of an evil queen. Since her struggle is with the queen, the conflict is **external**, character versus character.

Do you remember *The Story of Ferdinand*? It's about a young bull who does not like to fight like the other bulls. This bull prefers to sit under a tree and smell the flowers. Still, Ferdinand has to go to the bullring, a place where people expect him to be fierce. Rather than give in to the expectations of the world around him, Ferdinand remains true to himself and sits peacefully. Ferdinand faces a challenge from the world he lives in. That means the conflict is **external**, character versus society.

IDENTIFYING PLOT ELEMENTS

As we move on to other elements of plot, keep in mind that the conflict of the story is what directs the plot. What do the different stages of a story look like? There are some pretty fun words that describe the different parts of plot. And as you know by now, different people use different words when referring to the same thing. Those synonyms are noted for you!

Exposition is background information inserted into the story, often to give a character's backstory or provide other information important for understanding the story.

Rising action is the set of events that develop as a result of the conflict. Often things become more complicated before a solution to the conflict becomes clear!

Climax is the turning point in the story, the moment of drama. It's where you're really wondering—and even a bit nervous about—how things are going to turn out for this character. If the book is making your heart beat fast, it's beating its fastest at this time!

Falling action happens after the climax, as the conflict is starting to sort itself out. As a reader, you know what has happened. You see now whether the character is overcoming this particular conflict.

Resolution, or denouement, is the conclusion to your story. Any loose ends are wrapped up, or a cliffhanger is left, uh, hanging.

You can check out how to use these words with the short story "Thank You, Ma'm" by Langston Hughes.

> She was a large woman with a large purse that had everything in it but hammer and nails. It had a long strap, and she carried it slung across her shoulder. It was about eleven o'clock at night, and she was walking alone, when a boy ran up behind her and tried to snatch her purse. The strap broke with the single tug the boy gave it from behind. But the boy's weight and the weight of the purse combined caused him to lose his balance so, instead of taking off full blast as he had hoped, the boy fell on his back on the sidewalk, and his legs flew up. The large woman simply turned around and kicked him right square in his blue-jeaned sitter. Then she reached down, picked the boy up by his shirt front, and shook him until his teeth rattled.

EXPOSITION

- The large woman: we learn later in the story that this is Mrs. Luella Bates Washington Jones.
- The boy: his name is Roger.
- Setting: it's nighttime, probably in a city.

The beginning of a conflict happens when Roger tries to steal from Mrs. Jones.

RISING ACTION

- The boy is unsuccessful, and the woman gets a hold of him and won't let him go.

After that the woman said, "Pick up my pocketbook, boy, and give it here."

She still held him. But she bent down enough to permit him to stoop and pick up her purse.

Then she said, "Now ain't you ashamed of yourself?"

Firmly gripped by his shirt front, the boy said, "Yes'm."

The woman said, "What did you want to do it for?"

The boy said, "I didn't aim to."

She said, "You a lie!"

By that time two or three people passed, stopped, turned to look, and some stood watching.

"If I turn you loose, will you run?" asked the woman.

"Yes'm," said the boy.

"Then I won't turn you loose," said the woman. She did not release him.

"I'm very sorry, lady, I'm sorry," whispered the boy.

"Um-hum! And your face is dirty. I got a great mind to wash your face for you. Ain't you got nobody home to tell you to wash your face?"

"No'm," said the boy.

Roger apologizes, but Mrs. Jones keeps talking to him.

"Then it will get washed this evening," said the large woman starting up the street, dragging the frightened boy behind her. He looked as if he were fourteen or fifteen, frail and willow-wild, in tennis shoes and blue jeans.

The woman said, "You ought to be my son. I would teach you right from wrong. Least I can do right now is to wash your face. Are you hungry?"

"No'm," said the being dragged boy. "I just want you to turn me loose."

"Was I bothering you when I turned that corner?" asked the woman.

"No'm."

"But you put yourself in contact with me," said the woman. "If you think that that contact is not going to last awhile, you got another thought coming. When I get through with you, sir, you are going to remember Mrs. Luella Bates Washington Jones."

Mrs. Jones insists that Roger get cleaned up. Roger still wants to get away from her!

Sweat popped out on the boy's face and he began to struggle. Mrs. Jones stopped, jerked him around in front of her, put a half-nelson about his neck, and continued to drag him up the street. When she got to her door, she dragged the boy inside, down a hall, and into a large kitchenette furnished room at the rear of the house. She switched on the light and left the door open. The boy could hear other roomers laughing and talking in the large house. Some of their doors were open, too, so he knew he and the woman were not alone. The woman still had him by the neck in the middle of her room. She said, "What is your name?"

"Roger," answered the boy.

"Then, Roger, you go to that sink and wash your face," said the woman, whereupon she turned him loose—at last. Roger looked at the door—looked at the woman—looked at the door—*and went to the sink*.

Mrs. Jones drags Roger into her home while he struggles to get away.

"Let the water run until it gets warm," she said. "Here's a clean towel."

"You gonna take me to jail?" asked the boy, bending over the sink.

"Not with that face, I would not take you nowhere," said the woman. "Here I am trying to get home to cook me a bite to eat and you snatch my pocketbook! Maybe, you ain't been to your supper either, late as it be. Have you?"

"There's nobody home at my house," said the boy.

"Then we'll eat," said the woman, "I believe you're hungry—or been hungry—to try to snatch my pocketbook."

"I wanted a pair of blue suede shoes," said the boy.

"Well, you didn't have to snatch my pocketbook to get some suede shoes," said Mrs. Luella Bates Washington Jones. "You could of asked me."

"M'am?"

> While Mrs. Jones takes care of Roger, he explains that he was stealing because he wanted fancy new shoes.
>
> We are learning more about the conflict at this point. Roger is in conflict with himself—with his morality (his sense of right and wrong).

The water dripping from his face, the boy looked at her. There was a long pause. A very long pause. After he had dried his face and not knowing what else to do dried it again, the boy turned around, wondering what next. The door was open. He could make a dash for it down the hall. He could run, run, run, run, run!

The woman was sitting on the day-bed. After a while she said, "I were young once and I wanted things I could not get." There was another long pause. The boy's mouth opened. Then he frowned, but not knowing he frowned.

The woman said, "Um-hum! You thought I was going to say but, didn't you? You thought I was going to say, *but I didn't snatch people's pocketbooks*. Well, I wasn't going to say that." Pause. Silence. "I have done things, too, which I would not tell you, son—neither tell God, if he didn't already know. So you set down while I fix us something to eat. You might run that comb through your hair so you will look presentable."

Roger is tempted to escape.

He learns that Mrs. Jones has also made mistakes.

In another corner of the room behind a screen was a gas plate and an icebox. Mrs. Jones got up and went behind the screen. The woman did not watch the boy to see if he was going to run now, nor did she watch her purse which she left behind her on the day-bed. But the boy took care to sit on the far side of the room where he thought she could easily see him out of the corner of her eye, if she wanted to. He did not trust the woman not to trust him. And he did not want to be mistrusted now.

"Do you need somebody to go to the store," asked the boy, "maybe to get some milk or something?"

"Don't believe I do," said the woman, "unless you just want sweet milk yourself. I was going to make cocoa out of this canned milk I got here."

"That will be fine," said the boy.

She heated some lima beans and ham she had in the icebox, made the cocoa, and set the table. The woman did not ask the boy anything about where he lived, or his folks, or anything else that would embarrass him. Instead, as they ate, she told him about her job in a hotel beauty-shop that stayed open late, what the work was like, and how all kinds of women came in and out, blondes, red-heads, and Spanish.

Then she cut him a half of her ten-cent cake.

"Eat some more, son," she said.

When they were finished eating she got up and said, "Now, here, take this ten dollars and buy yourself some blue suede shoes. And next time, do not make the mistake of latching onto my pocketbook nor nobody else's—because shoes come by devilish like that will burn your feet. I got to get my rest now. But I wish you would behave yourself, son, from here on in."

She led him down the hall to the front door and opened it.

"Good-night! Behave yourself, boy!" she said, looking out into the street. The boy wanted to say something else other than "Thank you, m'am" to Mrs. Luella Bates Washington Jones, but he couldn't do so as he turned at the barren stoop and looked back at the large woman in the door. He barely managed to say "Thank you" before she shut the door. And he never saw her again.

CLIMAX

Mrs. Jones leaves Roger alone. He can steal her purse, and he can run away. But we see him changing (ahem, he is a *dynamic* character). He now wants to be trusted.

FALLING ACTION

- Roger does not take advantage of Mrs. Jones when given the opportunity!
- Mrs. Jones and Roger eat together, and she tells him a little about herself.

RESOLUTION

- Mrs. Jones gives Roger what he needs to get his new shoes.
- Her kindness affects him so much that he can barely speak.
- They never see each other again.

It's kind of like a puzzle the way all the parts of plot fit neatly together.

NOW YOU TRY!

Octopus Stew by Eric Velasquez is a funny story and a great way to get your feet wet identifying the elements of plot on your own. Remember to listen to your heart as you read—it will help you identify the climax.

TRY IT OUT: IDENTIFYING PLOT ELEMENTS

OCTOPUS STEW by Eric Velasquez	**IDENTIFY:** *Exposition, Rising Action, Climax, Falling Action, and Resolution*
1 When Grandma saw my painting of Super Octo, she got the idea to make pulpo guisado, octopus stew—not exactly my favorite dish.	
2 "But Dad makes that," I said.	
3 Grandma snapped at me, "I've been making pulpo guisado since your dad era un niño, since he was a boy."	
4 I didn't want to upset her, so I didn't ask any more questions.	
5 So later, while I was playing Super Ram with Chana, Grandma told me to get ready to go shopping with her.	
6 Grandma gave me a look and said, "¿Qué es esto? Boy, if you think I am going to the store with you wearing that silly cape, you've lost your mind."	
7 At the store, I saw lots of cool-looking fish. I took pictures so I could look them up later on.	
8 Grandma picked the biggest octopus in the store. She said it was the best of the bunch. It looked like it was still alive to me… and kind of creepy.	
9 I decided to do some web surfing when a warning popped up on my screen about octopuses.	

10	I tried to tell Grandma, but she wouldn't let me. "How often do I have to tell you to keep that thing in your pocket when you go out with me!" she said.	
11	Back home, Grandma unwrapped the octopus, gave it a good scrubbing, and put it in a pot of boiling water. I did my best to stay out of her way.	
12	Then Grandma came to sit with me while I did my homework. All of a sudden, strange noises started to come from the kitchen.	
13	**Blimp, Blump, Brr, Blimp, Blump, Brr.**	
14	"¿Qué será eso? What could that be?" Grandma asked. "Ramsey, quédate aqui. Voy a ver. Stay here."	
15	The sounds got louder.	
16	**Bloop, Bloop, Bloop, Brrrr. Bloop, Bloop, Bloop, Brrrr.**	
17	The octopus got so big it blew the lid off the pot.	
18	"¡Wela, tenga cuidado! Grandma, watch out!" I warned.	
19	"Escóndete!" Grandma hollered. "Hide!"	
20	**Thump! Thump! blop Thump! BRRRR! Thump! bloop blop Thump!**	
21	"¡Vámonos de aqui!" I yelled. "Let's get out of here!"	
22	But it was too late.	

23 I grabbed my phone and hid until I could figure out how to rescue Grandma.	
24 The octopus had to have a natural predator, something that it feared. I searched, and there it was: Sharks!	
25 I grabbed my drawing pad and markers and drew the biggest, meanest, scariest shark I could create.	
26 I put on my Super Ram cape and marched into the kitchen.	
27 "You put down my grandma," I yelled.	
28 The octopus dropped Grandma and attacked, spraying ink all over my drawing.	
29 Dad interrupted, "Okay, mijo, don't you think this is getting a little far-fetched? I mean like, really, Ramsey?"	
30 "Hey Dad, you broke my concentration! It's my turn to tell the story tonight. May I please finish now?"	
31 "Are you okay?" I asked Grandma.	
32 "¿Ramsey, qué pasó?" she said. "Voy a limpiar este desordeno. What happened?"	
33 She didn't seem to notice the twenty-foot octopus behind her.	
34 Then I remembered the warning that popped up on my phone and read it out loud. "Important, before cooking an octopus remove the eyes and beak..."	

35 WHAAAAAAAAAT! "Cook me? Take out my eyes and beak? Why?"	
36 "Basta ya. That's enough, Señor Pulpo," said Grandma. "I changed my mind. We are no longer having pulpo guisado. Instead we are having ensalada sin pulpo. Just salad, no octopus."	
37 And Señor Pulpo joined us.	

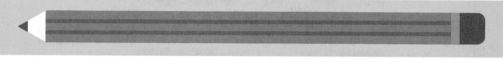

How did you do? What parts were easy to identify? What parts were more difficult?

PLOT DIAGRAMS

Here's what the plot of *Octopus Stew* looks like on a **plot diagram**, a way of showing the movement of the plot.

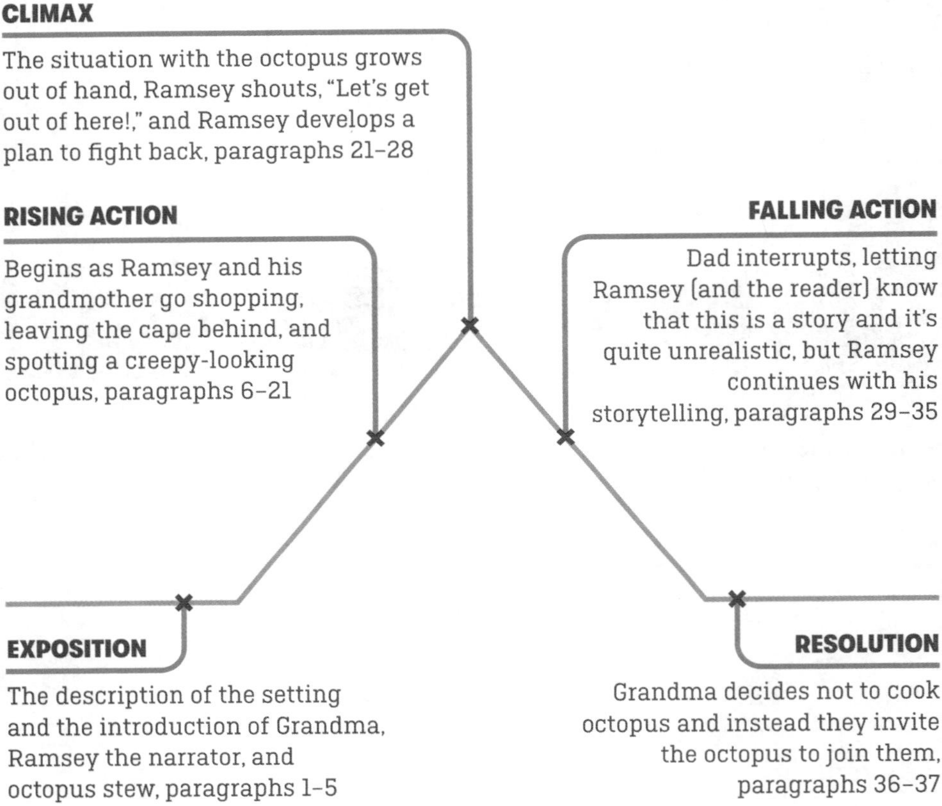

CLIMAX
The situation with the octopus grows out of hand, Ramsey shouts, "Let's get out of here!," and Ramsey develops a plan to fight back, paragraphs 21–28
RISING ACTION
Begins as Ramsey and his grandmother go shopping, leaving the cape behind, and spotting a creepy-looking octopus, paragraphs 6–21
FALLING ACTION
Dad interrupts, letting Ramsey (and the reader) know that this is a story and it's quite unrealistic, but Ramsey continues with his storytelling, paragraphs 29–35
EXPOSITION
The description of the setting and the introduction of Grandma, Ramsey the narrator, and octopus stew, paragraphs 1–5
RESOLUTION
Grandma decides not to cook octopus and instead they invite the octopus to join them, paragraphs 36–37

Great work following the plot of two texts. Now jot down one or two things about plot that will be good to remember for the next work of fiction you read:

WHO'S TELLING THE STORY?

When we were exploring the practices of expert readers, we talked about the perspective of the speaker. Now that we are navigating the world of fiction, we will consider **point of view**. The point of view is different from perspective because point of view is the way the author has decided to narrate, or tell, the story.

TYPES OF NARRATORS

One of the best things about fiction is that we get to see the world through the eyes of a stranger! Think about some of your favorite fiction books, or the stories we looked at together in this chapter. Who is telling each story? **Narrator** is the term we use to identify the voice telling the story.

Think of one of your favorite fiction books. Who told that story?

Was the narrator even a character in the book? Sometimes narrators of stories know more than any character. They get inside the heads of characters, or they tell us about the experiences of multiple characters, even when they are not a character in the story. We have language that helps us to describe the role of the narrator.

REVIEWING POINT OF VIEW

First-person point of view	The narrator is a person directly involved in the action. The narrator uses pronouns such as "I" and "we." **Example:** The smell of Grandma's peanut butter cookies was too tempting, and I snuck into the kitchen to grab one.
Second-person point of view	The narrator uses second person pronouns like "you" and "your." This pulls the reader in closer to the action. Second-person point of view is pretty rare. **Example:** The smell of Grandma's peanut butter cookies was so tempting that you snuck into the kitchen to grab one.
Third-person point of view	The narrator is a person outside the action. You will notice pronouns such as "he" and "she." Except in dialogue, the main characters are always referred to by name and pronouns such as "he," "she," and "they." **Example:** The smell of his grandmother's peanut butter cookies was too tempting, and he snuck into the kitchen to grab one.

As mentioned earlier, the first chunk of a book is where the author sets you up for what's to come. Noting the point of view in the first pages of a book will help you keep your bearings as you move through the pages.

NOW YOU TRY!

Below you will find the beginnings of three books. Practicing your expert navigation skills, you can identify which point of view the different authors employed. While you are taking notice of that, dig a little deeper to get a sense of the position from which the story is told. (Helpful hint: look for any emerging conflict!)

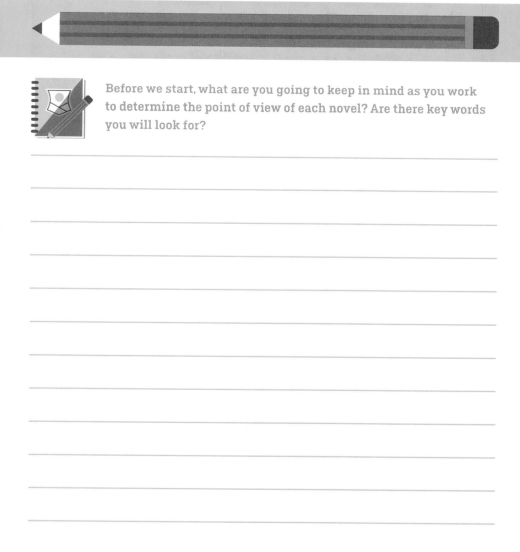

Before we start, what are you going to keep in mind as you work to determine the point of view of each novel? Are there key words you will look for?

Here is part of Kwame Alexander's *Booked*, a novel written as a series of poems.

Wake Up Call

After playing FIFA

online with Coby

till one thirty a.m.

last night,

you wake

this morning

to the sound

of Mom arguing

on the phone

with Dad.

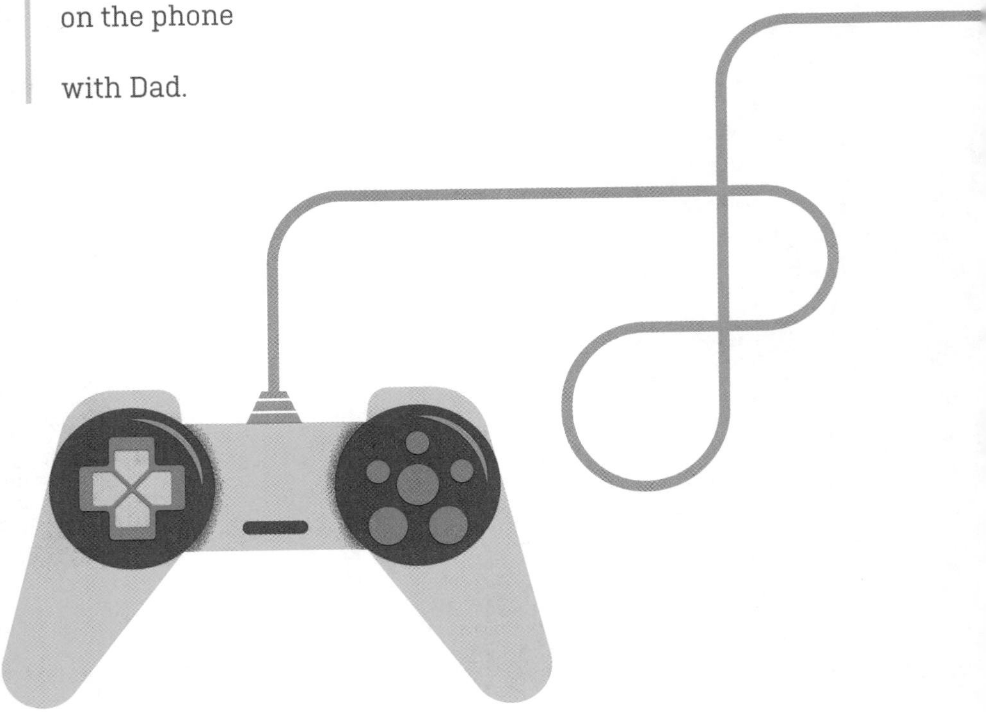

CLOSE READING FOR POINT OF VIEW

BOOKED

POINT OF VIEW:

Evidence:

OBSERVATIONS FROM A DEEPER DIG:

Evidence :

And here is an excerpt from *Journey to Topaz*, which is historical fiction by Yoshiko Uchida.

> **Strangers at the Door**
>
> It was only the first week in December, but already Yuki could feel the tingling excitement of Christmas in the air. There was, of course, no sign of snow, for it never snowed in Berkeley except for the winter when she was six and a thin flurry of flakes had surprised them all. Yuki remembered how she had run outside, stretched her arms wide and opened her mouth, thrusting her tongue out so she could feel the snow and taste it and gather it to her in any way she could before the flakes reached the ground and disappeared. Today looked like snow weather for the sky was gray and murky, but only with fog that blew in cold and damp from San Francisco Bay.

CLOSE READING FOR POINT OF VIEW

JOURNEY TO TOPAZ

POINT OF VIEW:

Evidence:

OBSERVATIONS FROM A DEEPER DIG:

Evidence :

Here is part of *For Black Girls Like Me* by Mariama J. Lockington.

> **Tumbleweeds**
>
> I am a girl but most days I feel like a question mark. People throw their looks at me. Then back at my mama sister and papa. Who are all as white as oleander. Then they look back at me. Black as a midnight orchard. And I see their puzzled faces trying to understand where I fit. People ask me where I'm from but I know they really mean
>
> *Who do you belong to?*

CLOSE READING FOR POINT OF VIEW

FOR BLACK GIRLS LIKE ME

POINT OF VIEW:

Evidence:

OBSERVATIONS FROM A DEEPER DIG:

Evidence :

How did it go? Take a look at the work of one expert reader.

BOOKED

POINT OF VIEW: Second-person point of view

Evidence: "...*you* wake / this morning..."

OBSERVATIONS FROM A DEEPER DIG: Emerging conflict: they may be dealing with some family stress.

Evidence : "...Mom arguing / on the phone / with Dad"

JOURNEY TO TOPAZ

POINT OF VIEW: Third-person point of view

Evidence: "...*Yuki* remembered how she had run..."

OBSERVATIONS FROM A DEEPER DIG: She is looking forward to Christmas.

Emerging conflict: there is concern it won't be as she wants it to be.

Evidence : "...Yuki could feel the tingling excitement of Christmas..."

"...There was, of course, no sign of snow..."

FOR BLACK GIRLS LIKE ME	
POINT OF VIEW:	First-person point of view
Evidence:	"*I* am a girl..."
OBSERVATIONS FROM A DEEPER DIG:	Immediately we see that this character is speaking from the perspective of being a Black child in a family where everyone else is white. Emerging conflict: feeling different and a sense of not belonging
Evidence :	"... mama sister and papa. Who are all as white as oleander. Then they look back at me. Black as a midnight orchard..." "*Who do you belong to?*"

CAN YOU TRUST YOUR NARRATOR?

Like people, narrators are funny beings. Make sure to examine your narrator closely. Like any great storyteller, narrators are guiding us through the experience they want us to have. If you are being told a story filled with suspense, the narrator may withhold certain details. Can you think of any other circumstances where a narrator may be somewhat unreliable or biased? (*Biased* means favoring one side or one point of view over another.)

Here are some things to consider when examining the reliability of your narrator:

- The motivations of the narrator
- What does this narrator know? What kinds of information might they not know?
- If you are reading a first-person narrative, then the narrator's experiences will affect how the narrator views things and what they understand.
- Sometimes the narrator in a third-person narrative might also have a specific viewpoint and only describe what one character sees and understands. That's called a third-person *limited* narrator.
- If the narrator knows and describes what every character understands, that's a third-person *omniscient* narrator (omni = all; scient = knowledge).

Remember, the writer created this narrator to tell the story. Why might a writer create a narrator who doesn't tell the "whole" story? Every different narrator will tell us their own version of events. Each narrator has **bias.** Can you think of a book you have read recently where a biased narrator told the story?

Be careful! Even when a book is written in first person, it's important to remember that the point of view of a narrator is not necessarily the same as the author's point of view.

What's one thing to consider when thinking about narrators?

In one sentence, summarize what you have learned about point of view:

Reflect on how thinking about the point of view helps you better understand the story:

THEME: WHAT IT'S ALL ABOUT

When you think about it, authors do a lot of work. They build setting, craft characters, develop plot, and define a point of view. Why? These elements give us clues about the **theme** of the book. *Theme* is a central idea, underlying meaning, or message you take from a piece of literature. (You'll see it pop up in other literary works, such as poems.) It's the hidden core in a story!

Imagine someone has given you a gift. It is wrapped in shiny, sparkly paper. It has ribbons, bows, even a card that explains the occasion and maybe hints at the nature of the gift. However, all of this wrapping is simply dressing for the gift inside. You don't know what that gift is until you have peeled off the layers of wrapping.

Just as there are all sorts of gifts, there are many themes. A few themes common to fiction are:

- Growing up
- Overcoming a fear
- Prejudice (unfairly judging someone or a group of people because of their skin color, where they come from, or some other reason)
- Being a hero
- Betrayal (harming someone else, often by letting them down or revealing a secret)

- Good versus evil
- Dealing with loss
- Finding courage
- Finding your voice
- Love
- Death

Thinking about books you have read, can you add to this list?

- ____
- ____
- ____

A theme is a universal statement. In other words, it is not just about the character—it's telling us something about the world or life in general. When you are naming the theme in a book, you won't use the characters' names. Instead, you will focus on the lesson learned.

IDENTIFYING THEMES

How can you determine and describe theme? It's kind of like a math equation where you think about the topics that are appearing in a text and combine them with what the author is teaching you about those topics. One more thing to note: stories may have more than one theme!

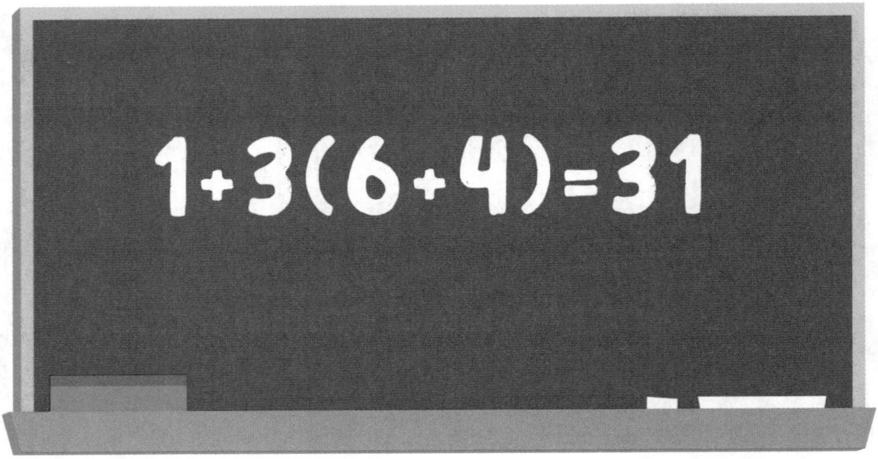

THE THEME EQUATION

Brainstorm topics from the text.

+

Ask yourself: what does the author want me to know about those topics?

+

Check for evidence.

=

A statement that combines the first two ideas

We can try it with this vignette written by Sandra Cisneros. (A *vignette* is a short, descriptive scene.)

> ### Hairs
>
> Everybody in our family has different hair. My Papa's hair is like a broom, all up in the air. And me, my hair is lazy. It never obeys barrettes or bands. Carlos's hair is thick and straight. He doesn't need to comb it. Nenny's hair is slippery—slides out of your hand. And Kiki, who is youngest, has hair like fur.

> But my mother's hair, my mother's hair, like little rosettes, like little candy circles all curly and pretty because she pinned it in pincurls all day, sweet to put your nose into when she is holding you, holding you and you feel safe, is the warm smell of bread before you bake it, is the smell when she makes room for you on her side of the bed still warm with her skin, and you sleep near her, the rain outside falling and Papa snoring. The snoring, the rain, and Mama's hair that smells like bread.

BRAINSTORM TOPICS FROM THE TEXT.		ASK YOURSELF: WHAT DOES THE AUTHOR WANT ME TO KNOW ABOUT THOSE TOPICS?		CHECK FOR EVIDENCE.
Individual differences	+	Our differences help make us who we are.	+	• "... Papa's hair like a broom..." • "... Carlos's hair is thick and straight..." • "... Kiki... has hair like fur..."
Family nurturing	+	Acts of love make us feel safe.	+	• "... sweet to put your nose into when she is holding you..." • "... the smell when she makes room for you on her side of the bed..."

=	A STATEMENT THAT COMBINES THE FIRST TWO IDEAS
=	Every person is an individual.
=	Small acts of love can make someone feel safe and like they belong.

NOW YOU TRY

Before we tie up all the ropes of fiction, let's use **close reading** to practice some of what we have learned. We can give it a try with this excerpt (small piece) from the novel *Piecing Me Together* by Renée Watson.

> The next morning I wake up before the sun. So early that only trucks and people up to no good are on the streets. There's nothing in the fridge but baking soda in the way back and half-empty bottles of ketchup, barbeque sauce, and mustard on the door. I drink a glass of water, take a shower, get dressed, and leave by six thirty so I can get to the bus.
>
> I ride the 35 through the maze of houses that all look like one another, like sisters who are not twins but everyone thinks they are. Living here means when people ask, "Where do you live?" and you say, "The New Columbia," they say, "You mean the Villa?" and remind you that your neighborhood used to be public housing for World War II shipyard workers, and they remind you how by the eighties a lot of those apartments were run-down and how really, they were just projects with a different name. At least that's what Mom says. She's always telling me, "I don't care if they give the 'hood a new name or not; it's still the 'hood."
>
> Lots of people can't find beauty in my neighborhood, but I can. Ever since elementary school, I've been making beauty out of everyday things—candy wrappers, pages of a newspaper, receipts, rip-outs from magazines. I cut and tear, arrange and rearrange, and glue them down, morphing them into something no one else thought they could be. Like me. I'm ordinary too. The only fancy thing about me is my name: Jade. But I am not precious like a gem. There is nothing exquisite about my life. It's mine, though, so I'm going to make something out of it.

READING 1

What's this passage mostly about?

What general observations can you make?

To do:

- Make initial observations.
- Jot down the gist of the excerpt.

YOUR NOTES:

READING 2

What do you notice about the author's craft and how she organized her ideas?

To do:

- Jot down standout words and phrases.
- Notice repeated ideas.
- Write down what the passage makes you "see."
- Look for point of view.

YOUR NOTES:

READING 3

What is the purpose of this excerpt?

To do:

- Look for the attitude of this speaker. How does she feel about her world and who she is?
- Note what is really going on in this text. Use the narrator's tone or attitude to help you.
- Note a theme from this excerpt.
- Check to make sure the evidence supports your ideas.

YOUR NOTES:

SUMMARIZE AND REFLECT

As you read all sorts of fiction, remember the most important lesson: fiction is a gift the world has given to you! Run to the middle-grade or the young adult section of the nearest library. Once you're there, take your time. Browse. Try out a graphic novel, then a mystery, and later a piece of dystopian literature. Somewhere in those stacks is the same comfort that Sandra Cisneros's *Hairs* offers, the passion for sports we saw in *Booked*, and the conflicted feelings of identity felt by the narrator in *For Black Girls Like Me*.

Before you go, let's **summarize and reflect**.

WHAT HAVE YOU LEARNED?

SUMMARIZE BY ANSWERING THE QUESTION:

What is fiction?

Reflect on fiction reading by choosing one of the following to write about:

- Something that surprised you
- Something that was challenging
- Something you want to try

AT A GLANCE: LEARNING THE ROPES OF FICTION

ELEMENT	BOOK NOTE	READER'S NOTE—what you want to remember
Genres	Categories of fiction	
Characters	Made up of protagonists, antagonists, and secondary characters	
Setting	When and where the story takes place	
Plot	How the events are organized—leading to the resolution of the conflict	
Point of view	The perspective from which the story is being told: first person, second person, or third person	
Theme	The underlying message of the story	

CHAPTER 2 VOCABULARY

antagonist: the character who works against the protagonist to prevent them from reaching their goals

climax: the turning point in a story

conflict: the battle or struggle between forces that oppose each other; conflict moves the story forward

dynamic character: a person or animal in a story who changes over the course of the story, either for better or for worse

exposition: background information inserted into the story, often to give a character's backstory or provide other information important for understanding the story.

external conflict: occurs when the struggle is with something outside of the character; external conflict includes:

> **character versus character:** one person's struggle is against another person in the story, battling for something like physical dominance or place in society
>
> **character versus nature:** a person is facing a struggle against the outside world, such as a desert, an ocean, or a natural disaster
>
> **character versus society:** a person is pushing back against a group of people or against people in general, perhaps in support of the person's own beliefs or sense of morality

falling action: events that happen after the climax of a story, as the conflict is starting to sort itself out

genre: categories of writing, including dystopian, fantasy, historical fiction, thriller, nonfiction, and more

graphic novel: a format that tells stories using a combination of words and pictures; sometimes called cartoons or sequential art

internal conflict: occurs when the character's struggle is within himself or herself; this may include figuring out emotional issues, a struggle about whether something is right or wrong, or ideas about the self

narrator: the voice telling the story

novella: fiction somewhere between the length of a short story and a novel

novel: a long fictional story with many chapters

play: fiction written to be performed on a stage; the format includes information about how people should move across the stage and lighting as well as what each character says (dialogue)

plot diagram: a visual way of showing the movement of the plot

plot: how the events and action of a story are organized

point of view: the format a writer has chosen for telling the story, or the way the story is narrated; point of view includes:

> **first-person point of view:** the narrator is a person directly involved in the action and uses pronouns such as *I* and *we*
>
> **second-person point of view:** the narrator uses pronouns such as *you* and *your*
>
> **third-person point of view:** the narrator is a person outside the action; you will notice pronouns such as *he*, *she*, or *they*

prose: regular writing made up of sentences and paragraphs, rather than poems, which are in verse

protagonist: the character you are rooting for; typically the character that undergoes the most change

resolution (also known as *denouement*): the conclusion (ending) to the story

rising action: the set of events that come out of the conflict

secondary characters: people or animals who play a supporting role in the text and often help you understand the main characters

setting: where and when a story takes place

short story: a brief work of fiction, in prose, that you can typically read in one sitting

static character: a person or animal who stays the same throughout the story

theme: the central idea, underlying meaning, or message you take from a piece of literature

THE
FACTS

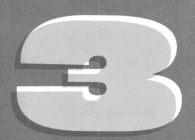

3 THE REAL TRUTH ABOUT NONFICTION

When we were little kids, we asked so many questions. Why do trees have leaves? How do planes stay up in the air? Why are my eyes brown? Adults answered these questions for us. But no adult (not even your teacher) knows *everything*. Luckily, a lot a people know about a lot of different things, and they wrote it all down for us to read and learn about. And all that stuff is what we call nonfiction. This chapter will teach you how to identify and decipher informative and reliable pieces of nonfiction text.

CHAPTER CONTENTS

INTRODUCTION TO NONFICTION

Nonfiction is text that is about real events and people. Remember, not all nonfiction looks the same. Also remember, there are a few very important strategies to use when you encounter nonfiction.

As you set out on your research, you're thinking, "Once I have the facts, I will be an expert on trees, planes, and eye color!" Well, the truth is trickier than you might think. Great readers of nonfiction use a critical eye as they select and read texts. By working with the five questions below, you too will become a great reader of nonfiction. And then . . . you will be able to announce, with authority, how it is that planes stay in the air!

What **type of nonfiction** am I reading?

What is the **author's purpose** in writing this text?

From what or whose **perspective** is this event or story being told?

Is this argument supported with strong **claims and evidence**?

Is this text **reliable**?

What do I already know about this subject that might help me understand this text?

You'll dive deeper into these questions over the next few pages as you practice them with different nonfiction pieces. While you consider and practice these questions, they will become the lens with which you view nonfiction. Analyzing text in this way will become as natural as reading left to right.

THERE ARE LOTS OF PLACES YOU CAN FIND NONFICTION.

- Magazines
- Newspapers
- Textbooks
- Primary documents (such as excerpts from legal documents, speeches, and other pieces of text that come to us directly from the event)
- Books created to share factual information about a particular topic
- Biographies and autobiographies
- Internet sources and materials

DIFFERENT TYPES OF NONFICTION

Nonfiction comes in all shapes and sizes. The first step in reading nonfiction is to recognize it and to name the category it mostly falls into, mostly because writers are sly creatures who sometimes merge different types of nonfiction into one piece of writing. You can begin by separating nonfiction into two main categories: literary and informational.

LITERARY NONFICTION

Literary nonfiction is written to engage and to spark emotion. It expresses feelings and opinions. You will likely notice more sensory detail in this type of nonfiction. That's because the writer is working to make sure you *feel* as though you are right there with them.

Forms of literary nonfiction include:

- Biography
- Autobiography
- Essays
- Opinion pieces
- Argument
- Exposition (writing that explains something)
- Letters
- Journals and diaries

INFORMATIONAL NONFICTION

Informational nonfiction is written to tell you something, or, um, to *inform* you.

Forms of informational nonfiction include:

- History books and articles
- Textbooks
- Pamphlets (thin, small books with paper covers)
- Newspapers
- Manuals
- How-to books
- Travel articles

TEXT FEATURES

Generally, informational text will include lots of **text features** to help you. Text features are elements that break down the information into smaller pieces. They organize the ideas and even illustrate some of them! This book is *absolutely littered* with text features. We even have text features about text features.

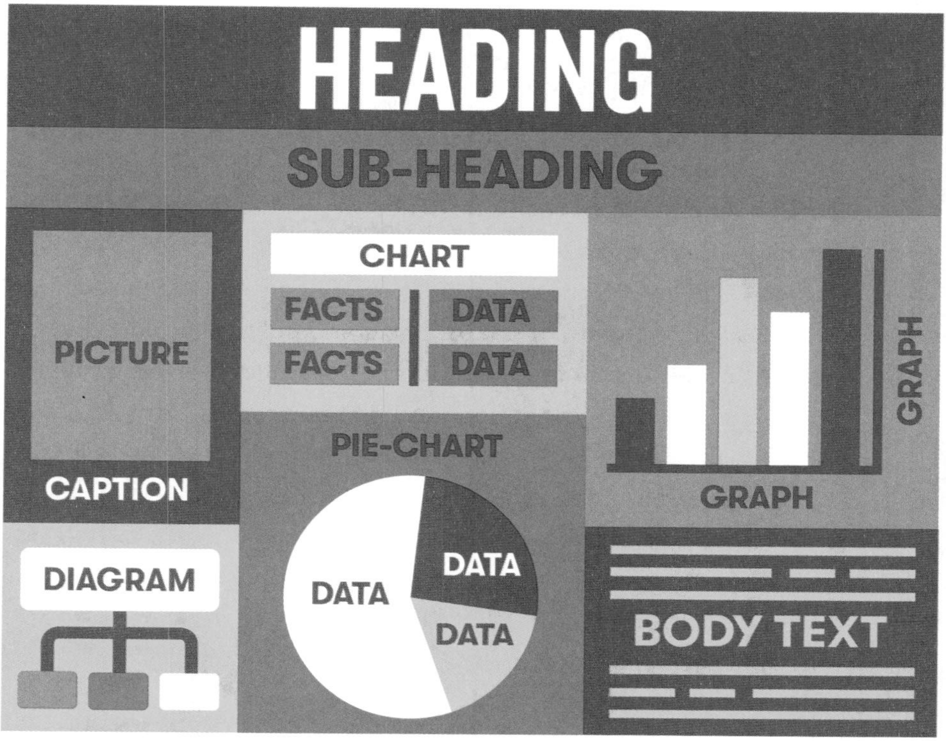

COMPARING LITERARY AND INFORMATIONAL NONFICTION

As someone who has been reading for a few years, you have probably figured out that text features make it so much easier to understand the information. Use them. But don't shy away from literary nonfiction. Informational nonfiction tends to sort out the details for you. It packs in facts and gives some order to the ugly mess that is, say, war. In contrast, literary nonfiction brings in the human-ness of it all. It can remind us why we care.

The two examples below are nonfiction pieces that explain parts of the Holocaust and World War II. As you prepare to read them, think about what you are likely to gain from each one. From the informational piece, you may hope to figure out some dates, specific events, and the places in which they occurred. From the literary piece, you can expect to learn someone's feelings or opinions on the subject.

THE CAMPS

The first camps were constructed in Germany and used by the **Nazi** regime to hold anyone that they wanted to remove from society. The first **concentration camp**, Dachau, was built in March 1933 when Hitler came to power. Others soon followed. They housed a variety of people, including political opponents such as **communists** and members of opposition parties in the former democratic government and Protestant and Catholic clergy who criticized him. Once Hitler started to attack those he believed to be inferior, the occupants of his camps included Jews, gypsies, homosexuals, and Jehovah's Witnesses (a religious sect). Anyone else who was careless enough to make critical remarks in the hearing of Hitler's secret police, the Gestapo, or their spies could also find themselves behind the barbed wire of camps.

By 1942, there were camps for a variety of purposes. As well as the concentration camps, there were forced labor camps and even more horrific, the **death camps**. As the Nazis overran Europe after 1939, the network of camps was extended into all occupied countries.

A VICIOUS ROUTINE

By 1942, there were an estimated 100,000 prisoners in the camps. By January 1945, it is claimed that there were around 700,000. But between 1933 and 1945, thousands more had passed through the camps and thousands had perished. The inmates of concentration and forced labor camps were either starved or worked to death. They could barely exist in the cramped and dirty conditions.

24 THE HOLOCAUST Susan Willoughby

Where do your eyes go first on the page? The title? The **boldfaced** words, or maybe the dates? People often use a quick scan as a first step when approaching nonfiction, looking over and around the page for what stands out and how it's organized. Some standout pieces of information in this nonfiction include:

- Germans built their first concentration camp in March 1933.
- The first people to be forced into these camps were those who opposed Hitler. Later, government officials forced Jews to go there.
- There were about 100,000 prisoners in these camps by 1942.
- By 1945, there were 700,000 prisoners there.
- At forced labor camps, people either worked until death or died from lack of food.

This page provides many **statistics**, or numbers that describe information. There are even some dates. It tells you the number of years the camps existed—more than ten—and the growing numbers of people present at the camps. You also learned that people were dying in these camps, but not how many. In sum, you gathered some facts.

Night by Elie Wiesel is an award-winning piece of literary nonfiction. While it is nonfiction, when you read it, it sounds like a story. It's autobiographical—he wrote it from his own experience about the Holocaust. This moment follows a separation from his father while they are in one of the Nazi camps.

From *Night*, by Elie Wiesel

> I walked for hours without finding him [Father]. Then I came to a block where they were distributing black "coffee." People stood in line, quarreled.
>
> A plaintive voice came behind me:
>
> "Eliezer, my son... bring me... a little coffee..."
>
> I ran toward him.
>
> "Father! I've been looking for you for so long ... Where were you? Did you sleep? How are you feeling?"
>
> He seemed to be burning with fever. I fought my way to the coffee cauldron like a wild beast. And I succeeded in bringing back a cup. I took one gulp. The rest was for him.
>
> I shall never forget the gratitude that shone in his eyes when he swallowed his beverage. The gratitude of a wounded animal. With these few mouthfuls of hot water, I had probably given him more satisfaction than during my entire childhood...

This excerpt from *Night* contains strong emotion. It reads in a style that seems like fiction more than nonfiction, including figurative language and sensory detail. *Figurative language* means words that create a picture in your mind. *Sensory details* are ones related to sight, sound, taste, touch, or smell. Because we know that this is a person's account of the events, told through the use of dialogue, description, and figurative language, we understand that this is literary nonfiction. (*Dialogue* is the term to describe the words people or characters speak to each other.)

Now that you have finished the excerpt, you know certain things:

- Some information about a camp—that food and drink were minimal

But more powerful is:

- A sense of the desperation for those there
- The need for basic supplies
- The camps did not destroy the need and ability for human connection, feeling grateful, and feeling needed and appreciated.
- That the love for family was unbroken

Throughout middle school and life, embrace both categories of nonfiction. They can work together to give you a deep understanding of the world. An informational text tells you facts and figures, while a literary form gives you an idea of how those events affected people in a personal way. Expert students strive for both understandings!

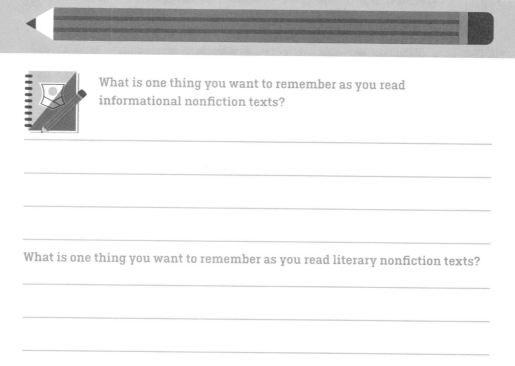

What is one thing you want to remember as you read informational nonfiction texts?

___

___

___

___

What is one thing you want to remember as you read literary nonfiction texts?

___

___

___

IDENTIFYING THE AUTHOR'S PURPOSE AND PERSPECTIVE

Anyone can write nonfiction. There's no special license or permit given to those who write nonfiction well. In fact, sometimes nonfiction may even be more fiction than fact. (You might have heard your family members grumbling about this when it comes to stories and articles about certain political figures.) So it's up to you to determine the value of the nonfiction texts you read. To do this, you will need to skillfully identify useful and reliable information. And here's how!

IDENTIFYING THE AUTHOR'S PURPOSE

After you have identified the type of nonfiction you are reading, ask yourself a very important question:

"WHY ON EARTH DID THE WRITER WRITE THIS?"

In other words: What is the **author's purpose** in writing this piece? When we talk about author's purpose, we are referring to why they wrote this piece—in other words, what they hoped to accomplish with this piece of writing.

Sometimes, a writer might have more than one purpose. Some of these reasons might be:

- **To persuade** or convince you to do something or to agree with a position
- **To inform** (tell) you about a real-world person, place, or thing by giving you some facts
- **To describe** something to you by including lots of details—often details that have to do with your senses
- **To explain or instruct** how to do something or how something is made
- **To compare or contrast** the similarities or differences of two topics
- **To narrate** a story, usually in an order that is chronological (also called time order)
- **To provide a solution** by presenting a problem and describing one or more ways to solve it

Why do we care about an author's purpose for writing a piece? Now that you're older, you have probably realized that things are not always what they seem. Sometimes writers will try to convince you that something is true, even though they have not included evidence for their reasoning.

EXAMINING VALIDITY

As an expert reader, after you have identified the purpose of the piece, you will want to dig beneath the surface of a text. That means you will check the validity of the text you are reading. Validity means the quality of the text. Is this piece accurate? When out in the wild, someone may use a pickaxe to identify what is under the topsoil. After identifying the author's purpose, your pickaxe will help you figure out how valid the text is. Imagine using your pickaxe to pull apart the text, looking for clues that help you identify what's beneath the surface. Is this text something you can really rely on? Is it actually what it seemed to be at first glance?

When you see that an author is trying to **persuade** you of something, right away, you can start searching the text for evidence. Great evidence will come in the form of facts that cannot be disputed and statistics. Keep in mind that some examples are just that—examples. They may not tell the whole story.

And when you notice that the author is **informing** you, check their facts. Did they include important facts and details? Is this information accurate, to the best of your knowledge? Can you use other sources to confirm it (in other words, show that it is correct)?

So many writers love to **describe** details. Make sure you are monitoring the relevance of those details. *Relevance* means relatedness. For instance, information about the writer's aunt may be funny without being related to the topic at hand.

Authors who **explain** how to do something or how something is made usually want to be clear. But are they? Check for clarity.

Often you will see that a piece of writing is **comparing or contrasting** two items, ideas, or events. Check to make sure that the similarities and differences make sense. Certain shopping websites like to compare items for us, but sometimes they have a bias—they're trying to persuade us to buy one thing instead of another. The same thing can hold true for comparison writing or contrast writing.

Narrative nonfiction is usually pretty engaging because it reads like a story. As you read, make sure that you know the difference between the parts that are subjective retelling and the parts that are more objective. Subjective means related to a person's own experiences and feelings. In a subjective retelling, the author's views and understandings, and their interest in engaging you, are driving the prose. The objective parts have dates and details that you can fact-check later.

And last, when reading a **solution to a problem**, treat it the same way you treat persuasive writing. Search for evidence, and check the trustworthiness of that evidence.

NOW YOU TRY!

On the next spread, there's a magazine article about food waste in schools that appeared in *Time for Kids*. From just this excerpt, can you determine the author's purpose in writing it?

WASTE *NOT*

April 19, 2019 | Shay Maunz

According to the U.S. Department of Agriculture (USDA), about $1.2 billion worth of school food is wasted every school year. Wasted food is money. It's also a missed opportunity to feed hungry people. And it's bad for the environment: Farming, packaging, and transporting food produces greenhouse-gas emissions, which pollute the air. Plus, food packaging often ends up in a landfill.

FIGHTING FOOD WASTE

Schools have developed strategies to cut back on waste. Since students are often hungrier after active play, scheduling lunch after recess can reduce the amount of food that's wasted by 30%, according to the USDA. Making lunch period longer also helps. It gives kids time to eat everything on their tray.

Many school districts follow government regulations requiring students to take a certain number of healthy food items at mealtime. Those rules were designed to ensure that kids get a balanced meal. But making kids take food they don't want leads to more waste.

That's why the Oakland Unified School District set up something called a share table. Students place untouched food on the table, and a student who wants it can take it. There are rules in place to make sure all food on a share table is safe for students to eat.

Clean, fully uneaten food that isn't taken from the share table is returned to the kitchen to be served another day. If the food can't be reused at school, it is donated to a charity. Food scraps that can't be reused are turned into compost. "It's about recognizing that food has value," [Nancy] Deming says. [Deming is the sustainability manager for the Oakland Unified School District.] Strategies like this have made Oakland a leader in the movement to reduce food waste.

TASTE TEST

Another reason students waste food is that they don't like how it tastes. Chef Sam Icklan wants to change that. He works with a program in Massachusetts called Chefs in Schools, which helps cafeteria staff develop recipes kids enjoy, using healthy ingredients. While working on recipes, Icklan conducts taste tests with students.

"It became this beautiful, vibrant dish that was delicious and packed with vegetables," Icklan says. "Who wouldn't eat that?"

"If they like it, great. If they don't, we keep working to find something they do," he told TFK.

In one school where kale often went uneaten, Icklan developed a recipe for pizza topped with kale, zucchini, and spinach. He called it Green Monster Pizza. Students polished it off. "It became this beautiful, vibrant dish that was delicious and packed with vegetables," Icklan says. "Who wouldn't eat that?"

JOIN THE FIGHT

You can fight food waste too. At the grocery store, look for "ugly" produce. Fruits and vegetables with irregular shapes are just as tasty as perfect ones but often go to waste. When choosing food at home, read safety labels. If a label says "best before," the food is still safe to eat for a little while after that date. (If the label says "use by," the food is no longer safe after that date.) At mealtime, start with small portions. If you're still hungry, you can take more later. And when you don't eat food, don't throw it away. Turn it into compost instead.

Let's first identify some facts. Jot down facts here:

____

____

____

____

Perhaps your list of facts looks something like this:

- A *lot* of school food gets thrown in the trash—$1.2 billion worth every year.
- Uneaten food wastes money.
- Uneaten food could be used to feed hungry people.
- Food waste harms the environment.

____

After reading just the title and first paragraph, you may feel quite informed about the harmful effects of food waste. So does that mean that the author wrote this to *inform* you? That paragraph certainly makes it seem so. But before you pass full judgment, pull out that pickaxe and take a closer look.

What's that in paragraph 5? **"Strategies like this have made Oakland a leader in the movement to reduce food waste."** *Suddenly, it seems as if the writer is trying to persuade you that there is a better way to manage food waste.* This brings up a new question: Can an informational text be persuasive? Or can a persuasive text be informational? Did this author pull a "bait and switch," reeling you in with a bunch of information only to persuade you and other readers to change your behavior? Why, yes, it does seem so. Now, you have a decision to make. Is the information that the writer chose to persuade you *valid*? Were you convinced? It's up to you!

The beauty in all this is that now you are ultra-informed. You understand not only the information that the writer is presenting, but how they are presenting it to you. That understanding is a kind of superpower. And now you can decide how you will respond to and work with the text.

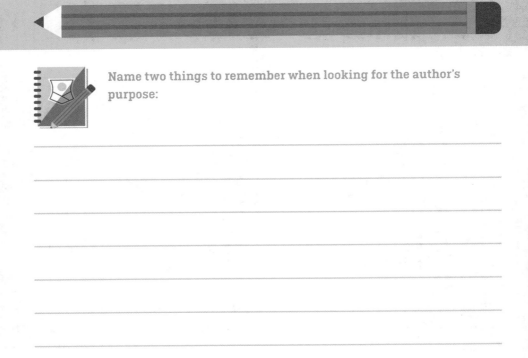

Name two things to remember when looking for the author's purpose:

SPOTTING AUTHOR BIAS

You've heard the saying, "There are two sides to every story." Well, guess what? There are more than two. Maybe hundreds. Or a gazillion. The numbers don't matter here—just the simple fact that writers, whether they want to or not, speak from a position or **perspective**.

As we critically examine a nonfiction text, we will consider the author's perspective. While we seek unbiased information, we must remember that we all have bias, writers included. Sometimes this is good. For example, it's great that some writers work to tell the story of the underdog, the lesser-known story. In other cases, it's not so good. We probably all know examples of how bias can work against members of minority races, or poor people, or people who come from other countries. Sometimes, a writer with a bias aims to convince us that his or her view is *the only* view. As a middle schooler with rapidly developing instincts for all that is amiss, you will not be fooled. Just do not forget to pull out your tools and use them:

From what or whose point of view is this story, idea, or event being told?

- Who benefits from this version of the story?
- Whose concerns are being represented?
- Whose concerns are *not* being represented?

WHOSE SIDE ARE YOU ON?

Or try it this way: ask yourself whose side this author would be on if the parties in the text were having a boxing match.

Here's one historian's account of the events that occurred as Christopher Columbus landed in the Americas. This is from *A Young People's History of the United States: Columbus to the War on Terror* by Howard Zinn, adapted by Rebecca Steffof.

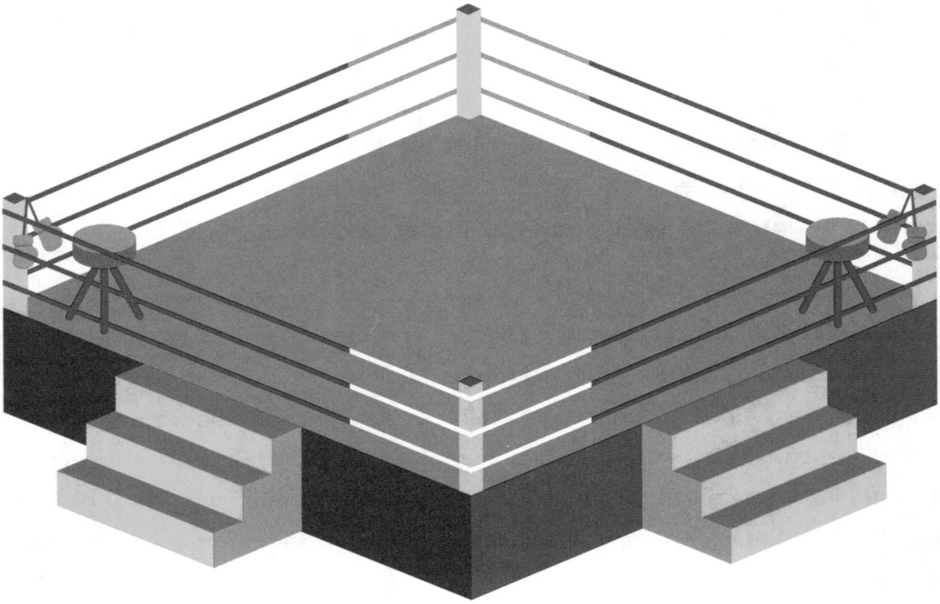

> The Arawak Indians who greeted Columbus lived in villages and practiced agriculture. Unlike the Europeans, they had no horses or other work animals, and they had no iron. What they did have was tiny gold ornaments in their ears.
>
> Those little ornaments shaped history. Because of them, Columbus started his relationship with the Indians by taking prisoners, thinking that they could lead him to the source of the gold.

Let's test out this boxing match theory. If Christopher Columbus is on one side of the ring, and the Arawak Indians are on the other, for whom is this author rooting?

GATHERING EVIDENCE TO SUPPORT PERSPECTIVE

CLUES THAT THIS AUTHOR IS ROOTING FOR THE ARAWAK INDIANS	EXPLANATION
"greeted Columbus"	Using the word "greeted" indicates that the Arawak were welcoming people.
"they had no iron"	The author is making it clear that the Arawak did not have advanced weaponry.
"Columbus started his relationship with the Indians by taking prisoners"	Columbus imprisoned Arawak people right from the start.
"thinking that they could lead him to the source of the gold"	Columbus wants gold, implying greed.

Once you've determined the perspective of the text, you have power over it. You can weigh the relevance and importance of that position. You can ask yourself deeper questions about what you read in texts that show other perspectives. You may look for texts that share other perspectives, and you may adjust your ideas about the reliability of the text. By simply understanding whose story is being told, or who is telling this story, you have strengthened your critical eye until it has hawklike vision.

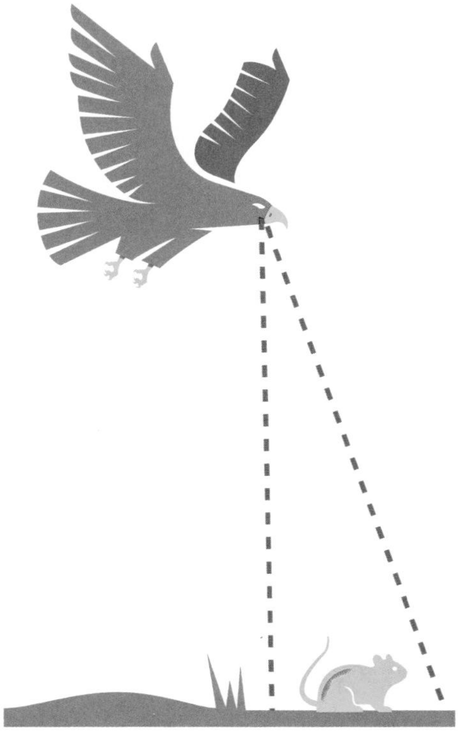

Why is it important to figure out an author's or text's perspective?

IDENTIFYING AND EVALUATING THE CLAIMS AND EVIDENCE

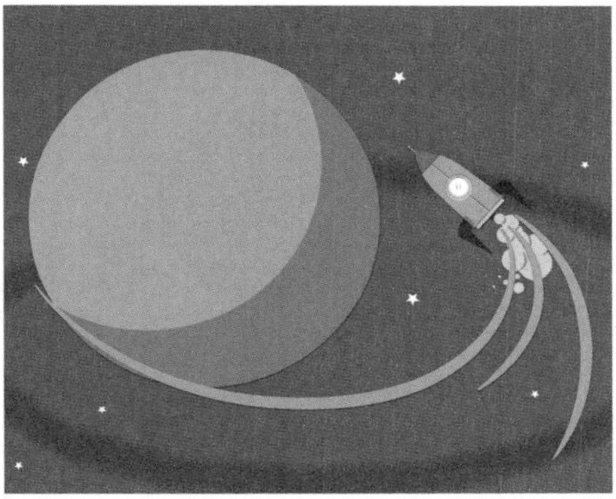

Now that you've established the writer's perspective, it's time to look for the **evidence**. In a text, evidence is the proof of the writer's **claim**—a statement that is presented as truth. Evidence is facts and details that help to prove something is true. Evidence may be quotations, statistics, facts, or events.

As expert, earthly navigators, let's explore the question: Should humans go to Mars?

First, let's orient ourselves to the question. Already, we see a yes-or-no question. This implies that someone is going to make an argument or claim. The person making that claim is arguing that it is a fact, so they had better use some great evidence to get us to believe them. Sometimes, a writer will acknowledge the opposing side of an argument—and show why it is wrong! This technique of introducing the opposing view and disproving it is called a **counterclaim**.

Back to our question at hand:

Should humans go to Mars?

EXAMINING AN ARGUMENT

Breakfast on Mars: Why We Should Colonize the Red Planet (Part 1, Argument)

The author's claim is: yes, humans should go to Mars.

Now let's see if this author supports this claim with solid evidence.

When we look back at the twentieth century, there's one obvious milestone that stands out for our species as a whole: We left Earth for the first time and even sent people to the moon. (Though only a dozen walked on the surface, and they were all men.) **In the twenty-first century, Mars can and should be our next milestone...**

In 1962, President John F. Kennedy, Jr., gave a speech at Rice University that kicked off the race to put men on the moon. JFK told the American people we should go to the moon, "not because [it is] easy, but because [it is] hard." As a society, we need to challenge ourselves to do what is hard in order to make progress. If we simply choose the easy stuff, we'll never achieve anything great. Getting to the moon was arduous—**eight American astronauts died in training accidents.**

Wait, what's this? This writer was arguing that sending people to Mars is a good thing. But before he even gives his evidence, he tells us that eight people died in training for the lunar landing. That doesn't seem to support his argument.

This must be a counterclaim where the writer introduces the opposing view. People were killed, so this is a pretty serious counterclaim!

But what we gained from the mission to the moon was immense: safety gear for firefighters and race car drivers, freeze-dried food used for soldiers' rations, and even technology that powers credit card transactions. We had no idea all those inventions would spring from the lunar missions, but now they're part of daily life.

I can check my idea that this is a counterclaim by looking for a place where the writer begins to disprove this counterargument.

There it is! That's some evidence that the counterclaim is outweighed by the author's argument.

Evidence #1. It will spur new inventions.

What's more, Americans were inspired by the challenge of putting men on the moon, and that inspiration drove a generation of innovators to try what was previously thought impossible...

As we look to the future, we need to plan for our children, and their children, and there simply isn't enough room on Earth to keep growing as we have. **By establishing a colony on Mars, we open up an entire planet's worth of room for people to live. This is the single best land investment we can make, especially since there is hardly any unclaimed land left on Earth, no stretch of new frontier into which we can explore. Mars is there for the taking.**

Evidence #2. There will be more room on Earth for humans.

And what's most enticing is that we could actually put humans on Mars within a few decades. Elon Musk (creator of PayPal and founder of the space exploration company SpaceX) says he plans to retire on Mars. His retirement is only about twenty years away. It's easy to imagine what this means—people will be on Mars, and soon. Wouldn't you like to be one of them?

—Chris Higgins

And at the end of our own voyage into this author's claim, we see that he brought us back to his original claim!

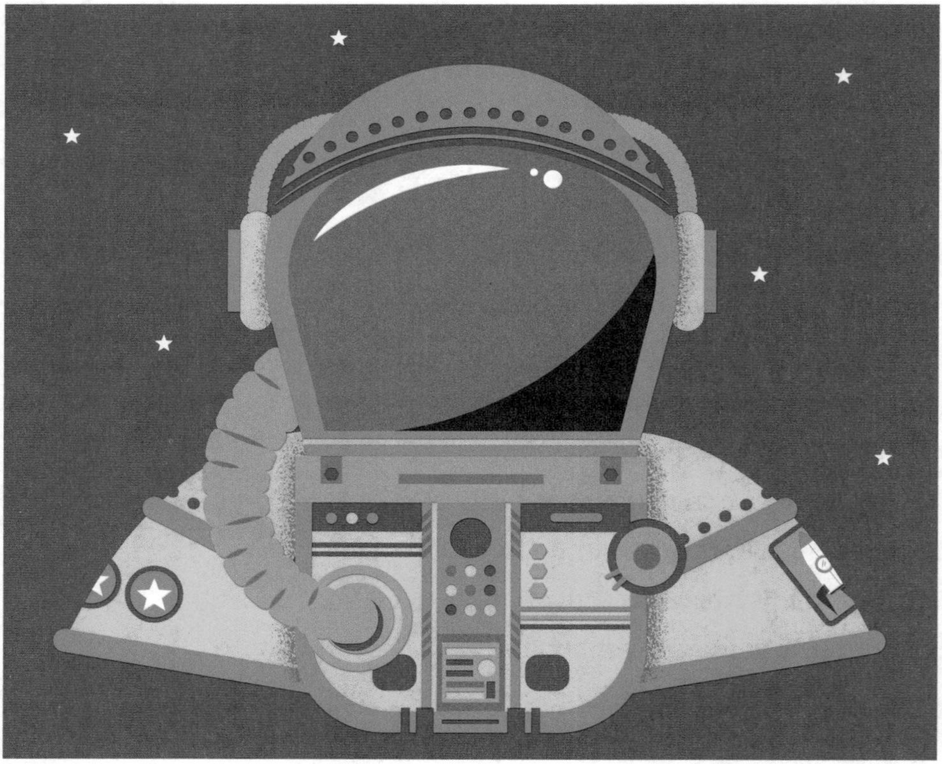

Let's huddle up. What do you think about Chris Higgins's claim that humans should go to Mars? Did his evidence convince you?

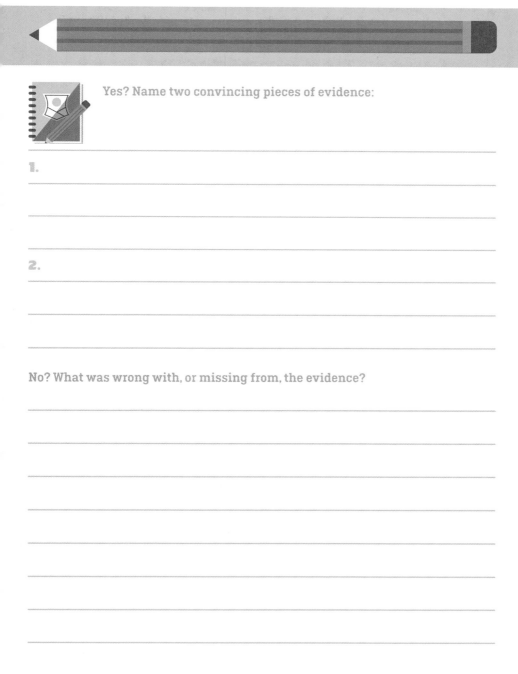

Yes? Name two convincing pieces of evidence:

1.

2.

No? What was wrong with, or missing from, the evidence?

Navigating the seas of the argument can be tumultuous. Regarding Mr. Higgins's argument, you might want to say "maybe." That's OK.

Huh? Here you are in a forest of claims and evidence, and you don't know what way is north. How can that be good? Well, as you wrap up your journey into nonfiction, remember that in the world of nonfiction, you can always check for *reliability* (keep reading for more on this).

CHECKING SOURCES FOR RELIABILITY

The **reliability** of a text is the degree to which people can trust it as a source. You already know how to identify the author's purpose and perspective in a text—those are important steps in determining reliability! If a text is valid, it's more likely to be reliable. If a text is unfairly biased, it is probably not reliable. But there's a lot more to it than that! To check for reliability, you need to learn more about the text you're evaluating.

- **Author's purpose**: Is this text written to express a view, to get you to buy something, to offer knowledge, or for entertainment?
- **Author**: Can you identify the person who wrote this? What about an editor who organized this? What is their potential bias?
- **Dates**: Can you find a year of publication? Is the text older than you are?
- **Sources**: Does this writer refer to other sources? Are those sources current?
- **Publisher**: Who produced this information? If it is from a website, what kind of website is it?

Since you may not have been fully convinced we should pack our space travel bags and get on a rocket ship to Mars, let's keep exploring. The essay we just read is actually from a book of essays, and this writer argued both sides of the question. We haven't gotten to the "con" side yet—that sending people to Mars is unwise. Let's take a look at that now.

Robots Only: Why We Shouldn't Colonize Mars (Part 2, Counterpoint)

Everyone is curious about Mars, our red neighbor in the solar system. We want to know how much water is there, and we want to dig into Martian rocks, looking for fossils of life that may have existed in the distant past. It is true that to get this information, we need to have some presence on the ground there. But just because we're curious about a place does not mean we should try to colonize it...

As I write this essay (in early 2012), two robotic rovers are already sitting on Mars, hibernating during the Martian winter. The twin rovers are called Spirit and Opportunity, and they arrived on Mars way back in January 2004. They were designed for a mission lasting only 90 sols (days are called "sols" on Mars), but the rovers lasted far longer than expected—Spirit finally failed in 2010 (six years after its initial mission ended), and Opportunity is still running. These two rovers, along with satellites armed with cameras and other gear, have given us an up-close view of Mars—something we can't do well using telescopes on Earth. And what's remarkable is that they've done the job cheaply, by space exploration standards. Spirit and Opportunity have so far cost about $900 million, which is the cost of two shuttle launches.

This essay is inspired by the scholarly paper "Fast, Cheap and Out of Control: A Robot Invasion of the Solar System" by MIT scientists Rodney A. Brooks and Anita M. Flynn, published in the *Journal of the British Interplanetary Society*, vol. 42, pp.478–485, 1989. Please read the paper for more specifics on building robots for space exploration.

The most costly parts of space missions are building things to send into space, and then launching them. Humans are very heavy—we're basically big, weighty bags of water—and the life-support systems needed to keep us alive are heavy too. We need food, we need liquid, and we need air to breathe. But robots don't have lives that need support, and they can be built at any imaginable size or weight. Furthermore, designing life-support systems for long-term human colonies requires lots of unbelievably expensive experiments. The enormous Biosphere 2 experiment in Arizona (3.14 acres in size—the same number as pi) was partly envisioned as one such test for a human settlement on Mars. Yet, after twenty years in operation, it is now considered a massive failure…

Sending humans to Mars and building a settlement for them would be a colossal waste of money and would entail terrible danger for our astronauts, our space program, and our own planet. Earth is our home, and here we should stay. But we can—and should—send our robot emissaries to Mars and beyond, to learn and to send back pictures, sounds, and data of places where human feet may never tread.

—Chris Higgins

Now that you've read both sides, consider the reliability of the essays by whipping out your *reliability checklist*. You'll need to know things like publication date and sources, so look around for that information as well.

MY RELIABILITY CHECKLIST

QUESTION	YES	NO	NOTES
Can you find a date of publication?	x		I see in the second paragraph that it was written in 2012. Older publications can have out-of-date information or views. This is somewhat recent, but I might want to check newer sources as well.
Did the author(s) cite any sources?	x		Yes, he cites an article by an expert.
Can you identify the author's purpose?	x		To show two sides of an argument—encouraging us to agree or disagree as to whether humans should go to Mars.
Can we identify the author?	x		There is just one. We don't know much about his background. I might want to see what experts like the scientists at NASA have to say about this subject as well.
Is there an identifiable publisher?	x		Both essays were published in a book by a mainstream publisher.

Overall, these two pieces look reliable. Two sides of an argument are presented. They both use valid logic. There's an authoritative source cited. What's a nonfiction reader to do to determine what to believe?

(A) Read more.

(B) Use your good judgment.

(C) Accept that sometimes there are no clear answers.

(D) Any or all of the above

The correct answer is—drumroll please—D! The world is full of nuance. It's beautiful and confusing and annoying and comforting. Often, there is no one right answer, and that's the real truth about nonfiction!

TAKING YOUR NONFICTION SKILLS INTO THE REAL WORLD

You can put some of these skills to use right now! Take a look at the text below. It's from the introduction to a book called *Made You Look* by Shari Graydon, and it was published in 2012. As you read it, you will want to find answers to the following questions:

- What type of nonfiction is this?
- What is the author's purpose?
- From what perspective or position was this piece written?
- Are there strong claims and evidence?
- Is this text reliable?

Ads Unlimited—from *Made You Look*, by Shari Graydon

People in Ghana, a country in West Africa, have a saying: *To the fish, the water is invisible.* In other words, when you're surrounded by something all the time, you don't notice it. You take it for granted and assume that it's natural, or that it's always been there. You don't think about whether it's good or bad, or how it's affecting your life.

In parts of the world where people have a lot of modern conveniences and up-to-date technology, you could say that advertising has become "the water in which we swim." There's so much of it that we hardly notice it anymore. In fact, some experts estimate that a young person growing up in North America is likely to see between 20,000 and 40,000 TV commercials every year. When you add in all the advertisements from other media—up to 16,000 a day!—it's easy to see how you'd begin to stop noticing, and just keep swimming.

ASKED AND ANSWERED

QUESTION	YOUR THOUGHTS OR ANSWERS	EVIDENCE FOR YOUR ANSWER
What type of nonfiction is this?		
What is the author's purpose?		
From what perspective or position was this piece written?		
Are there strong claims and evidence?		
Is this text reliable?		

As you worked to understand this nonfiction piece, what was pretty easy? What was more difficult?

CHAPTER 3 VOCABULARY

author's purpose: why someone wrote a piece of nonfiction

bias: thoughts or opinions that can consciously or unconsciously push you toward one side of an issue or argument

claim: the basis of an argument; a statement that the writer believes is true

counterclaim: the technique of introducing the opposing view to the writer's own and disproving it is called a counterclaim

evidence: proof of the writer's claim—may be quotations, statistics, facts, or events

nonfiction: text that is about real events and people; nonfiction includes:

> **informational nonfiction:** factual information mainly meant to inform and teach, such as textbooks or manuals
>
> **literary nonfiction:** nonfiction written to bring up emotions, with tools such as sensory details helping the writer express feelings and opinions

reliability: how trustworthy something is

statistics: numbers that show patterns or changes or that provide information about larger issues

text features: elements such as headings, charts, and graphs that help you organize information, break down information into smaller pieces, or emphasize the most important points

4 PICTURES FROM WORDS: READING POETRY

The world of poetry is vast. As you move through this world of rhyme and form, you undoubtedly will find a poem that speaks to you. This chapter will help you read poems with a critical eye. But here's the real secret: Expertly reading poems is going to help you expertly examine all texts. The poetic devices in poetry are also woven into fiction and nonfiction. So while you are becoming a more sophisticated reader of poetry, you are also becoming an expert at recognizing the poetry hidden within prose.

CHAPTER CONTENTS

HOW TO UNDERSTAND POETRY

Sometimes people think that poetry isn't for them. They may get intimidated by poems. Here's a little secret: There are poems for everyone, and poetry can be appreciated by everyone. Each of us brings our own experiences and knowledge to the poems we read.

Poets brilliantly craft poems so that every reader may see something different in them. Our goal is to get as much from each poem as we can. To do this, we look at the elements of poetry, peeling back layers of meaning until we have our own informed interpretation of the words on the page.

Let's start with this poem by Maya Angelou.

> **Caged Bird**
> by Maya Angelou
>
> A free bird leaps
> on the back of the wind
> and floats downstream
> till the current ends
> and dips his wing
> in the orange sun rays
> and dares to claim the sky.
>
> But a bird that stalks
> down his narrow cage
> can seldom see through

his bars of rage
his wings are clipped and
his feet are tied
so he opens his throat to sing.

The caged bird sings
with a fearful trill
of things unknown
but longed for still
and his tune is heard
on the distant hill
for the caged bird
sings of freedom.

The free bird thinks of another breeze
and the trade winds soft through the sighing trees
and the fat worms waiting on a dawn bright lawn
and he names the sky his own
But a caged bird stands on the grave of dreams
his shadow shouts on a nightmare scream
his wings are clipped and his feet are tied
so he opens his throat to sing.

The caged bird sings
with a fearful trill
of things unknown
but longed for still
and his tune is heard
on the distant hill
for the caged bird
sings of freedom.

Imagery is a poetic device where the poet uses words to create pictures in your mind. When you read this poem, what do you "see"?

Or, if you'd like, sketch what you "see":

Perhaps you visualized something like this:

UNDERSTANDING FIGURATIVE LANGUAGE

When Maya Angelou uses words such as "narrow cage" and "fat worms waiting on a dawn bright lawn," you can imagine a picture. Writers might also include details that appeal to your other senses, such as smell or taste, when creating sensory details.

But is this poem really just about a bird stuck inside a cage? What if the bird represents something else? And the cage? When analyzing poetry, we call this **figurative language**—ways writers use words to mean something more than their literal meaning, helping the reader to gain new insights into the topic.

EXAMPLES OF FIGURATIVE LANGUAGE

EXAMPLE	**I saw red.**
LITERAL MEANING OF EXAMPLE	My eyes noticed a color.
FIGURATIVE MEANING OF EXAMPLE	I was furious.
EXAMPLE	**I was stuck in a cage.**
LITERAL MEANING OF EXAMPLE	Metal bars surrounded me.
FIGURATIVE MEANING OF EXAMPLE	I felt trapped and confined.

Figurative language can include metaphor, simile, and symbolism. Let's look at each of these terms, one at a time.

METAPHOR

A **metaphor** is a comparison. When the writer compares an idea to something else, when the object or action written in the poem actually represents another idea, that is a metaphor. When you think about it like that, could a bird in a cage be a metaphor? Could these words represent a bigger idea?

What if the poet wants that bird to represent a person who is not allowed to move about freely or express himself or herself freely, and the cage represents that which oppresses the bird? This is just one theory, and there is no single "correct" interpretation of a poem. Still, we can get a deeper understanding of the poem by using our pickaxe to look for evidence that supports what we think the poem is saying.

UNDERSTANDING METAPHORS

WHAT THE METAPHOR MIGHT REPRESENT	EVIDENCE	EXPLANATION
In this metaphor, the bird in the cage could represent a person who is oppressed.	"... a bird that stalks / down his narrow cage / can seldom see through / his bars of rage"	The reference to the bars of rage shows us that there is anger about being in the narrow cage.
	"his wings are clipped and / his feet are tied"	The clipped wings and feet tied indicate that a human is responsible for the caged bird's situation. We know that humans oppress other humans.

SIMILE

Other poems use **simile**, a comparison that uses the words "like" or "as." Looking at similes and metaphors side by side can give you a sense of the different impact of each.

SIMILE	METAPHOR
Hope is *like* a spring day.	Hope is a spring day.
He is as hungry *as* a lion searching for prey.	He is a hungry lion searching for prey.
Now try writing a few of your own.	
Love is like ...	Love is...
School is like...	School is...

Here is part of a poem that has both metaphor and simile. Can you find them?

I Am Who I Am, So What

by Raquel Valle Sentíes

(Translated from the Spanish by Raquel Valle Sentíes)

I'm a grafted flower that didn't
take, a Mexican without being one,
an American without feeling like one.

The music of my people fills me.
The huapangos, rancheras,
and the Mexican National Anthem
give me goose bumps, a lump
in my throat. They make my feet tap
to the beat. But I feel as if I'm wearing
a borrowed hat.

Mexicans stare as if saying,
"You're not a Mexican!"...

As you read poems and other texts, you may come across words that you don't know, especially if you are reading about a culture other than your own, or reading a translation from a different language, like the poem above. You can always start by using your tricky word solutions and using definitions, synonyms, antonyms and inferences to figure out the meaning, but sometimes you might need to look further. It's a good idea to try searching online or in a dictionary (you can find dictionaries that translate from a different language to English)! In the poem above, you might need to look up words like:

Huapango: a Mexican folk dance and music style
Ranchera: a genre of the traditional music of rural Mexico

ANALYZING A METAPHOR OR SIMILE

LINE FROM THE POEM	SIMILE OR METAPHOR?	AN EXPLANATION
"I'm a grafted flower that didn't / take,"	Metaphor	A gardener creates a grafted flower by joining two plants, taking a cutting from one and attaching it to another plant to make something new. She feels like a person who was pieced together but didn't grow, perhaps wilted.
"But I feel as if I'm wearing / a borrowed hat."	Simile	A hat is a personal item of clothing that can express the wearer's personality. If she feels as if she's wearing a borrowed hat, she's letting us know that she doesn't feel comfortable in that activity.

How are metaphor and simile similar? How are they different? Is there a reason a poet may choose to use one or the other?

SYMBOLISM

When a writer uses an object to represent an idea or a quality, that is called **symbolism**. Sound familiar? Metaphor is a type of symbolism. We can return to Maya Angelou's poem to look at how to unpack symbolism and adapt our original question: Is this poem really just about a bird stuck inside a cage?

New questions:

- Is the caged bird *really* a bird?
- Is the cage *really* just a birdcage?
- What ideas might these objects represent?

EXPLORING SYMBOLS

SYMBOLS	LINE OR LINES FROM TEXT	POSSIBLE MEANINGS
Bird	"The caged bird sings / with a fearful trill / of things unknown / but longed for still" "for the caged bird sings of freedom"	A person The person has both fear and hope. Maya Angelou—is this autobiographical? Is this a commentary on the Black experience in America? The person wants freedom.
Cage	"can seldom see through his bars of rage" "for the caged bird / sings of freedom"	Oppression Slavery and systemic racism

In this poem, the poet has woven a symbol throughout. To identify it, keep your eye out for an object.

> **Mother to Son**
>
> by Langston Hughes
>
> Well, son, I'll tell you:
> Life for me ain't been no crystal stair.
> It's had tacks in it,
> And splinters,
> And boards torn up,
> And places with no carpet on the floor—
> Bare.
> But all the time
> I'se been a-climbin' on,
> And reachin' landin's,
> And turnin' corners,
> And sometimes goin' in the dark
> Where there ain't been no light.
> So boy, don't you turn back.
> Don't you set down on the steps
> 'Cause you finds it's kinder hard.
> Don't you fall now—
> For I'se still goin', honey,
> I'se still climbin',
> And life for me ain't been no crystal stair.

You probably noticed that the "crystal stair" is an object that stands out in this poem, and you probably found yourself wondering if the speaker is *really* talking about a crystal stair.

Get out your pickaxe to dig through the lines, so you can see what ideas may be underneath this object.

SYMBOLS	LINE OR LINES FROM TEXT	POSSIBLE MEANINGS
Crystal stair	"Life for me ain't been no crystal stair."	Comparing life to a crystal staircase—but not her life. Since crystal is a delicate and expensive type of glass, we get the sense that a crystal staircase is something that would be beautiful to walk on, to go up. The crystal stair symbolizes the easy path or access that some people in society get. **Dig a little deeper to get ideas as to who uses the crystal stair and who in our society uses the torn-up, splintered staircase. This poem is making some big observations about the world!**

How does digging into the symbolism of the crystal stair help you understand the poem's message? The speaker is climbing a different type of stair—one with hardships such as tacks and splinters. She keeps going, but she recognizes the injustice. Not only do you better understand the poem, but also you begin to learn about the world and people's experiences in it. Recognizing and interpreting symbols makes you a better reader—a reader who sees beyond the words in front of you.

UNDERSTANDING LITERARY DEVICES

As you can see, poets often use colorful, artful expressions. Aside from figurative language, another category of poetic devices are literary devices. These are ways writers convey meaning through creative language. We've already talked about imagery, which is one **literary device** that helps readers visualize the text. But there are a lot more you can try!

THE ART OF HYPERBOLE

We all exaggerate sometimes. In other words, we make statements that heighten or overstate reality. You might say something like, "I am so hungry I could eat a horse!" Writers have a fancy word they use to describe this device: **hyperbole**.

The poem below is filled with hyperbole. You may be aware something is going on with the language as you read, and when you get to the end you know for sure that it's a poem of hyperbole.

Louder Than a Clap of Thunder

by Jack Prelutsky

Louder than a clap of thunder,
louder than an eagle screams,
louder than a dragon blunders,
or a dozen football teams,
louder than a four alarmer,
or a rushing waterfall,
louder than a knight in armor
jumping from a ten-foot wall.

Louder than an earthquake rumbles,
louder than a tidal wave,
louder than an ogre grumbles,
as he stumbles through his cave,
louder than stampeding cattle,
louder than a cannon roars,
louder than a giant's rattle,
that's how loud my father SNORES!

There's no way a man snores louder than a cannon! Prelutsky has used hyperbole to poke fun at a snoring dad. The tone there is happy and silly. Could a writer use hyperbole to push forward other emotions and more serious ideas?

"Perhaps the World Ends Here" by Joy Harjo offers us a different look at hyperbole. You'll notice some metaphor too. Read the poem, underlining examples of hyperbole, metaphor, and any other poetic device you see. Take notes on the side to record your ideas and questions.

Perhaps the World Ends Here

by Joy Harjo

The world begins at a kitchen table. No matter what, we must eat to live.

Hyperbole-the world begins at the kitchen table.

The gifts of earth are brought and prepared, set on the table. So it has been since creation, and it will go on.

Could this also be an exaggeration? Have kitchen tables existed since the beginning of humankind? Do all gifts from nature get placed on the kitchen table?

We chase chickens or dogs away from it. Babies teethe at the corners. They scrape their knees under it.

The poet returns to everyday experience, using imagery to help us visualize the table.

It is here that children are given instructions on what it means to be human. We make men at it, we make women.

At this table we gossip, recall enemies and the ghosts of lovers.

Our dreams drink coffee with us as they put their arms around our children. They laugh with us at our poor falling-down selves and as we put ourselves back together once again at the table.

This table has been a house in the rain, an umbrella in the sun.

Metaphor showing how the table—a place where we come together—protects us from the world.

So if the kitchen table is a metaphor, what does it represent?

Wars have begun and ended at this table. It is a place to hide in the shadow of terror. A place to celebrate the terrible victory.

We have given birth on this table, and have prepared our parents for burial here.

At this table we sing with joy, with sorrow. We pray of suffering and remorse. We give thanks.

Perhaps the world will end at the kitchen table, while we are laughing and crying, eating of the last sweet bite.

When you think about Joy Harjo's first line, how does her use of hyperbole feel compared to "Louder Than a Clap of Thunder"?

As you read the rest of the poem, what is Joy Harjo really saying about a kitchen table? Is she speaking about ideas bigger than a table? What could those ideas be?

ANALYZING POETIC DEVICES

Poetic devices help turn language into art. We can paint with all sorts of colors, but when an artist adds certain techniques, such as shapes, lines, and shadows, that paint turns into artwork—something that brings out many emotions. The same thing happens when a writer uses poetic devices—the words become artful.

You have seen a few poetic devices in action, including figurative language and literary devices. But there are many more. Here's a quick reference list.

POETIC DEVICES YOU SHOULD KNOW

FIGURATIVE LANGUAGE

Ways writers use words to mean something more than their literal meaning, which helps the reader gain new insights into the topic

LITERARY TERM	EXPLANATION	EXAMPLE
Metaphor	A comparison that uses an object in place of an idea	He has a heart of stone.
Simile	A comparison that uses an object in place of an idea and uses "like" or "as"	Brave as a lion
Symbolism	When an object is being used to represent something other than itself	Writers and visual artists often use an apple to represent education or a dove to represent peace.

LITERARY DEVICES

Ways writers convey meaning through creative language

LITERARY TERM	EXPLANATION	EXAMPLE
Imagery	Descriptive language that appeals to any of the five senses	The sparkling city lights were reflected in the river that moved below it.
Hyperbole	An exaggeration	I told you a million times to clean your room!
Personification	The writer gives human characteristics to a non-human object.	The last piece of coconut cake was calling her name.
Repetition	The writer draws attention by repeating words, phrases, or lines.	The mother said to her child, "I love you, I love you, I love you."
Allusion	A writer alludes (or refers) to another literary work.	You poor Cinderella, being forced to clear your plate from the table!

SOUND DEVICES

Ways writers affect the sound of their texts

LITERARY TERM	EXPLANATION	EXAMPLE
Alliteration	Two or more words have the same beginning consonant sound—these words are usually in a row.	The **d**irty **d**og **d**ove into the water.
Assonance	Two or more words have a repeating vowel sound.	Gl**ee**ful and f**ee**ling fr**ee**, the children ran to the playground.

Onomatopoeia	When the word itself makes its own sound	Clap, shriek, ring, meow
Rhyme	When the endings of words sound the same—often in the final word in lines of poetry	She combed her hair Then braided it tight With the greatest care To look great that night
Rhythm	The beat of the poem, the patterns made by the syllables—some syllables get more stress or emphasis, while others get less—similar to how you can hit a drum with a big bang (DUH) or a lighter tap (duh)	I am here duh duh DUH Without exception duh-DUH duh-DUH-duh

Now that you're savvy to a whole bunch of poetic devices, you will start to see them in poems and other literature. Noticing that artistic language will transform your understanding! Don't get caught up in figuring out exactly which device you noticed. Instead, look for the layers of meaning hidden in the words, and appreciate the artistry.

FINDING POETIC DEVICES

You can practice thinking about these devices with a few poems.

In this one, look for rhyme, repetition, and imagery. But also think about the speaker. From whose perspective is this story being told?

Life Doesn't Frighten Me

by Maya Angelou

Shadows on the wall
Noises down the hall
Life doesn't frighten me at
all
Bad dogs barking loud
Big ghosts in a cloud
Life doesn't frighten me at
all

Mean old Mother Goose
Lions on the loose
They don't frighten me at all
Dragons breathing flame
On my counterpane
That doesn't frighten me at
all.

I go boo
Make them shoo
I make fun
Way they run
I won't cry
So they fly
I just smile
They go wild
Life doesn't frighten me at all.

Tough guys fight
All alone at night
Life doesn't frighten me at all.
Panthers in the park
Strangers in the dark
No, they don't frighten me at all.

That new classroom where
Boys all pull my hair
(Kissy little girls
With their hair in curls)
They don't frighten me at all.

Don't show me frogs and snakes
And listen for my scream,
If I'm afraid at all
It's only in my dreams.

I've got a magic charm
That I keep up my sleeve
I can walk the ocean floor
And never have to breathe.

Life doesn't frighten me at all
Not at all
Not at all.
Life doesn't frighten me at all.

What did you notice in "Life Doesn't Frighten Me"?

What phrases did the poet repeat? In repeating those phrases, what is she trying to emphasize in this poem?

Describe something you "saw" as you read this poem.

For you, what is this poem mostly about? What is its message?

FEELING POETIC DEVICES

The poem "maggie and milly and molly and may" includes rhyme, alliteration, and personification. And don't miss the similes at the end! (The word *languid*, in stanza three, may be new to you. It means "slow or lazy.")

maggie and milly and molly and may

by E. E. Cummings

maggie and milly and molly and may
went down to the beach(to play one day)

and maggie discovered a shell that sang
so sweetly she couldn't remember her troubles,and

milly befriended a stranded star
whose rays five languid fingers were;

and molly was chased by a horrible thing
which raced sideways while blowing bubbles:and

may came home with a smooth round stone
as small as a world and as large as alone.

For whatever we lose(like a you or a me)
it's always ourselves we find in the sea

Lots of sound devices are present in this poem. As with repetition, these devices may emphasize key ideas. Keep track of sound devices by jotting them down, along with your impressions of the poem:

DEVICE	EXAMPLE	WHAT IT MAKES YOU THINK OR FEEL
Rhyme		
Alliteration		
Assonance		

How did it go? Do you like this poem? What about it did you like or dislike?

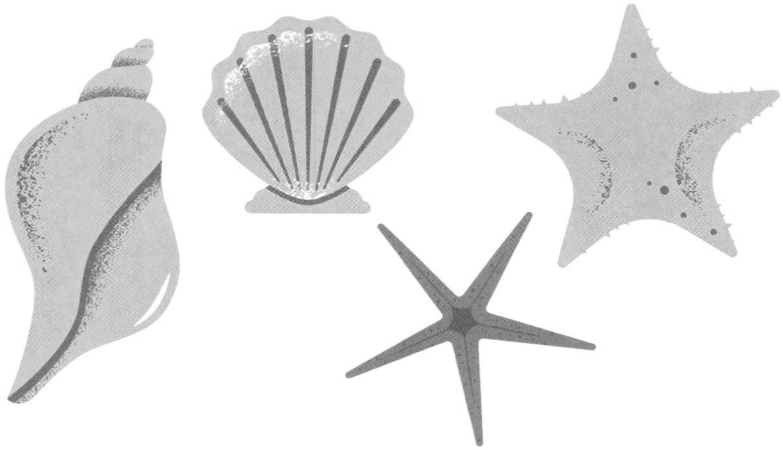

Were you able to find the bits of personification? The "shell that sang" and "befriended a stranded star" give us ideas about these girls' relationships with the seaside objects. What have you learned about these young people? How has the use of rhyme and alliteration affected the tone, or feeling of the poem? (In other words, what *feeling* did this poem leave you with?)

HEARING POETIC DEVICES

Below is one stanza (section) from a famous poem. You will find onomatopoeia, repetition, rhyme, and rhythm. This poem has some splendid words, including *merriment* (which means fun), *melody* (a song or tune), *Runic* (written with ancient symbols), and *tintinnabulation* (ringing or tinkling).

The Bells

by Edgar Allan Poe

Hear the sledges with the bells—
Silver bells!
What a world of merriment their melody foretells!
How they tinkle, tinkle, tinkle,
In the icy air of night!
While the stars that oversprinkle
All the heavens, seem to twinkle
With a crystalline delight;
Keeping time, time, time,
In a sort of Runic rhyme,
To the tintinnabulation that so musically wells
From the bells, bells, bells, bells,
Bells, bells, bells—
From the jingling and the tinkling of the bells.

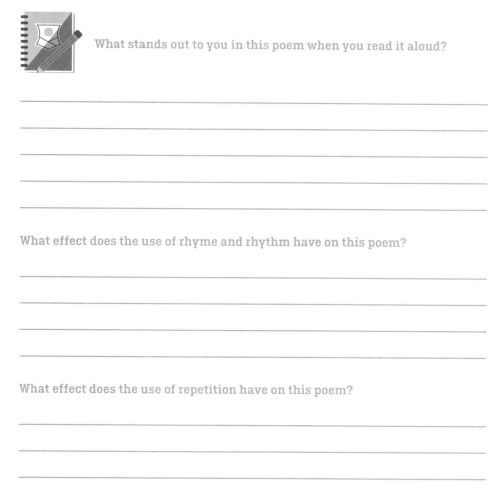

What stands out to you in this poem when you read it aloud?

What effect does the use of rhyme and rhythm have on this poem?

What effect does the use of repetition have on this poem?

EXPLORING FORM

You have probably noticed that the poems we have looked at in this chapter have come in all sorts of shapes and sizes. Poets use the term **form** when discussing how a poem looks—how it is constructed.

Some poems, such as "Life Doesn't Frighten Me," have stanzas. **Stanzas** are to poems what paragraphs are to prose. There is no set number of lines for a stanza, but a four-line stanza is called a **quatrain**, and a two-line rhyming stanza is called a **couplet**.

Poems that don't follow a particular structure or style are called **free verse**. You won't see one rhythm or rhyme scheme that exists throughout the whole poem in these poems. "Mother to Son" is in free verse.

Haikus were born in Japan. They consist of three lines. Usually, the first line has five syllables, the second has seven syllables, and the third has five syllables. They are usually written in the present tense.

> **"The Old Pond"**
>
> by Matsuo Basho, translated by Harry Behn and Peter Beilenson
>
> *An old silent pond...*
> *A frog jumps into the pond,*
> *splash! Silence again.*

Does Matsuo Basho's haiku make you stop and think about something deeply, or does it give you more of a feeling of being present at a particular time and place?

Before you wrap up this journey into poetry, let's use close reading to try out *all* that you've learned. This poem has so much going on that three reads might not even be enough! As with all poems, feel free to come back to it.

The First Book

by Rita Dove

Open it.

Go ahead, it won't bite.
Well… maybe a little.

More a nip, like. A tingle.
It's pleasurable, really.

You see, it keeps on opening.
You may fall in.

Sure, it's hard to get started;
remember learning to use

knife and fork? Dig in:
you'll never reach bottom.

It's not like it's the end of the world—
just the world as you think

you know it.

READING 1

PURPOSE AND GUIDING QUESTIONS:

A relaxed reading

What does this poem seem to be about?

What general observations can you make?

To do:

- Make initial observations.
- Jot down what you understand and your questions.

READING 2

PURPOSE AND GUIDING QUESTIONS:

Looking for the writer's craft

What devices do you notice?

What words and language stand out to you?

Who is speaking?

What powerful images do you "see" as you read?

READING 3

PURPOSE AND GUIDING QUESTIONS:

Finding meaning

What is the deeper meaning of this poem?

Is there more than one big idea?

To do:

- Look for the attitude of this speaker.
- Note what is really going on in this text—use your knowledge of poetic devices.
- Check to make sure the evidence supports your ideas.

USING WHAT YOU KNOW ABOUT POETRY TO UNDERSTAND PROSE

One last thing: Expert readers of poetry apply these skills to *all* that they read. Take a look at this piece of prose. It's the first couple of paragraphs from the book *The Marrow Thieves* by Cherie Dimaline. Read it using your poet's lens.

> Mitch was smiling so big his back teeth shone in the soft light of the solar-powered lamp we'd scavenged from someone's shed. "Check it out." He held a bag of Doritos between us—a big bag, too.
>
> "Holy, Mitch! Where'd you get that?" I touched the air-pressurized bag to confirm it was real. My dirty fingers skittered across the shiny surface like skates. It was real. My mouth filled with spit, and a rotten hole in one of my molars yelled its displeasure.

What stood out to you? Did you notice:

- Imagery
- Alliteration
- Personification

Could the Doritos be a symbol? That might be something to look out for if you choose to read further into the book.

What have you learned about reading poetry that will make you a better reader of whatever texts you encounter?

CHAPTER 4 VOCABULARY

figurative language: ways writers use words to mean something more than their literal meaning, helping you gain new insights into the topic; figurative language includes:

> **metaphor:** a comparison that uses an object in place of an idea without using the words *like* or *as*; for instance, "The raindrops were arrows striking the ground."
>
> **simile:** a comparison that uses an object in place of an idea and uses the word *like* or *as*; for example, "The raindrops were like arrows striking the ground."
>
> **symbolism:** the poetic or artistic use of an object to represent something other than itself; for instance, a flower might symbolize spring, or red might symbolize blood

form: how a poem is constructed and how it looks on the page

> **free verse:** poems that don't follow a particular structure or style
>
> **haiku:** a specific type of poem that originated in Japan and that usually has three lines: one with five syllables, the next with seven syllables, and the last with five syllables

literary devices: The ways writers show meaning through creative language. These include:

> **allusion:** a reference to another literary work
>
> **hyperbole:** an exaggeration used for comedic or emotional effect, such as "I've told you that a million times!"
>
> **imagery:** the use of words to create vivid pictures in your mind
>
> **personification:** giving human qualities or characteristics to a

non-human object, such as "The car's engine growled."

repetition: drawing your attention by repeating words, phrases, or lines

sound devices: ways writers affect the sound of their texts through word choice and structure

alliteration: when two or more words have the same beginning consonant sound—these words are usually in a row, as in "gorgeous gray goose"

assonance: when two or more words have a repeating vowel sound, as in "the night's bright firelight"

onomatopoeia: when a word itself makes its own sound, such as buzz, bang, whoosh, or murmur

rhyme: a sound device in which the endings of words sound the same—particularly in the final words in lines of poetry, such as "Good night/Sleep tight"

rhythm: the beat of a poem, the patterns made by the syllables; some syllables naturally get more stress or emphasis, while others get less

stanzas: the building blocks of a poem; they are to poems what paragraphs are to prose

couplet: a two-line rhyming stanza

quatrain: a four-line stanza

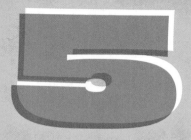

5 USING THE PRACTICES OF EXPERT WRITERS

Life as an early teen can be interesting. You're more aware than ever of the sociopolitical world. Your peer relationships may be shifting in big ways. Even your way of interacting with your family is different. You are getting wiser every minute. You probably already *feel* wiser. Adults are less likely to change their voices to a whisper when you walk into a conversation on politics, health, or social issues. You see, hear, notice, and think so much more.

CHAPTER CONTENTS

WRITE POWERFULLY!

Writing is power. It's a form of communication in which you can explain your ideas, request change, share emotion, and *challenge the thinking of others*. The power of writing, though, is twofold. Not only is it a tool with which you can change your world, but also the act of writing will change you. Writing is like a super-powerful sifter for your ideas. As your ideas move through that super-powerful sifter, the writing process, you will find that you are left with some real golden nuggets.

DEVELOPING POWERFUL WRITING PRACTICES

The first order of business is to write! As with everything, spending time writing will help you become a better writer. You will strengthen that writing muscle. To start, pay attention to two things:

- The amount of **time** you spend writing
- The **quantity** you write (how many words or pages)

Keep track of how much you write and how much time you spend doing it. You may notice that you become more efficient. Or you may notice that some days you spend a lot of time writing, but you write less. It's *all OK*. The point is that you are carving time out of your week to write. Some days you just may have more to say than you do on other days.

As you get started nurturing the writer inside you, consider what and where you will write.

ARE YOU SOMEONE WHO LOVES PENS AND PAPER?

You like to watch the trail of letters come from your pen. You may try out different types of handwriting, looking for new ways to make that perfect lowercase "g." Perhaps you have a collection of colored pens, or pens with different-sized tips. Or maybe you love paper. You collect journals. These are signs that you may want to write on paper—either loose paper or in a journal.

IS TECHNOLOGY MORE YOUR THING?

You like the sound your fingers make as they press the keys on the keyboard. You may like to select fonts to match your mood. Perhaps you organize your work into electronic folders. Maybe you just prefer to type. In this case, you will want to work on a computer or similar device.

It doesn't matter what you use to get your writer wings in the air, so select whatever feels comfortable. And feel free to mix it up if you'd like.

Now that you've selected your writing medium—pen or keyboard—you're set to start writing. What? You don't know *what* to write? The options are vast. Here are a few.

KEEP A JOURNAL

Many people find writing a journal or diary to be rewarding. It's a chance to reflect on your day, record your hopes and concerns, and jot down what you have experienced.

Here are some prompts and topics to get you started:

- Describe your day. Include sensory details to elongate your writing—sounds, tastes, smells, sights, and textures that relate to your experiences.
- Write about memories you have. Describe them in detail. If you wish, explain why they matter to you.
- List your favorites—music, foods, athletes, artists, video games, and so on. You can stretch this writing by explaining what qualities about each gets it onto your list.
- Write about current events. Include your concerns, frustrations, and hopes.
- Write about what you hope for yourself and the world.
- Document your family's history. Interview family members, gather their stories, and record them. Every family needs a great storyteller, so why not let it be you?
- Try any of these prompts as a **freewrite**. This means you don't have to worry about grammar, punctuation, or structure. Instead, just write what comes into your mind as quickly as you can.

Remember, it's *your* journal. Inside of it, write about what matters to you.

WRITE STORIES

You enjoy reading them, so why not write them? Your stories can be completely made up, or you can take some truth and stretch it into something new. Unless you want to show them to someone else, they are private. So give it a try. Write that romance or mystery or fantasy story that's been in the back of your mind!

In case you need an idea to get started:

- Think of a lyric from a song, and use it as the first line of dialogue in a new story.
- Choose a secondary character (possibly an antagonist) from a book you love, and tell that character's story.
- Put a character in a mode of transportation, and tell their travel story.
- Write from the perspective of an object in your home.
- Write about you from the perspective of the fly on your wall.
- Write the sequel to a favorite book or movie.

WRITE POEMS

You know that poems can look all sorts of ways. They can be about absolutely anything. Why not write a poem or two? Or three or more. Poems can provide information or tell a story. They can also use words to paint a picture of an idea or feeling. Each line is like a brushstroke that you can admire alone or as a part of the whole picture.

Below are some ways to ignite the poet in you:

- Write a poem about an object or feeling.
- Write a haiku.
- Use a poem you like to get you started—borrow its title or first line.

- Describe something you feel strongly about by writing a list of things about it.
- Write poetry that is social commentary, sharing your opinions about what is going on in the world.
- Write poems about yourself!

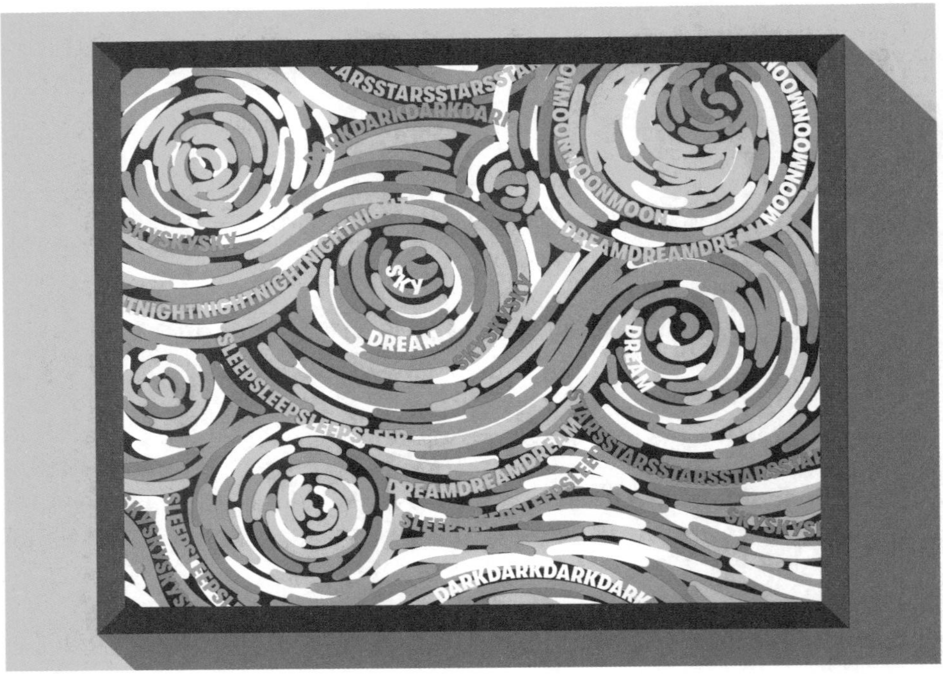

These are just a few ways to develop a daily writing practice. The key thing is to write!

INCREASING YOUR WRITING STAMINA

How does a person become a writer? By writing. It's as simple as that!

You want to be the strongest writer possible. To do that, you'll want to develop your **writing stamina**—your ability to write for lengths of time, to write longer pieces, and to be able to work on one writing project over several days.

You can monitor your stamina using the charts below. If you are writing on a computer, you may want to use the number of words as your measure. If you're writing in a notebook, you will probably just want to count pages. Your writing goal: to average at least three hours of "just for you" writing per week. You can organize this any way you want, but starting with small blocks of writing time for yourself might be the way to go. As you write, fill in what you accomplished to collect evidence of your progress!

YOUR PERSONAL WRITING LOG

WEEK 1

	S	M	T	W	T	F	S	TOTALS
Minutes spent writing								
Amount written (pages or words)								

WEEK 2

	S	M	T	W	T	F	S	TOTALS
Minutes spent writing								
Amount written (pages or words)								

What do you see happening to your writing over time? Why do you think that is?

If you found that logging your writing is helpful, keep that up by making your own writing log.

THE WRITING PROCESS

There will be times when you want to polish your writing. Perhaps one of your daily writing pieces is something you want to develop and refine. Maybe you have a piece of writing that you will submit to a teacher or coach or for a contest. When you are working to create a finished piece of writing, you follow the **writing process**. That is the set of steps you take to help you end up with a piece of writing you feel great about. Dividing a big task into smaller parts makes it less daunting.

THE SIX STEPS OF WRITING

Step 1: Brainstorming

Step 2: Collecting and Sorting Information

Step 3: Drafting

Step 4: Revision

Step 5: Editing

Step 6: Publication

You can use the writing process with all types of writing. Let's practice the writing process by writing a poem.

BEFORE YOU WRITE

Sometimes, we think of writing as something that happens to us. An idea might hit you like a lightning bolt, or a perfect sentence might just pop into your brain fully formed, and you can barely write it down fast enough to keep up with your mind. But the truth is that writing doesn't just happen . . . you have to make it happen! Before you even write the first word, there are some steps you have to take to get yourself ready.

First, you need an idea that will hold your attention—what would be fun or interesting to write about? Is it something people you know would want to read about? Chances are that if you're really enthusiastic about a subject, you can make it interesting for other people to read about. Then, you need to collect and sort the information you will use before you write it down. So before you write your poem, let's think about where you want to start.

STEP 1: BRAINSTORMING TO FIND A TOPIC

Writers need to find or narrow their ideas. When you brainstorm, you come up with as many ideas as possible—everything you can think of that fits your writing goal. Then narrow your ideas, testing them out.

Start by listing possible ideas. For your poem, you will be writing something personal, so list topics that matter to you. (If you are writing an opinion piece for a newspaper or magazine, list topics that matter to both you and the community. If you are entering a short story contest, list ideas for your short story.) No matter what form your writing will take, brainstorming will help you find a topic that is just "write" for you!

BRAINSTORMING IDEAS

SAMPLE TOPIC IDEAS FOR A POEM	*Topic ideas for a poem—things that matter to me, things I think about*
Social media	
City life	
Basketball	
School	
Courage	
Bullying	
Climate change	
Popular dances	
Pizza	
Friendship	

Next, read your list and identify your favorite topics. This narrows your list.

SAMPLE TOP CHOICES	*My top choices*
Courage Pizza Friendship	

TEST YOUR IDEAS BY FREEWRITING

To find the absolute best topic for this writing project, test out an idea and make sure you are comfortable with it. To do this, we briefly freewrite on your idea. Remember, that means writing down whatever comes into your head about your idea *without stopping*. If you have enough to write about for two minutes or so, you probably feel strongly enough about the topic to move forward. If you find that you don't have much to say about it, try freewriting with another top choice. *Remember: your goal is to find the best topic for yourself, so take your time making sure it suits you!*

TESTING OUT YOUR IDEA

SAMPLE TWO-MINUTE FREEWRITE ON ONE TOPIC	*My two-minute freewrite on one topic*
I have been thinking a lot about courage lately. I see some very courageous people standing up for what they believe is right. Sometimes their friends and family don't agree with them. Sometimes they risk getting hurt for stepping up. I admire those people so much. Once, someone acted courageously for me. Someone was picking on me, and even though that person was their "friend," they stepped in.	

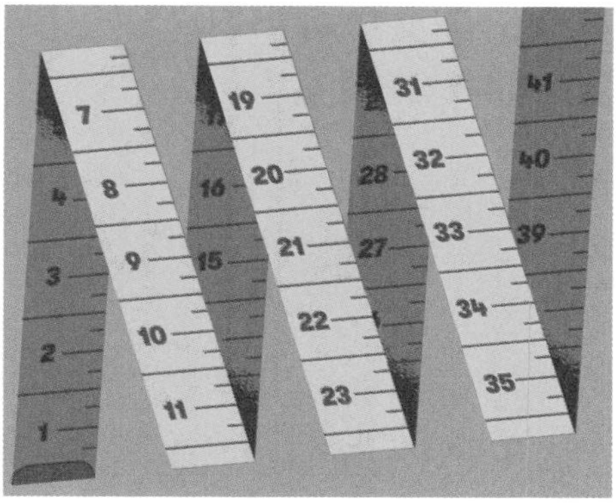

- Is this topic a good fit for me?
- Did I have something to say?
- Could I have written for more than two minutes?

If you answer "yes" to those questions, you are ready to move on to the next step.

STEP 2: COLLECTING AND SORTING INFORMATION

This step will look different depending on the kind of writing you are producing. For your poem, you may choose not to do formal research and write just from personal experience. However, you may want to add some researched evidence into your poem. For other types of writing, you certainly may need to collect notes. Remember, when conducting research, always record where you found your information!

WHAT YOU KNOW FROM PERSONAL EXPERIENCE

SAMPLE ANSWER—WHAT I KNOW ABOUT MY TOPIC	WHAT DO YOU KNOW ABOUT YOUR TOPIC?
Courage is like being brave.	
People who take a risk to stand up for what they believe are courageous.	
That type of courage is called moral courage.	
There are examples of courage everywhere.	
Courage is stepping up.	
Courage is something that makes the world better.	
I have seen big acts of courage in person—mostly around bullying and showing kindness.	
I have seen lots of acts of courage on the news—mostly people demanding equal rights.	
Lions are a symbol of courage.	

If you are doing research, you may use a note catcher, which can look something like this:

SOURCE	NOTE	WHAT IT TELLS YOU OR WHAT IT MAKES YOU WONDER

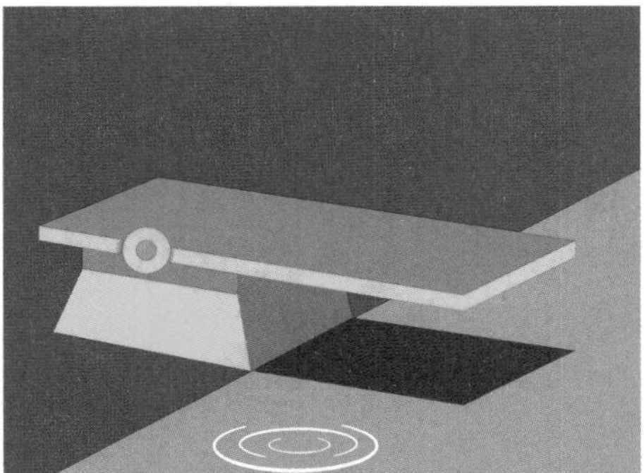

For certain types of writing, you will need to sort or organize your ideas. You may create an outline or use another means of planning your writing. (An **outline** is a list of the most important parts of your writing. It's almost like a skeleton that you will flesh out or the support beams of a house you will build.) To write this poem, you won't plan. Instead, you will just dive right into writing.

DRAFTING AND REVISING

Now that you have completed the first two steps, you are ready to start writing your poem! This stage is about actually putting pen to paper. First you will let your ideas flow until you have your first draft. Then, you get to make it even *better* by revising. Writing isn't like taking a picture where one click freezes the image in place forever. It's like a painting—you get to add details and color whenever you want, or even paint over an old part with something new!

STEP 3: READY, SET, DRAFT

It's time to write your poem's first **draft**. At this stage, you are more worried about getting your ideas down than you are with details such as wording and punctuation.

draft: an early version of a piece of writing before it has been fully edited

Sample poem's first draft

If I were courageous, would it matter?
Would people listen?
Would things change?

If I were courageous,
Would the bullies
Stop dead in their tracks
Change their sneers to sorries?

If I were courageous,
Would the world change
And become stronger
And kinder?

If I were courageous,
Would I speak up
When you need me
And make you feel
Like you matter?

When I am courageous,
I show
How strong I am.

Your poem's first draft

Whew! Writing a poem is fun and hard. That first draft was all about getting ideas down. What was it like for you?

STEP 4: REVISION

The revision step is where you take a critical look at your writing and ask yourself: how can I make this piece stronger? Outlining what you've said and looking at word choice are revision strategies that you can use across all types of writing.

revision: reviewing your writing and making changes to improve it

OUTLINING IN REVERSE

You may have created an outline *before* you wrote. This **outline in reverse** is an opportunity to check how you did with that. What, you didn't make an outline first? Even better—using this method will allow you to see what ideas you have included and the order in which you shared them.

To outline in reverse:

1. Jot down the purpose of your piece—what you want it to mostly be about.
2. Look at each paragraph or section separately. Ask yourself: what is this part mostly about?
3. Look over your outline in reverse with eagle-eyed vision. Make sure you are expressing exactly what you want—neither too much nor too little—and that you're staying on topic. Take notes on anything you want to improve.
4. Make any needed changes. These may include:
    - Changing the order of ideas (use arrows on your draft, or number the paragraphs)
    - Adding in something that is missing
    - Taking out something that doesn't fit

OUTLINE IN REVERSE IN ACTION

Purpose of this piece:

To express personal feelings about courage, how when we have courage, we can change things around us. To express that it's scary to have courage.

DRAFT 1	THE MAIN IDEA	ANNOTATIONS ON THE OUTLINE	NEW IDEAS AND CHANGES
If I were courageous, would it matter? Would people listen? Would things change?	Questioning effects of courage	Opening—like an intro	Would it change things?
If I were courageous, Would the bullies Stop dead in their tracks Change their sneers to sorries?	Can courage make bullies change?	Tells who	
If I were courageous, Would the world change And become stronger And kinder?	Can courage make the world better?	Doesn't really fit with the rest of the poem, which focuses on changing things that are close	Take out this part.

If I were courageous, Would I speak up When you need me And make you feel Like you matter?	Courage to show compassion	Not sure about the question	I would speak up.
When I am courageous, I show How strong I am.	Courage shows strength.	Kind of like a closing Focus is on speaker	Add: And how much I care.

Second draft of the poem:

If I were courageous, would it matter?
Would people listen?
Would it change things?

If I were courageous,
Would the bullies
Stop dead in their tracks
Change their sneers to sorries?

When I am courageous,
I speak up
When you need me
And make you feel
Like you matter.

When I am courageous,
I show
How strong I am
And how much I care.

Try outlining in reverse with your own poem. Purpose of this piece:

NOW YOU TRY!

DRAFT 1	THE OUTLINE	ANNOTATIONS ON THE OUTLINE	NEW IDEAS AND CHANGES

Your poem's second draft

What did you notice about your draft as you worked on your outline in reverse?

WORD CHOICE

While you are revising, you will also want to take a close look at word choice. To do this:

1. Read your work, and circle or underline words that are a little weak given what you are trying to express.
2. Use a **thesaurus** (book or online version) to look for words that may better express your ideas.
3. Rewrite the line or sentence with the new word.
4. Decide if the new word improves your poem or if it was better before you changed it.

thesaurus: a resource that lists word synonyms and antonyms to help you find the best word to express an idea

Go back and mark up your second draft with the words you think you might be able to improve.

SPICE UP YOUR WORD CHOICE!

WORD FROM SECOND DRAFT	SYNONYMS (TWO TO FOUR)	FAVORITE NEW WORD	LINE REWRITTEN WITH THE NEW WORD	DO I LIKE THE NEW WORD BETTER?
change	Amend, replace, recast, transform	Replace	Replace their sneers with sorries?	No
sorry	Apologetic, contrite, rueful, remorse	Remorse	Change their sneers to remorse?	Yes
strong	Tenacious, tough, mighty, powerful	Mighty	How mighty I am.	Yes

WORD FROM SECOND DRAFT	SYNONYMS (TWO TO FOUR)	FAVORITE NEW WORD	LINE REWRITTEN WITH THE NEW WORD	DO I LIKE THE NEW WORD BETTER?

SAMPLE POEM'S THIRD DRAFT	YOUR POEM'S THIRD DRAFT
If I were courageous, would it matter? Would people listen? Would it change things? If I were courageous, Would the bullies Stop dead in their tracks Change their sneers to remorse? When I am courageous, I speak up When you need me And make you feel Like you matter. When I am courageous, I show How mighty I am And how much I care.	

CHOOSING A TITLE

Now that you've read your work critically a couple of times, you are ready to title it. The formula for titling a piece of writing changes depending on form and audience. In all cases, it sets the stage for your piece of writing.

Key ideas for choosing titles:

- May acknowledge or support the point or argument you are making
- May acknowledge the overall assignment
- Captures the reader's interest
- May have a main title and a subtitle separated by a colon
- Language is captivating

For this poem on courage, the title will need to match the topic and hopefully generate some curiosity about the poem it comes before.

SHOW OFF YOUR NEW TITLE

What do you think of "Becoming Mighty" as a title for the courage poem? Does it make you want to read more? Do you have an idea for your poem's title? Write a few down below!

As you practice specific forms of writing in the next few chapters, you will try out a few more revision strategies. In this chapter, you tried two. How did these revision strategies transform your poem?

POLISHING AND SHARING YOUR WRITING

The reason most of us write is to share ideas with others. Publishing is the final step in the writing process, but not before we give our work one last critical read-through—the final edit.

STEP 5: EDITING

When you edit your writing, you make small corrections. You check for punctuation, spelling, capitalization, and grammar (these are covered in Chapter 10). The best tool for this step is . . . *you*! Read your writing out loud. As you do so, you will notice errors in punctuation and typos. It's at this point that you double-check to make sure you are using all words correctly. Some people call this step **proofreading.** You may want to get someone else to read your work. It's easier to see small errors in work that is not our own.

Writers carefully craft sentences and phrases. Poets and other writers often get creative with language. You can use the checklist below with all forms of writing. However, if your poem or other writing is *intentionally* being creative with capitalization or any other element of writing, just check to make sure your adjustments work, and move on!

YOUR EDITING CHECKLIST

		COMPLETED	NEEDS A SECOND READER
PUNCTUATION AND GRAMMAR	While reading my work out loud, I check that I used commas, semicolons, periods, question marks, or exclamation points to show places where I want the reader to pause.		
	I am happy with my verb tense and agreement. For example, I don't switch from present tense to past tense in my writing unless it makes sense to do so.		
	I used commas to divide items in a list. I used quotation marks around dialogue.		
CAPITALIZATION	I used capital letters at the beginning of all sentences.		
	I capitalized all proper nouns (examples: Maya, Istanbul, Buddhism).		
SPELLING	I have double-checked homonyms (example: *there, their, they're*).		
	I have checked and fixed words that don't "look just right" and words that have those dotted red lines underneath in an electronic document.		
STRUCTURE	My paragraphs are indented.		
	My title is centered at the top of my piece. It is properly capitalized, and there is a space between it and the first paragraph.		
	I have included my name and the date.		

STEP 6: PUBLICATION

It is time to create your final draft and share it. “Share” can mean almost anything. Maybe that means sending it in to a writing contest, turning it in to a teacher, showing it to someone you respect, or hitting “send” on an email. Or maybe it’s simply placing it in a folder or box that’s labeled “My Favorite Writing Pieces.”

Now that your creation has been edited, revised, and has a title, it is fully ready for publication. Congratulations. Here’s a place for you to publish the poem you just wrote:

TITLE:

What are a few things you want to remember about the writing process?

MAKING A LONG STORY SHORT: SUMMARIZING

Writing a **summary** is a skill that you will use often. A summary is when you briefly retell something. Sometimes you may need to put lots of ideas into one sentence. In that case, a summary tells your audience the main idea. Other times you will need to give more of an overview that includes the most important details. A summary does not include your ideas or opinions. It is just a brief retelling of a text or event.

Steps to summarizing:

- Identify the main idea.
- Identify the key points.
- Put the idea and points into your own words.

Remember, summaries are much shorter than the original text or event. You can practice summarizing with this article titled "Kid Heroes for the Planet." As you read, jot down the main idea and key points from the article.

> Isabel and Melati Wijsen were 10 and 12 when they learned about Nelson Mandela and Martin Luther King, Jr. These change-makers inspired the sisters to think about how they could make a difference in the world. They decided to focus on the plastic pollution affecting Bali, Indonesia,

where they live. "Growing up on the island of Bali, we already had a strong connection to the environment," Melati told *Time Edge*.

Melati and Isabel created Bye Bye Plastic Bags in 2013. The group's initial goal was to have single-use plastic shopping bags banned across Bali. It succeeded: Bali's governor introduced a law banning the bags beginning in 2019.

Now the group has 25 locations worldwide. It raises awareness of plastic's impact on the environment. Melati hopes more kids will be inspired to speak up. "You have a voice, so use it," she says.

KEEP YOUR NOTES NEAT

MAIN IDEA	
KEY POINTS	

Maybe your notes look something like this:

MAIN IDEA	Young girls made big changes.
KEY POINTS	10 and 12 years old Inspired by Nelson Mandela and Martin Luther King, Jr. Plastic was affecting Bali's environment Created a program that led to a change in law and had an international impact

Write a summary. A good rule of thumb is that your summary should be no more than one-quarter the length of the original text. Your summary for this text should be one to three sentences.

Your summary might look something like this:

"Kid Heroes for the Planet" is about two girls, inspired by Martin Luther King, Jr. and Nelson Mandela, who set out to change their world. They began a movement to ban the use of plastic bags in their home, Bali—a movement that had international impact.

Write a summary of this chapter on the practices of expert writers:

Which practices were most surprising to you?

CHAPTER 5 VOCABULARY

draft: an early version of a piece of writing before it has been fully edited

freewrite: an exercise where you write continuously for a set amount of time

outline: a list or description of the most important topics of a piece of writing, organized in order and by level of importance

proofreading: reading back over your writing (often aloud) to check for errors

revision: reviewing your writing and making changes to improve it

summary: a brief retelling of the most important points of a story

thesaurus: a resource that lists word synonyms and antonyms to help you find the best word to express an idea

writing process: a set of steps you can take to help you create a finished piece of writing

writing stamina: your ability to write for lengths of time, to write longer pieces, and to be able to work on one writing project over several days

6 SPOTLIGHTING THE STORYTELLER IN YOU: NARRATIVE WRITING

How often do you find yourself telling a story? You might be recapping what you did last weekend, describing your descent down a double-diamond ski slope, or recollecting details about how the perfect cannonball created a tidal wave in the local pool. At these times, you are speaking in *narrative form*—an account of events, a story with a beginning, middle, and end. A narrative can be about an imagined or real event—or real with some stretching of the truth!

CHAPTER CONTENTS

SHARING PERSONAL NARRATIVES

These moments you share, the stories you tell at the dinner table at night or by your locker in the morning, make up who you are and how you experience the world around you. Writing them down is recording part of your story, your history. Of course, you may also tell some made-up stories, and those are also narratives. A **narrative** is a story where a character or individual faces a problem. In this chapter, we will look at ways to get the most out of your own moments by using strategies to write powerful **personal narratives**. A personal narrative is written from personal experience. Its intent is usually to amuse or teach a lesson. Writing personal narratives is something you will need to do in applications for schools, scholarships, and other programs. Also, you might write them as a family member who wants to be a keeper of history and as a person with insights worth sharing.

HOW TO BE A STRONG STORYTELLER

Before we start, think about the great storytellers you know. Think about what it is that makes them great storytellers. Is it the subjects they talk about, or is it the *way* they tell the story? Here's the secret: anyone can tell a great story—it's all in the way you tell it.

This example, written by Dan Carroll, shows us how we can turn a pretty common occurrence—attending a high school dance—into a powerful story. Its title, "Practical Dance Theory," gives us little insight into what this story may *really* be about.

Pull out your pickaxe to look at his craft—*how* he is telling this story. While you examine the story, look for details, especially ones that really stand out. You can even use your pickaxe to sift through those details and begin to explain how they affect the story.

READING AS A WRITER:

TEXT

Practical Dance Theory

by Dan Carroll

In a dingy boy's bathroom at a high school dance, my friends—we're closer to a zombie apocalypse survival crew than we are to friends—are scribbling our latest theories onto the cold walls. This new one has often been questioned but is still undisputed. It's that no one between 13 and 18 can dance. They are too self-aware, sober, and scared. But it's not their fault. Those rooms are filled with way too many watching adults and pushed-aside lunch tables. The whiplash of country songs and trap music don't help much, either.

Despite this, they jump and flail like they see adults do in TV and movies. It can be hard to watch. See the children jumping and grinding, all bare stomachs and sharp elbows slamming against fabric scented heavily with body spray. Watch them thrash through each number and sing along for every word, including the slurs. Watch them try and move like the math teacher that just gave them a 67% on a test isn't standing twenty feet away. Watch them attempt to use their bodies for themselves.

You may have missed the corner table, however. Far away from the huddled masses sit a humble few underclassmen who already used up all their confidence convincing

WHAT DO YOU SEE

YOUR ANNOTATIONS—*observations, noticing what works well in this narrative*

themselves to go to the dance, and now have none remaining to dance with. I am fiercely protective of these people, because I was one of them, and I am sure some of you were too. When I was a freshman, the other closeted kids and I sat around that table and dreamed up a safe and fictional place where there were more of us than them and none of us would have to be afraid. Go ahead, make whatever jokes you want about gay kids not dancing to the Beyoncé songs, but a person just doesn't forget about the long line of dead queers who chose to slow dance with the wrong people. Besides, we had already collectively decided we were different. We were not like Them.

Because being in high school often means only being able to define yourself against things. Sometimes that requires running away from the group and then wearing that separation as a badge of honor. Sometimes it means looking in the mirror and only finding a rough silhouette of yourself built from the negative space of everything you are not.

At some point a dance circle will simultaneously open up and close off. The dance circle is a perpetual embarrassment machine into which students are pulled, pushed, and peer-pressured at ever changing intervals. It is like Soul Train except so much worse because no one can dance. So you make the fated jump into the center and hopefully onto the beat, and it doesn't matter whether you stay on it or not because everyone will forget about you

YOUR ANNOTATIONS—*observations, noticing what works well in this narrative*

by the end of the song. Or maybe you never step inside, because anxiety, a term you do not fully understand, is racking around your body to the tune of every song you don't know the words to.

This, by the way, is high school; when every moment and song is the most important of your entire life until the next one proves it wasn't. Or until the next song leaves you missing the previous one, even if that means longing for a past you never had—one where you danced better or held on to someone longer.

If you really want to make sense of high schoolers, then it can only be understood by watching the dance floor at any dance in America. I know this sounds obvious: by meeting the people who shape high school culture and are shaped by it, you'll absorb its ethos. But you don't actually need to meet them. Just watch them. And watch yourself watching them, unable to look away, even for a moment, even to hide in the bathroom or to pretend that somebody is texting you.

In reading this narrative, you may have noticed a few interesting things:

- The moment he focuses on is rather common: a high school dance.
- It's grounded in a short period of time—not a two-week vacation or the first two years of piano lessons.

YOUR ANNOTATIONS—*observations, noticing what works well in this narrative*

- What makes this moment significant is how the school dance tells a bigger story, one of exclusion and fear.
- There's descriptive language, such as "zombie apocalypse survival crew" and "whiplash of country songs and trap music," that helps you *feel* as if you're there with them.
- There's tension around how the narrator views the high school experience.

A STRONG PERSONAL NARRATIVE WILL:

1. Zoom in on one small moment.

2. Include sensory detail and a small amount of dialogue.

3. Have conflict or a feeling of tension.

That's it? Well, pretty much. So let's revisit the writing process so you can produce a strong personal narrative.

BUILDING YOUR STORY

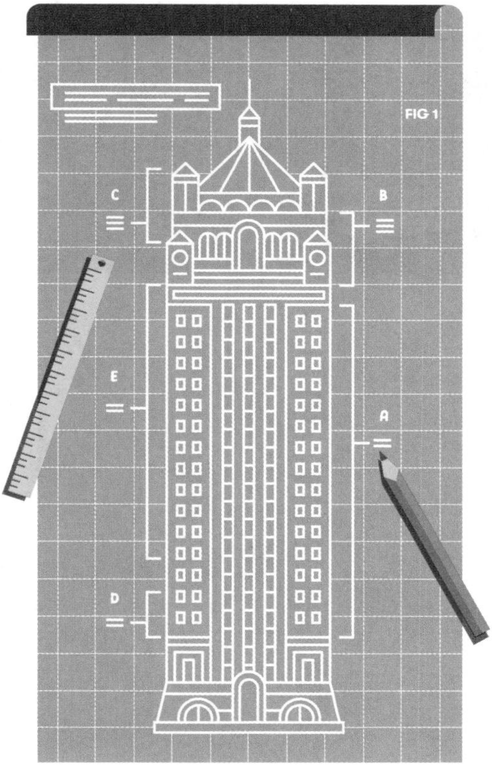

Since personal narratives are stories that tell something about your personal life, you can root around in your memory to find a good story to tell. Don't try to tell the story of your whole life! Focus on something small but interesting (or important, or funny).

Did you ever take a trip that changed you or turned out differently than you thought it might? Help an injured animal? Eat something that turned out to be not what you thought it was?

These are the kinds of events, small and large, that can make a good story.

BRAINSTORMING AND CHOOSING YOUR TOPIC

We talked about brainstorming as the first step in the writing process, or a way to choose your writing topic. To find an idea for a story about you, you will want to brainstorm about you! Try making lists in any or all of the columns below.

ALL ABOUT YOU

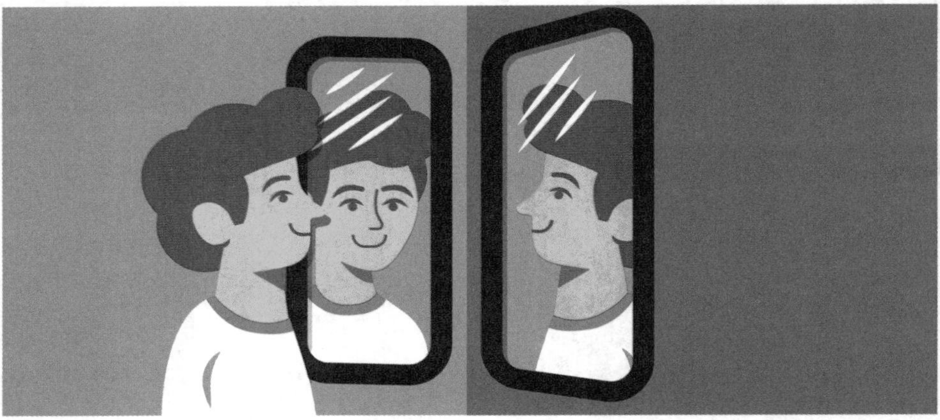

PEOPLE WHO MATTER TO YOU IN BIG OR SMALL WAYS (Hint: You may want to include people whose names you don't even know—the gentleman who sells you your egg sandwich, the new girl who moved in next door...)	
LOOK AROUND YOU. LIST OBJECTS THAT HAVE MEANING TO YOU—things you want to keep, things you find special.	
MOMENTS WHERE YOU LEARNED SOMETHING—in "Practical Dance Theory," we saw how one writer based his narrative off of a common, relatable event: the high school dance.	

THINGS YOU DO ALL THE TIME— martial arts, drawing class, making breakfast on Saturdays, walks after dinner	
SIGNIFICANT MOMENTS— · first experiences · the last time you... · embarrassing moments · standout memories	
STRONG FEELINGS—feelings or emotions you have for people, things, places, or events	

If Dan Carroll were using this strategy, he may have circled "being closeted in high school" in the "strong feelings" column. In his free writes, perhaps he would have tested out a couple of different moments—perhaps a school lunch or a family trip—or he may have included this dance in the "moment where you learned something" column.

Now that you've got a bunch of ideas, you will narrow your list. Read your ideas, and circle the three that you feel most strongly about. Test them out. Do your two-minute freewrites on your ideas.

FREEWRITE TOPIC	TWO-MINUTE FREEWRITE

After you are done, you will use your key questions:

- Is this topic a good fit for me?
- Did I have something to say?
- Could I have written for more than two minutes?

If you answer "yes" to those questions, you are ready to move onto the next step.

Before you move on, revisit the goals of narrative writing.

A STRONG NARRATIVE WILL:

1. Zoom in on one small moment.
2. Include sensory detail and a small amount of dialogue.
3. Have conflict or a feeling of tension.

In thinking about your topic, ask yourself:

- Does it focus on a short period of time?
- Can you include details that help your reader really feel like they are in the moment with you?
- Is there some tension or conflict?

If you answered "yes" to these questions, you are ready to move on. If you didn't, try:

- Adding to your freewrite
- Choosing another topic to freewrite on
- Rereading "Practical Dance Theory" or other personal narratives for some inspiration

EXAMPLES OF GREAT PERSONAL NARRATIVES

"Eleven" by Sandra Cisneros

"The Jacket" by Gary Soto

The Hero Next Door edited by Olugbemisola Rhuday-Perkovich

The House on Mango Street by Sandra Cisneros

DEVELOPING DETAILS

Now that you have a story or moment you are interested in writing about, move on to step 2 in your writing process: collecting and sorting information. When writing a personal narrative, you must decide what details or events you are going to talk about and how you are going to tell the story. There are a few ways to do this.

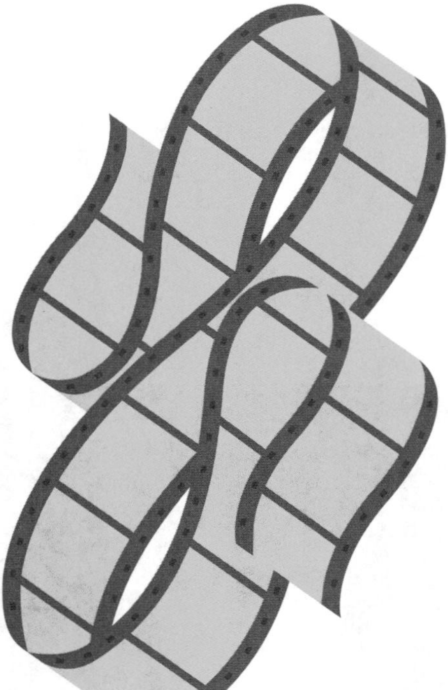

DEVELOPING YOUR STORY OPTION #1:

Write about one instance as if it were being played in slow motion.

For example, imagine you wrote this during a freewrite: "We ate our codfish fritters."

What if you took this moment and rewrote it frame by frame, as if your brain was replaying it slowly. It might turn out something like this.

FRAME BY FRAME

1 The codfish fritters were medium brown with crunchy bits sticking out.	2 I went to grab a fritter.	3 It was too hot, so my fingers jumped away.	4 I found the fork hidden beneath the plate.
5 I stabbed the fritter.	6 The fritter made a cracking sound as the fork pierced its crunchy exterior.	7 A plume of steam rose from the opening.	8 To dip or not to dip? My fork paused over the sauce.
9 Then it detoured straight for my mouth.	10 Ouch!	11 Hot!	12 I had to leave my mouth open to let the steam escape.
13 Finally I could chew—crunch, crunch.	14 The buttery soft interior was salty and delicious.		

Give it a try! Choose a sentence from your freewrite, and write about it frame by frame to collect more details.

1	2	3	4
5	6	7	8
9	10	11	12
13	14		

How did your language change when you put your sentence or sentences into slow motion? What kinds of extra details did you come up with?

DEVELOPING YOUR STORY OPTION #2:

Make a list. Think about the idea you want to share with your reader. Then ask yourself: What is *everything* someone needs to know about this?

Here's an example. Again, we are talking about codfish fritters.

THE ULTIMATE LIST OF EVERYTHING

MY IDEA	Codfish fritters are my all-time favorite food.
EVERYTHING MY READER SHOULD KNOW	They are made with dried cod. They are fried, so they are crunchy on the outside. They are pale yellow inside with red flecks. I think the red flecks are red pepper. They are spicy only if you add the spicy sauce. My great-grandmother used to make them for us. My great-grandmother died. Now we get them as take-out from a restaurant. We sit at old wooden picnic tables outside and eat our fritters. We eat them once a year, when we visit my grandmother over summer vacation. When we eat them, we talk about all the other summers we spent eating fritters at those tables or in my great-grandmother's kitchen. We all love them, but I love them the most. My grandmother knows everyone at the restaurant where we get them—they call her "Miss T." I also see my cousins in the summer.

Give it a try:

YOUR IDEA	
EVERYTHING YOUR READER SHOULD KNOW ABOUT YOUR IDEA	

Look over your last steps. How many more details were you able to get from yourself? Which strategy worked better for you?

WRITING YOUR FIRST DRAFT

Now that you have activated your memory to collect more details, you are ready for step 3 of our writing process. It's time to write your first draft! No pressure here—just sit down and write your story. You've collected some details, so let them appear in this draft.

Your goal: Get your story written down. Aim for more than one page.

Don't worry about: paragraphing, mechanics, spelling

This is an *ideas* draft. It does not need to contain your best writing. You will work on that in the next steps.

MAKING SUBSTANTIAL REVISIONS

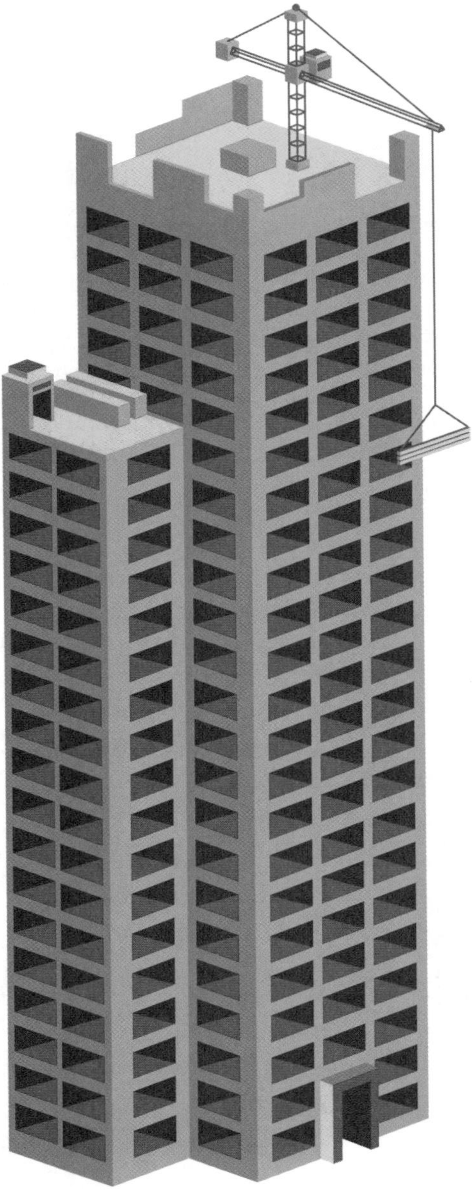

Now that you have chosen your topic and written down your ideas, it's time to move on to step 4 of the writing process: revision. In this step, you will take some time to work on the craft of your writing. Revisions and editing differ. When you revise your writing, you can take risks, try new things, and make your work very different. Revision will make your personal narrative stand out as you artfully express your ideas. You will use a few strategies:

- Shine a spotlight on the deeper meaning in what you are writing or experiencing.
- Diagram your plot.
- Try out different ways to open your narrative.
- Use a mentor text.

Don't understand some of these terms? Don't worry. We'll go through each step by step.

SPOTLIGHT THE DEEPER MEANING

This two-step revision strategy will ensure that your story has meaning and that the meaning shines through. Let's think about "Practical Dance Theory." That story had a big idea that was important to its narrator: realizing that high school dances highlight teenagers' feelings of acceptance, exclusion, comfort, or discomfort! You can imagine Dan Carroll thinking about that idea, its importance, and his need to make sure the reader can understand that importance.

STEP 1: READ YOUR DRAFT, LOOKING FOR YOUR STORY'S DEEPER MEANING.

Great writers ask great questions of themselves and their writing. Read your draft with a strong guiding question: *What is this piece really about?*

What is your piece really about?

STEP 2: REDRAFT

You've identified the point to your story—whether it's to make your reader laugh, teach a lesson about forgiveness, or express a new understanding. Now you will want to make sure that this meaning comes through clearly in your piece. Your challenge here is to write a new draft, holding that deeper meaning in your head while you do it. This is still a rough draft, so don't worry about spelling, punctuation, or paragraphs.

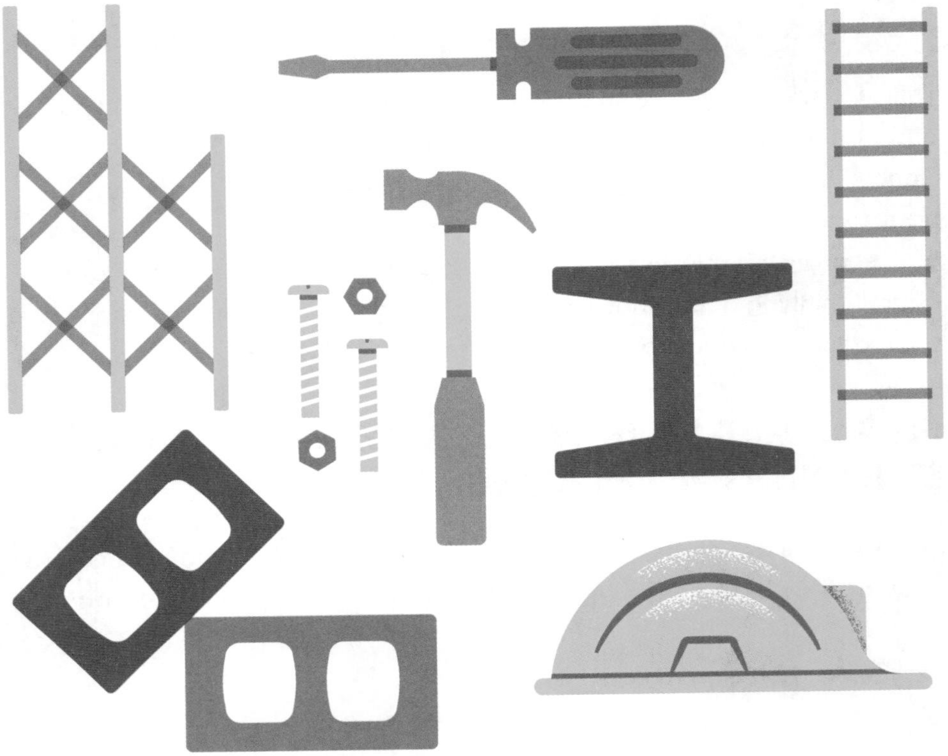

This draft will spotlight the deeper meaning by:

- Elaborating on actions that relate to it
- Including dialogue that relates to it
- Adding symbolism
- Not looking at your first draft

It may be helpful to brainstorm some additions before you start. See what you can think of to weave into your story. Here's what it looks like using the codfish fritter idea:

SPOTLIGHT THE DEEPER MEANING BY ADDING IDEAS

What is your piece really about? The codfish fritter piece is really about family traditions and how they help us feel and show love.

STRATEGY TO SPOTLIGHT THE DEEPER MEANING OF YOUR STORY	WHAT YOU MAY LOOK FOR	IDEAS YOU CAN ADD
Elaborating on action that relates to it	*Identifying important moments, adding details, or expanding that moment*	I want to write about my great-grandma's smiling eyes locking with mine as I bite into my fritter. Her eyes, focused only on me, sparkled with love.
Include dialogue that relates to it.	*Think about conversations that show the conflict or resolution around the deeper meaning you are trying to convey.*	The conversation we had about great-grandma's fritters as we sat at the take-out table
Add symbolism.	*See if there's an object that can symbolize the big idea you are trying to convey.*	The table can symbolize our togetherness.

You can give it a try with your story:

STRATEGY TO SPOTLIGHT THE DEEPER MEANING OF YOUR STORY	WHAT YOU MAY LOOK FOR	IDEAS YOU CAN ADD
Elaborating on action that relates to it.	*Identifying important moments, adding details, or expanding that moment.*	
Include dialogue that relates to it.	*Think about conversations that show the conflict or resolution around the deeper meaning you are trying to convey.*	
Add symbolism.	*See if there's an object that can symbolize the big idea you are trying to convey.*	

Write this draft with laser focus on that deeper meaning.

As the writer redrafts the piece about codfish fritters, the bigger meaning is beginning to shine through. For example, this is an added part where there's effort to bring out the idea of the table as a symbol of family:

> My youngest sibling swung his legs over the picnic bench first. He was followed by my younger sister, who hopped up on the bench, did a quick twirl, then scrunched herself close to my little cousin. Before I knew it, all the cousins, an aunt, and two uncles squeezed their way into the table benches. My mom pulled up a chair at the end for my grandmother, who sat quietly, looking at each one of us. Then she rested her hands on the table and smiled.

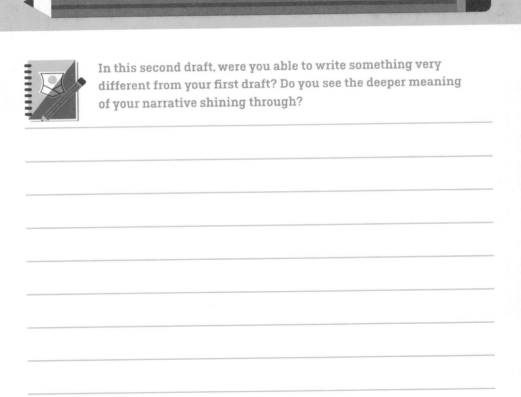

In this second draft, were you able to write something very different from your first draft? Do you see the deeper meaning of your narrative shining through?

DIAGRAM YOUR PLOT

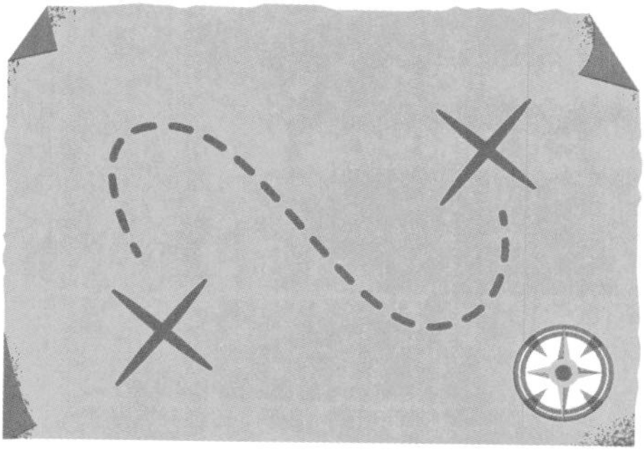

Now that you have identified the deeper meaning of your story, you will want to take a look at its arc. (An arc is a curve. To writers, an arc is the path a story takes as it develops.) Writers can use the same plot diagram that readers use. As a writer, though, you will use it to check your story, identifying places where you may need to elaborate and places where you may need to take something away.

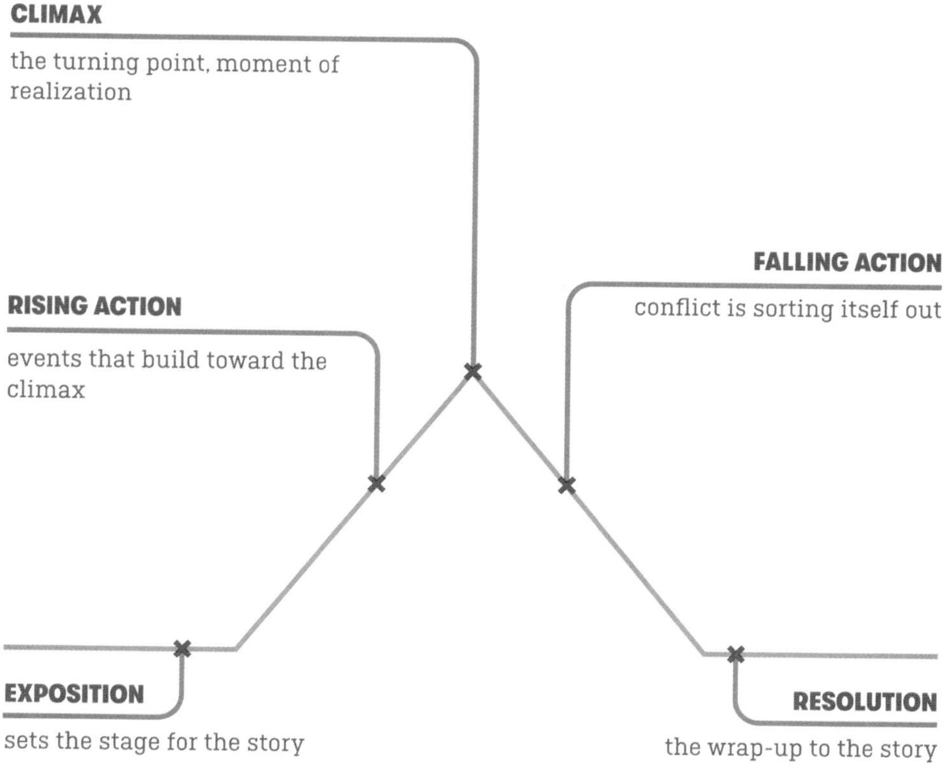

Dan Carroll's "Practical Dance Theory" is a fully revised short personal narrative. Let's take a look at how this narrative looks on a plot diagram.

PLOT DIAGRAM OF "PRACTICAL DANCE THEORY"

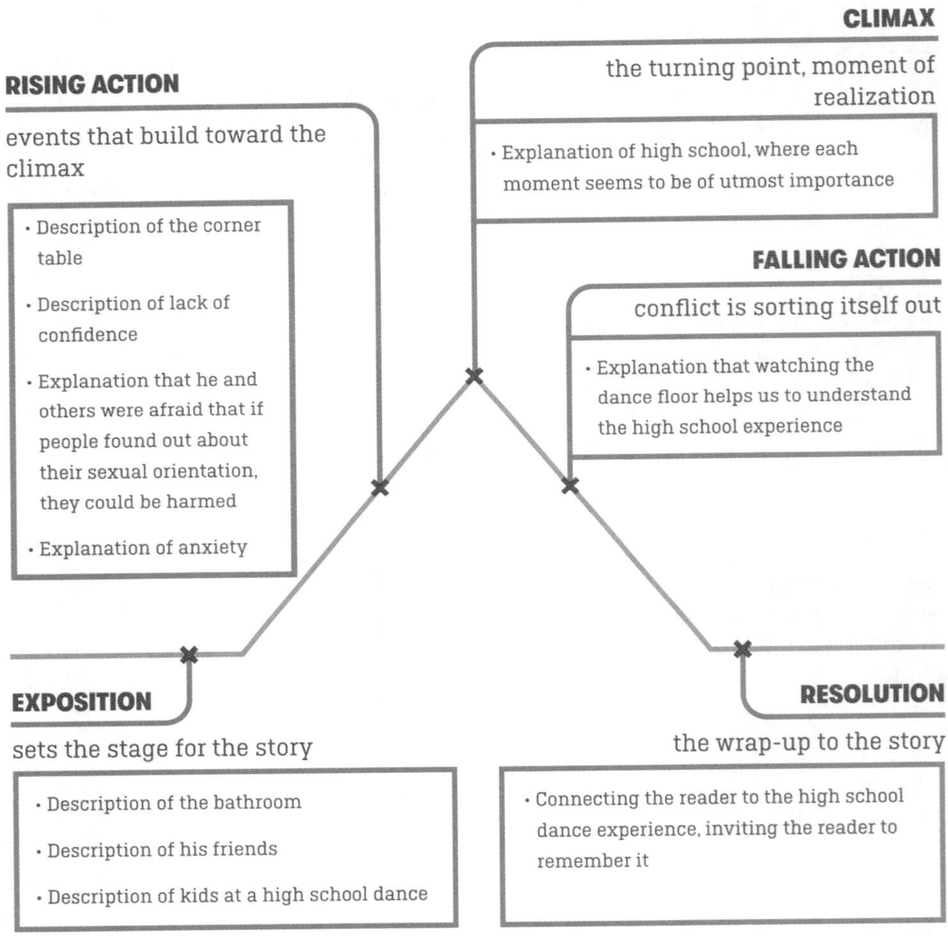

CLIMAX
the turning point, moment of realization
• Explanation of high school, where each moment seems to be of utmost importance
RISING ACTION
events that build toward the climax
• Description of the corner table
• Description of lack of confidence
• Explanation that he and others were afraid that if people found out about their sexual orientation, they could be harmed
• Explanation of anxiety
FALLING ACTION
conflict is sorting itself out
• Explanation that watching the dance floor helps us to understand the high school experience
EXPOSITION
sets the stage for the story
• Description of the bathroom
• Description of his friends
• Description of kids at a high school dance
RESOLUTION
the wrap-up to the story
• Connecting the reader to the high school dance experience, inviting the reader to remember it

When you look at the completed diagram chart, you can see that most of the story is in the rising action, the build toward the climax. In the conclusion, you can see that the narrator has learned something.

Read over your second draft, and fill in the plot diagram with moments and lines from your story.

PLOT DIAGRAM OF MY STORY

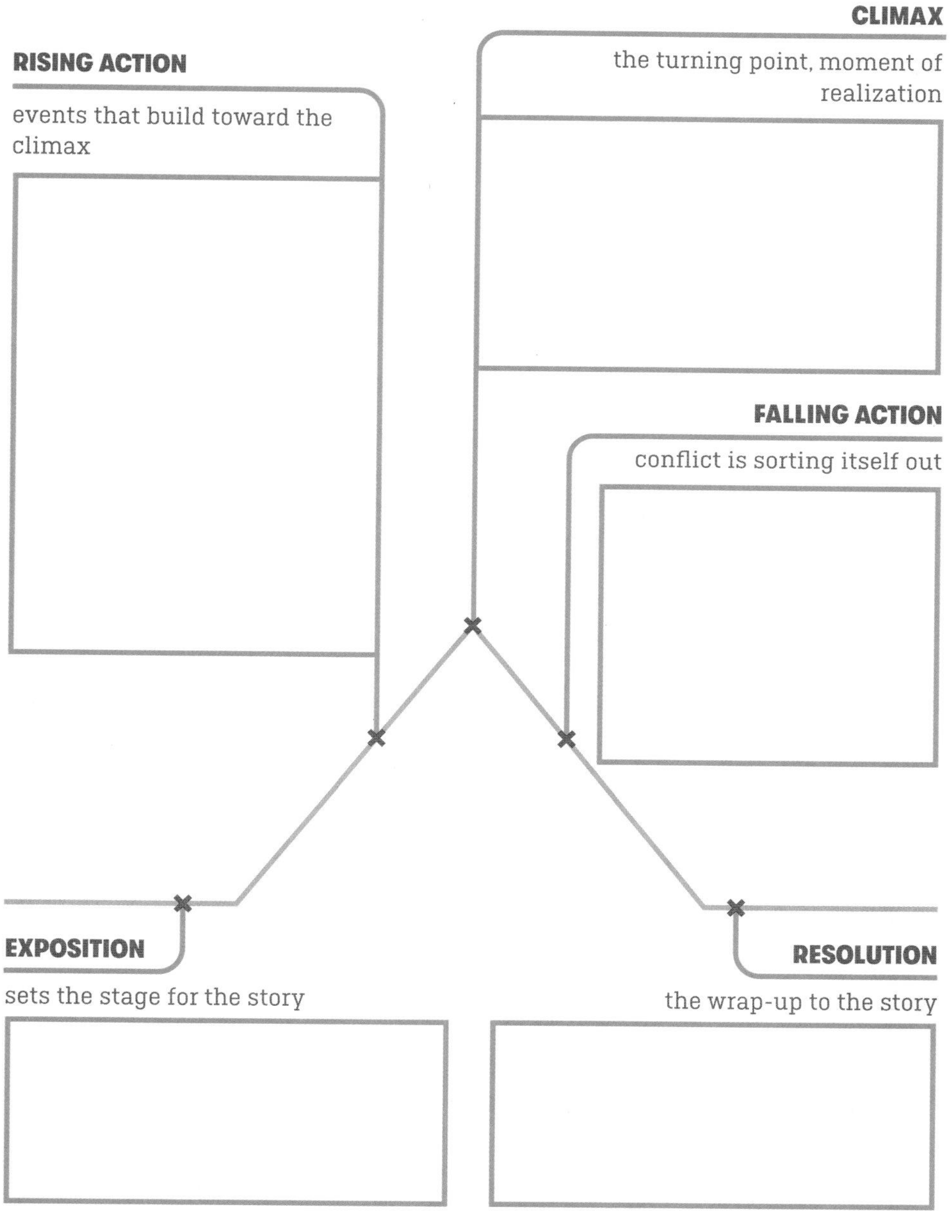

Write your new ideas into your plot diagram above. You will refer to this when you write your next draft.

Take a look. How is the pacing? Do you have all of the components? What do you need to add or take away?

STARTING STRONG: TRY DIFFERENT LEADS

You know how adults always say breakfast is the most important meal of the day? Well, the opening of your story is one of the most important parts of your personal narrative. Personal narratives can begin in all sorts of ways, but they all aim to capture the reader's interest right away and get them to keep reading. Writing an opening that deliberately draws in the reader is called writing a lead. The chart on page 272 lists some strategies writers use to draw in their readers.

READ THIS

EXAMPLES OF DIFFERENT LEADS

LEAD	EXAMPLE	IMPACT IT HAS
Question	Have you ever had a conversation with your pet goldfish?	Engages reader right away
Dialogue	"You're going to be late for the ceremony."	Pulls the reader into the character's world right away
Sound or onomatopoeia (a word that imitates a sound, such as *buzz*, *slurp*, or *squeak*)	BOOOOOM! The sound of the thunder jolted me awake.	Brings the reader right into the moment
The end	Learning to ride my bike taught me the biggest lesson I ever learned.	Gets the reader wondering how the narrator got to this point, wondering what happened
Action	Racing home, I could feel the repeated whacks of my backpack against my back.	Pulls the reader right into the action and sets the tone
Character description	And in walked our new teacher, not much older than we were, a bit messy, but with an enormous smile.	The reader immediately sees a character through the narrator's eyes, making the reader curious about the character.
Setting description	Through the front window of the old Jeep, I could see miles of gray and dusty road ahead.	Has the reader visualize the setting right away
A memory/ flashback	I was five years old, on an enormous stage, and terrified.	Brings the reader to the moment when the event started.

IDENTIFYING DIFFERENT TYPES OF LEADS

Below, you can see examples of how some of these strategies look in published work. Take a look, and identify the type of beginning, or lead, in these stories.

AUTHOR AND TITLE	LEAD	TYPE OF LEAD—*is it a combination?*	YOUR NOTES—*how does it affect the opening?*
I Am Malala, Malala Yousafzai with Christina Lamb	I come from a country that was created at midnight. When I almost died it was just after midday.		
"Papa Who Wakes Up Tired in the Dark," Sandra Cisneros	Your *abuelito* is dead, Papa says early one morning in my room.		
"One Wish," Ronald L. Smith	"Got a piece of corn bread, cuz?"		
"Home," Hena Khan	A blast of heat hits my face as I walk out of our hotel room into the fierce sunlight.		
"All Talk and No Action," Elizabeth Thompson	Have you ever spent hours and hours every night talking on the phone with someone?		

Rewrite your opening by trying out a couple of new leads. Put a star next to the one you like best—your just-right opening!

TRYING NEW LEADS

TYPE OF LEAD YOU ARE TRYING	NEW OPENING

What type of lead works best for your narrative? Why do you think that is?

USING A MENTOR TEXT

Great writers look at how other great writers solved problems and try to use their strategies. We call this using a **mentor text**. The mentor text acts like a role model for what you are writing. You find something you like about the mentor text and create something similar in your own piece with your own words.

Let's look at some great writing and see if you can borrow from some of these writing moves.

SECRET TRICK OF WRITERS:

Read with your writing lens. Read looking for techniques, writing moves, and models that you like. You can even copy favorite phrases into your writer's notebook for safekeeping.

From "Eleven" by Sandra Cisneros:

> My face all hot and spit coming out of my mouth because I can't stop the little animal noises from coming out of me until there aren't any more tears left in my eyes, and it's just my body shaking like when you have the hiccups, and my whole head hurts like when you drink milk too fast.

ANALYZING A MENTOR TEXT

This is one juicy sentence. Instead of saying, "I cried," the narrator used descriptive language and comparisons to make us really feel the act of crying. She used phrases such as:

- Little animal noises
- Aren't any more tears left in my eyes
- My body shaking like when you have the hiccups
- Whole head hurts like when you drink milk too fast

Sandra Cisneros streeeeetched the idea of crying, using descriptive language and comparisons to help the reader really feel the act of crying. The writing move: **Show, don't tell, using descriptive language and comparisons.**

Did you notice anything interesting about the way this sentence is built? The voice that is used?

You may have noticed the *voice*, the way words are put together, in this sentence is more conversational than formal. This sentence is rich not just in details but in its use of English. It honors the way this speaker may put together words rather than an artificial voice that most of us do not use in conversation.

INCORPORATING A MENTOR TEXT INTO YOUR OWN WRITING

Here's an example of borrowing from Sandra Cisneros's style:

Draft 1: I laughed really hard.

Revision: My face pulls up tight, my cheeks pushing up into my eyes and I can't stop the bark bark coming out of my chest, tears run down my face, and my body dances, and I gasp for new air between bursts of Earth-moving laughter.

Now let's try it again!

From "Minnows and Zombies" by Rita Williams-Garcia:

> We walk like a school of fish in our aqua-blue t-shirts.

Rita Williams-Garcia took a simple idea—they walked together in a group—and made it more interesting by incorporating a simile, "like a school of fish." (Remember, a simile is a comparison that uses the word "like" or "as.") This simile shows the way the people are walking together by comparing them to a school of fish. Here's something else you can try: **Use figurative language, such as a simile, to describe something.**

Here's an example of how to revise a straightforward sentence by adding figurative language in the style of Rita Williams-Garcia:

Draft 1: I saw her walking slowly toward the group of bigger girls.

Revision: She approached the bigger girls like a lamb trying to join the flock.

HELP YOUR READER VISUALIZE THE TEXT

Another revision technique you can find in a mentor text is to **include the narrator's inner thoughts, and use details to help the reader visualize the narrator's experience.** Look at this example from "Blue-Sky Home" by Lisa Papademetriou:

> "What is it, to be American?" Grandfather snorted. "No. You are Greek." Phoebe didn't want to tell Grandfather that Greece didn't feel like her country. The sky was so blue it hurt her eyes, for one thing. The toilets had buttons instead of handles. And she could hardly even talk to people.

In this passage, Lisa Papademetriou lets us know the narrator's inner thoughts. She also helps us visualize the narrator's experience by listing details.

Here's what it might look like to use these few lines by Lisa Papademetriou as a mentor text:

Draft 1: "Why didn't you clean your room?" my dad asked. I didn't answer him.

Revision: "Why didn't you clean your room?" my dad asked. I didn't want to tell him that my new room in our new house didn't feel like my own. The floor was carpeted, not wood. The window only had a view of another building, not the tree with the purple flowers in spring. And my older brother's bed was now two rooms away in his own room, not two feet away like it used to be.

USE MENTOR TEXT TO REVISE YOUR STORY

Try this revision strategy with your draft. Choose one of the examples above to rewrite a sentence or two from your own personal narrative.

DRAFT 1 OF YOUR SENTENCE(S)	
MENTOR TEXT—SENTENCE(S)	
MENTOR TEXT—SENTENCE(S)	
YOUR REVISED WORK	
HOW DID IT GO?	

WHAT HAVE YOU LEARNED ABOUT REVISION STRATEGIES?

In this section, you have explored a few different ways you can work on strengthening your narratives through revisions. What stood out to you, and what do you want to remember? Write down anything you would like to use in your own writing.

STRATEGY	EXPLANATION	YOUR NOTES
Spotlight the deeper meaning	Identifying the real meaning in your story and revising to highlight it	
Diagramming your plot	Using the diagram to check and adjust the pacing of your narrative	
Try out different ways to start your narrative	Replacing your opening with different leads to identify the just-right lead	
Using a mentor text	Rewriting a section of your text by imitating the writing moves of another author	

How have parts of your personal narrative changed under the revision process?

THE HOME STRETCH: FROM DRAFT #3 TO PUBLICATION

At this point, you have done a lot of work on your personal narrative. You collected a range of ideas and then narrowed your focus to one topic. You collected details related to your topic, wrote a rough draft, and put that draft through a set of revisions. Wow! That's quite a journey. You are now ready to write Draft 3. Use a clean sheet of notebook paper for this one.

HOW TO WRITE A REVISED DRAFT

For this draft, you will take all the work you have done and mold it into a piece of art. This step will require more deliberate writing as you:

- Follow the flow of your plot diagram.
- Refer back to Drafts 1 and 2.
- Include all your revisions.
- Write while paying attention to paragraphs and sentences.

How has your piece changed?

ADDING A TITLE

Before you finish revising, make sure you have given your personal narrative a title.

Need ideas for choosing a title? Let's look back at some of the narratives explored in this book and consider how the authors may have arrived at those titles.

TITLE	HOW IT RELATES TO THE STORY
"Practical Dance Theory"	This title hints at the big gap between "theory," or what goes on in people's minds, versus what's "practical"—what takes place in the real world, as the reader watches an awkward high school dance alongside the writer.
"Eleven"	This is a piece about birthdays, and in it our speaker turns eleven. The piece shares ideas about what being eleven, or any age, is and isn't.
I Am Malala	This is an autobiography. The title is an introduction. It also tells us who is telling this story.
"Blue-Sky Home"	The sky in this story is a symbol. At first, the speaker is uncomfortable with the blue sky of Greece. But over the course of the piece, she finds comfort in it.

Titles may express, in just a word or two or three, a key idea of your narrative.

You can make these changes in your third draft.

EDITING YOUR WORK

Editing is your last step before publication. This is where you read your work with attention to detail. Editing reminders:

- Read your work out loud.
- Double-check spelling and punctuation (refer to your editing checklist on page 229).

PUBLICATION

You have accomplished so much! Let's celebrate! To get your writing dressed for the party, you will make your final draft. Think about how you want to present it. Do you want a typed version, or do you want to handwrite it on nice clean paper?

However you choose to document this final draft, remember:

- Put your name and the date on it.
- Make sure it has its title.
- Make sure it is neat.

SHARING YOUR WORK

Next, how will you share your piece? Since it's a personal narrative, you probably will want to have someone you know read it. Or, you could even read it out loud. And no matter what you do, put it in a safe place, so you have it forever!

Collect some feedback from the people you shared your piece with, and write down their comments. You might want to ask them about:

- Something they enjoyed
- Something that stood out to them
- A feeling they had while reading your personal narrative

Reflecting on your process as a writer, what two things do you think are most important to remember when writing a narrative?

CHAPTER 6 VOCABULARY

lead: an opening that deliberately draws in the reader

mentor text: an example text by a great writer that can act as a role model for your writing

narrative: an account of events with a beginning, middle, and end

personal narrative: a narrative written from your experience, drawing on your own life

7 WRITING TO SHARE KNOWLEDGE: INFORMATIONAL WRITING

Now that you're in middle school, you know so much more than you used to. Others also expect you to share what you know more than ever. But how? Well, luckily, the writer in you has just the tools! In this chapter, we will look at a few forms your informational writing can take. You will learn some tricks you can use for writing pieces that clearly share information.

CHAPTER CONTENTS

WHAT TO KNOW ABOUT INFORMATIONAL WRITING

Writers share facts and details through **informational writing**, or writing that informs readers about a topic. What makes this type of writing exciting is that it's your opportunity to share your knowledge.

- Informational writing uses facts or opinions to inform, teach, entertain, or persuade.
- There are no fictional characters (though informational writing might be about people).
- Informational writers share facts on a topic.
- Informational writing is nonfiction.
- It may use features such as headings and subheadings.
- Informational writing can be structured in different ways.

DECIDING WHAT TO TEACH

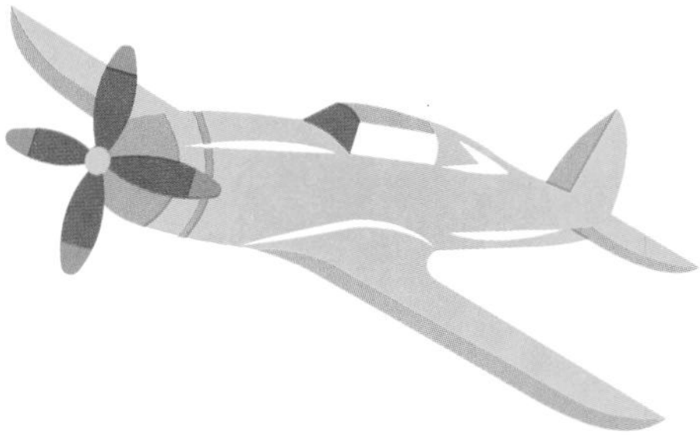

As with your other writing, when you start writing an informational piece, you will need to select a topic. What, you've been told to write a paper on World War II? You feel like you don't have a *choice*. Here's the truth of the matter: Unless your teacher expects you to write a 400-page book on all aspects of World War II, you do have a choice. There's so much power in that choice because you will use it to teach something you find important—something that matters to you.

Literally everything there is to know about WWII

BRAINSTORMING A TOPIC

Before you choose a topic, take a step back. List general things you are interested in and things that matter to you. You can add to and adjust these lists at any time. They are a great resource for you when you need to choose a topic.

BRAINSTORMING GUIDE

THINGS I AM INTERESTED IN	ISSUES THAT MATTER TO ME
Dance	The environment
Baseball and softball	Racism
American Indians	Children's rights
Cooking	
My city's history	
Fashion	
Reading	

Your next step will be to find subtopics that connect to your interests and to the larger topic at hand. You may need to do a little research to get there.

DOING RESEARCH TO FIND SUBTOPICS

You may be thinking that there's no way your passion for baseball can tie into World War II. Here's the thing: Baseball has been around since long before World War II. So with a little bit of research, you might be able to find a link! To find subtopics that connect to both your interests and your larger topic, a quick Internet search can help you find topics you wouldn't have known about. The search recipe is your interest + the big topic.

This is what it looks like if your topic is World War II.

YOUR INTEREST	+	THE BIG TOPIC	=	A POTENTIAL SUBTOPIC
Dance	+	World War II	=	Dances popular in World War II era: jive, swing, jitterbug
Baseball				Why baseball players left their teams to go to war
American Indians				Navajo Code Talkers
Race in America				Tuskegee Airmen
Reading				Distribution of books to American soldiers
Environment				Environmental effects of the atom bomb

But this would never work with science . . . or would it? Let's try it using ecosystems as our topic.

YOUR INTEREST		THE BIG TOPIC		A POTENTIAL SUBTOPIC
Cooking	+	ecosystems	=	Sustainable food sources
American Indians				The role of the Akwesasne Mohawk people in protecting black ash trees
American Fashion				How the fashion industry affects the environment
Pollution				The effect of the BP Deepwater Horizon oil spill in the Gulf of Mexico

There will be other times when you have the freedom to choose any topic. In that case, you can start with the brainstorming you did about your interests and the things that matter to you.

EVALUATING A TOPIC

To narrow these ideas, you can freewrite on your topics, as you did in the previous two chapters. Or, since your ultimate goal is to inform, you may want to check your level of interest and background knowledge. Do this by recording what you know and want to know on a topic.

A person really interested in travel and the environment may choose the Galápagos Islands as their topic. Testing it out may look like this:

TESTING YOUR TOPIC

TOPIC: Galápagos Islands	
WHAT I KNOW	**WHAT I WANT TO KNOW**
In the Pacific Ocean	How do you get to the islands?
Off the coast of Ecuador	What animals are unique to the Galápagos Islands?
Many interesting species live there	How many species are there?
Blue-footed boobies live there	Does pollution affect the animals there?
Near the equator	

Is this a good topic for this person? It seems like they have some general knowledge of the Galápagos Islands. They have listed quite a few questions. So this person seems to have enough interest to do their research.

NARROW YOUR FOCUS

However, this topic needs to be narrowed a bit. How could this person find a focus? Let's identify the subtopics that came up:

- Travel to the Galápagos
- Species living in the Galápagos Islands
- The environment

This narrowed list allows the writer to select a focus and develop a line of inquiry. (That means a series of questions the person wants to answer.) Even after that, the writer may want to narrow their focus. For example, instead of writing about *all* the species, this person may choose one species to research.

Here are some possible inquiry questions:

- What are the feeding habits of the blue-footed booby?
- What's so special about the blue-footed booby?
- Why are their feet blue?
- Does climate change affect this bird?

Give it a try with your own topic:

TESTING YOUR TOPIC

TOPIC:	
WHAT I KNOW	WHAT I WANT TO KNOW

What are two things you want to keep in mind when you are trying to find a topic for your own informational writing?

Which topic did you select for your practice draft? Why?

RESEARCH AND NOTE-TAKING

Once you settle on your topic, you will need to collect information. While doing this, you will **conduct research** and **keep organized notes**. A few tricks of the trade will help you expertly collect information.

Perhaps you are a collector. Maybe you collect rocks, or seashells, or baseball cards. The thing about collecting is that you are focused. Your collection is all about one thing. Maybe you just collect by color—your favorite color is orange, so you collect all things orange. In your effort to build this collection, you look in all sorts of places: clothing stores, thrift shops, toy stores, and so on, for orange items. You may sort your items. Maybe orange shirts go in the closet, orange animals and figurines are on one shelf, and orange office supplies sit on your desk. Researchers are a bit like collectors. They use a range of sources to seek out information on a topic, and then they place that information where it is easy to find.

YOUR SOURCES MATTER!

Remember to ask questions of your sources to check for reliability:

- Is this source relevant? In other words, does it connect to my topic?
- What is the purpose of this source? Does the writer want to convince me of something, share information, or entertain?
- Who is responsible for this source? Is it from a trustworthy publisher? Is it from a blog? (Remember that anyone can blog, post anything, and call it true!)
- When was this information shared? Does my topic require recent publications? Am I using primary evidence from a historical event? (Primary evidence comes from documents and interviews that took place at the time the event happened.)
- Can I double-check the accuracy of this information? If so, where?
- Does this source present just one side of an argument, or does it present multiple sides?

BEST RESEARCH PRACTICES

There are a few rules to follow to make your research as good as it can be:

1. **Use a range of sources**. Even a very short paper should include information from a variety of sources. This gives your work validity—in other words, improves its quality. This means that your diligent, hard work will result in sharing information that is accurate.

2. **Make sure your sources are reliable**. Double-check your information. Use trusted sources—your teacher or a librarian can help you find these. Collect facts and primary (firsthand) accounts. See if you can find the same facts in multiple sources.
3. **Don't rely only on the Internet**. Use books, magazines, and journals, too. Expert writers use many types of sources.
4. **Keep track of all the sources you use**. You will create a list of your sources, called a bibliography, at the end of your paper.
5. **Focus on recording facts, statistics, and direct quotations from people**. Including specific information will strengthen your writing.
6. **Ask a librarian for advice**. Librarians are wonderful resources!

ORGANIZING YOUR NOTES

As you collect information, you will want to keep it organized. This will help you later, when you write. Some people like to take notes on index cards, others on notebook paper, and some people like to type their notes into a document on their computer. There are advantages to each type. Do you have any thoughts on these methods? Practice taking notes on note-taking below!

TYPES OF NOTE-TAKING

MATERIAL FOR NOTE-TAKING	BENEFITS	TO REMEMBER	YOUR THOUGHTS
Index cards	Can be color-coded for easier organization Easy to reorganize when it is time to plan your paper	It's best if you put just one note per card. That way you can more easily organize your information later. Cite your source on every card.	
Loose-leaf paper or notebook	Less paper to manage Can stay in a notebook until needed	Can list the source once and have several notes from that source below Best to use just one side in case you want to cut up your notes to reshuffle them when it's time to organize	
Computer document	Can copy and paste your quotation directly into your paper or organizer	Do more than Internet research! It's easy to fall into the Internet-only trap when you are already online. Don't do it!	

CITATIONS

When you are taking notes, collect all the bibliographic information you will need to properly cite your sources later. (*Cite* is a fancy way of saying "list" or "refer to.")

Bibliographic information means details about your source. These include the author's name, title of the source, name and location of publisher, and page number.

Citing your source means explaining where your information comes from. By doing this, you give credit to other authors. Also, you make your own writing stronger and more trustworthy when you share your sources.

Wherever you are taking your notes, you'll want to make sure you include information such as:

- Author
- Title
- Publisher
- Publication date
- Page number
- Website address (also called URL) and the date you accessed it
- Magazine title

Researchers organize their notes before they even start. They go in with a plan. What's your plan? What sounds like it will work for you? Why?

ANALYZING A QUOTATION

Topic: Blue-Footed Booby; focus of notes: Feeding

SOURCE

"Blue-footed Boobies" by Ellen Lambeth. *Ranger Rick*, March 2010.

PAGE(S)

Not applicable, from a website

RELEVANT PASSAGE

> Boobies have an impressive fishing style. They usually fly high above the waves, on the lookout for schools of small fish below. When they see one, they tilt downward, fold back their wings, and pierce the water's surface headfirst. Boobies also have excellent vision, so their aim is dead-on as they nab their underwater targets. Splash—gotcha!

SIGNIFICANCE OF QUOTATION IN YOUR WORDS

Details about how they fish for food:

- They look for schools of small fish while flying.
- They dive headfirst to catch fish.
- They use their excellent vision to aim for their targets.

ORGANIZING YOUR NOTES

As you read your sources and collect your notes, you will want to organize those notes into categories. If you are using index cards, you can do that by sorting your notes into stacks. If you are writing your notes into a notebook, create subtopics so that you can group like ideas together. For example, research on the blue-footed booby may look like this:

ORGANIZING YOUR RESEARCH

Topic: Blue-Footed Booby

Categories:

PHYSICAL CHARACTERISTICS	HABITAT	EATING
• Blue feet that are webbed	• Live along the coast, from southern North America down to northern South America • Spend most of their time at sea but come ashore to breed	• Prey on schools of small fish • Dive to catch food

Source: "Blue-footed Boobies" by Ellen Lambeth. *Ranger Rick*, March 2010.

In this example, the researcher has sorted the notes into different categories. You may do this as you take notes, or you may sort your notes after doing a bit of research. The important thing is to have organized notes!

RESEARCH AND NOTE-TAKING REMINDERS:

- Use multiple sources.
- Keep accurate records of where your information comes from.
- Organize your notes into categories.

What part of research and note-taking do you expect to be the most challenging? Which system is most appealing to you?

CHOOSING THE RIGHT TEXT STRUCTURE

Great research deserves celebration! Writers celebrate their knowledge by . . . writing! To best celebrate and highlight your great work in an amazing piece of informational writing, you will decide on a structure for presenting it. You can structure informational writing in a few different ways. Some are:

- Sequence (also called time order)
- Compare and contrast
- Cause and effect

Each of these formats gives your readers a different view of your subject. To make the best choice, think about which format best suits your research, your audience, and what you want to say.

DIFFERENT CHOICES FOR TEXT STRUCTURE

TEXT STRUCTURE	BENEFITS	TO REMEMBER	YOUR QUESTIONS
Sequence	Tells things in order Lists the steps of something	When you want to explain something in chronological order	
Compare and contrast	Discusses the similarities and differences of two different objects, events, places, people...	When you want to make connections between things or ideas When you want to explore the relationship between two things or events	
Cause and effect	Explains the reasons or the outcomes of something	When you want to explore why something happened or the changes that happened because of something	

Each of these structures looks a little different, requiring certain planning and writing moves.

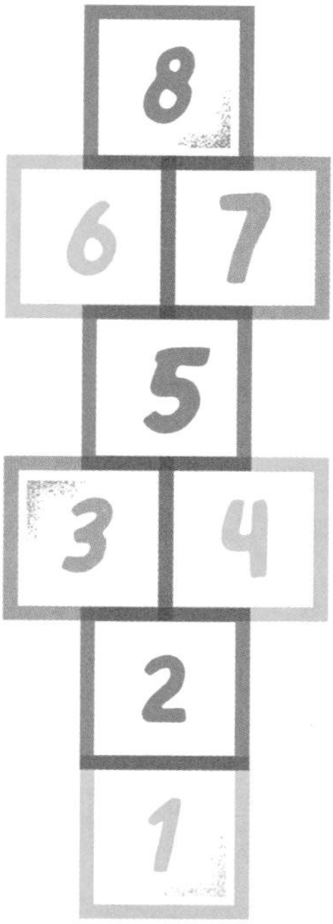

SEQUENCE STRUCTURE

Choose this structure when you want to make sure to include the order of things and describe a sequence of events. Perhaps you are writing a piece that tells how to do something, such as how to tie-dye a shirt. Or maybe you want to share information about an event by discussing the order in which things happened, such as the building of the Brooklyn Bridge.

Below is an example of the sequence structure. Let's take a close look at how the author used a sequencing structure to share information about events. While reading, mark the events in order using numbers. Also, jot down the words that indicate the order of events.

PRACTICING SEQUENCE STRUCTURE

Your sequential writing may look something like this:

From *14 Cows for America*, a story about how a group of Kenyans responded to the events of 9/11

> "*Súpa*. Hello," Kimeli hears again and again. Everyone wants to greet him. His eyes find his mother across the *enkáng*, the ring of huts with their roofs of sun-baked dung. She spreads her arms and calls to him, "*Aakúa*. Welcome, my son."
>
> Kimeli sighs. He is home.
>
> This is sweeter and sadder because he cannot stay. He must return to the faraway country where he is learning to be a doctor.

He thinks of New York then. He remembers September.

A child asks if he has brought any stories. Kimeli nods.

He has brought with him one story. It has burned a hole in his heart.

1 But **first** he must speak with the elders.

2 **Later**, in a tradition as old as the Maasai, the rest of the tribe gathers under an acacia tree to hear the story.

There is terrible stillness in the air as the tale unfolds. With growing disbelief, men, women, and children listen.

Buildings so tall they can touch the sky? Fires so hot they can melt iron? Smoke and dust so thick they can block out the sun?

3 The **story ends**. More than three thousand souls are lost. A great silence falls over the Maasai.

Kimeli waits. He knows his people.

They are fierce when provoked, but easily moved to kindness when they hear of suffering or injustice.

4 **At last**, an elder speaks. He is shaken, but above all, he is sad. "What can we do for these poor people?"

Nearby, a cow lows. Heads turn toward the herd.

"To the Maasai," Kimeli says softly, "the cow is life."

Turning to the elders, Kimeli offers his only cow, Enkarûs. He asks for their blessing. They give it [their blessing] gladly.

SEQUENCE SIGNAL WORDS

Writers use words to signal order and time. You will use these words when you are writing a piece that shows sequence.

Here is a list of words that signal sequence. There's space for you to add some of your ideas.

- First, second, third. . .
- Next
- Then
- Additionally
- Last
- Afterward
- Later
- ____________________
- ____________________
- ____________________

Writers may also use familiar markers of time the way "in the second quarter" might be used in a story about a basketball game. A writer might include terms such as "in the afternoon," "on Monday," or "in the third scene" to make sure readers understand the order.

GRAPHIC ORGANIZERS

Before writing a draft, writers often plan out what they are going to say using graphic organizers or outlines. Graphic organizers help you make sure you have all the elements of your piece, and they lay out for you how you will write it.

Take a look at the examples below. What do they have in common?

A.

Topic:

Write down the events in the order in which they occur.

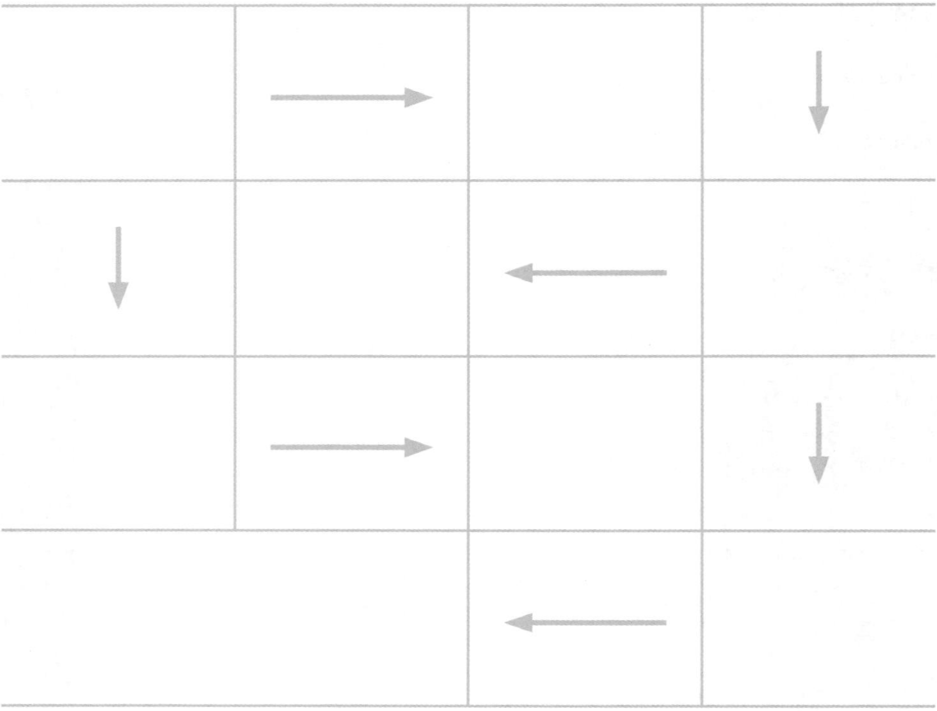

B.

Topic:

List the events in order.

FIRST	
SECOND	
THIRD	
FOURTH	
FINALLY	

C.

Topic:
Write down events in the order they occur. Jot down other information to include.

	EVENT	EVIDENCE, DETAILS
↓		
↓		
↓		
↓		

All three graphic organizers offer a way for you to put information in order. B uses numbers, while A and C use arrows. A looks more like a storyboard than B or C. C has a place to add details or research. These are examples, so use what works for you and the piece you are creating. You may need to add in or take away from the organizer. The important thing is that you are making sure you have your details in order.

Let's take a look at how the writer might have used a graphic organizer for *14 Cows for America*.

Topic: Telling the story of 9/11 to the Maasai people

	EVENT	EVIDENCE, DETAILS
	Arrives home	Sees mom Thinks of NY Sees a child
↓	Must speak with the elders	
↓	Tribe gathers.	Acacia tree Sadness and disbelief
↓	Retelling of 9/11 ends.	People are sad, quiet, including Kimeli
↓	Elder speaks.	"What can we do for these poor people?"
	Cow is donated.	Kimeli hears a cow and is reminded of the importance of the cow. Kimeli donates his cow.

An advantage to graphic organizer C is that it lets you keep the events separate from the details you want to add in.

List a few writing topics that would work great with the sequence structure.

COMPARE AND CONTRAST

Compare and contrast is a writing structure that explores the similarities (comparisons) and differences (contrasts) between two things. It's a great option to use when you are looking at two pieces of literature or two different characters. But it's also smart to use with ideas related to science and history. You can compare and contrast environments, animals, historical leaders, wars, cities, anything!

USING A VENN DIAGRAM

Many researchers and writers use a Venn diagram when they are developing the ideas to compare and contrast. The shape shows you that you are identifying both similarities and differences. See the overlapping part of the two circles? That's where the similarities go.

VENN DIAGRAM #1

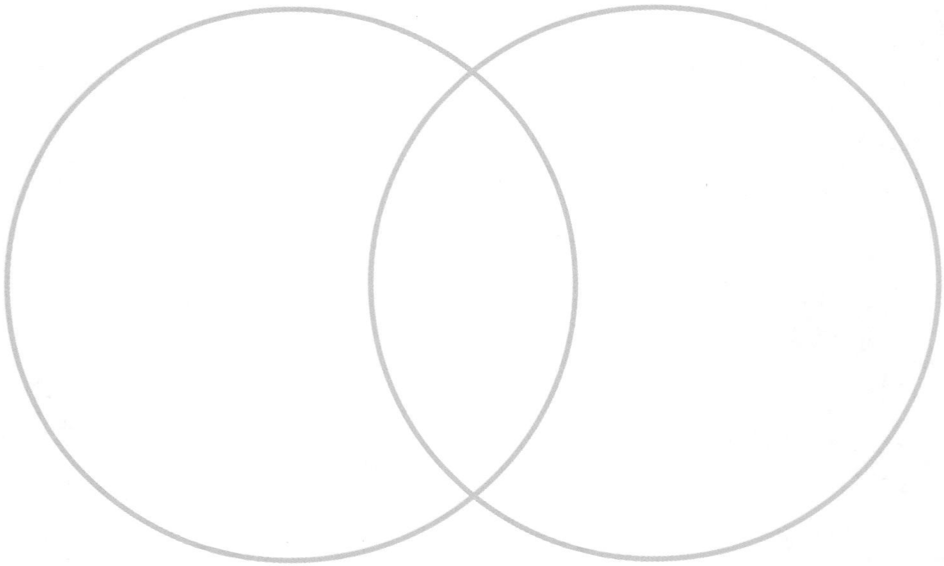

VENN DIAGRAM #2

It can be tricky fitting words into that overlapping part, so another version might look something like this:

THINGS UNIQUE TO OBJECT 1	THINGS IN COMMON	THINGS UNIQUE TO OBJECT 2

If you are comparing two foods, such as hamburgers and hot dogs, this graphic organizer might look something like this:

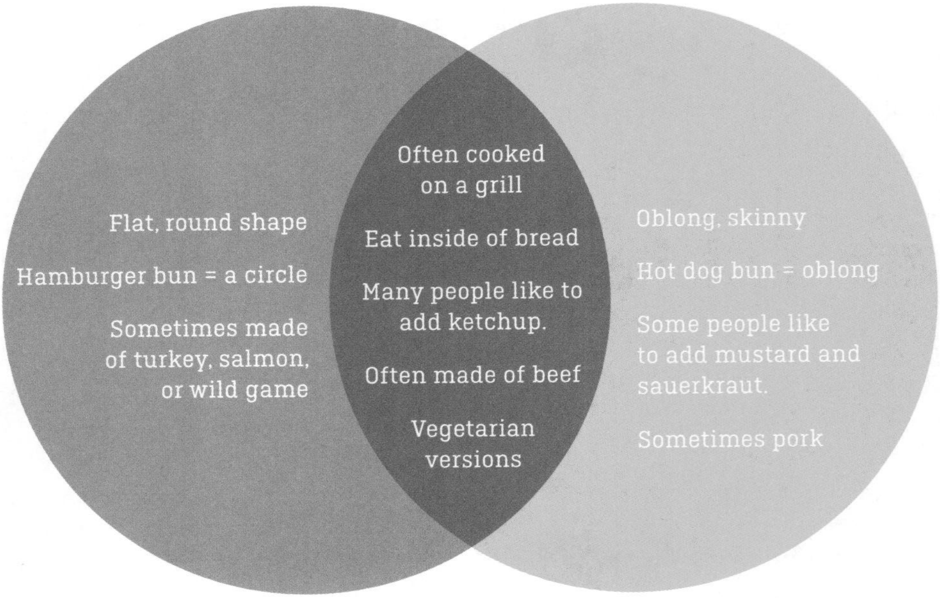

Give it a try! You can compare anything: foods, characters, vacation spots, or swimming pools versus the beach.

YOUR VENN DIAGRAM

THINGS UNIQUE TO OBJECT 1	THINGS IN COMMON	THINGS UNIQUE TO OBJECT 2

This step, of sorting your ideas into similarities and differences, helps ensure that you have two ideas that you can put together into a compare-and-contrast piece. You will need to further organize these ideas before putting them in your paper.

ORGANIZING YOUR COMPARE AND CONTRAST ESSAY

When you looked at the sequencing structure, you probably noticed there was one way to write it: in chronological order. For compare and contrast, you have a couple of options for how to format your essay. Take a look at the outline for a typical five-paragraph essay below. Then think about how that same structure might work using different forms of compare-and-contrast essays.

STANDARD FIVE-PARAGRAPH STRUCTURE

¶	TYPE OF PARAGRAPH	WHAT IT INCLUDES
1	Introduction	"Hook" that makes the reader want to keep reading Connection or supporting information Main idea
2	Body	Claim that supports main idea Evidence or example and explanation
3	Body	Claim that supports main idea Evidence or example and explanation
4	Body	Claim that supports main idea Evidence or example and explanation
5	Conclusion	Restate main idea Give context, explain why this topic matters Possibly include a call to action (a strong suggestion to do something or believe something)

OPTION 1: SUBJECT BY SUBJECT

One option is to write about each object separately, and then follow up with a paragraph in which you point out their similarities. Here's how this may look using the subject of hot dogs and hamburgers:

¶	PURPOSE OF PARAGRAPH	DETAILS TO INCLUDE
1	Introduction—introduces the two objects	Hamburgers and hot dogs are two foods that people often serve together.
2	Describes what's unique about **hamburgers** 	Circles served in circular buns Usually beef, but sometimes made of other meats, such as turkey or salmon Some favorite toppings are cheddar cheese and bacon.
3	Describes what's unique about **hot dogs** 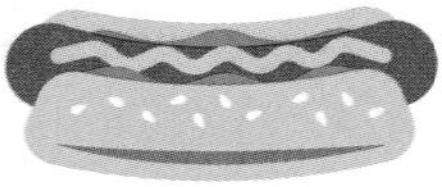	Skinny, cylinder shape served in oblong rolls to match Usually made of pork or beef Some favorite toppings are mustard and sauerkraut.
4	Describes what hamburgers and hot dogs have **in common** 	Served at cookouts Cooked on the grill 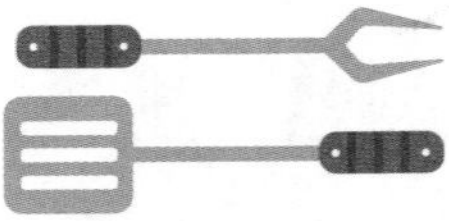 People often want ketchup for them Both have meatless alternatives, so there's something for everyone.
5	Conclusion—wraps up your paper	From coast to coast, people enjoy these popular cookout foods, but they are just a small part of a great cookout. What are your favorite cookout foods?

Another way to format your compare-and-contrast paper is to organize it point by point.

For this format, you need to make sure your information is organized into subtopics, or categories. Think about the information you are sharing about hot dogs and hamburgers. What categories does that information fall into?

- Contents (what they are made of)
- Condiments and toppings
- How people cook and serve them

It might look something like this:

OPTION 2: POINT BY POINT

¶	PURPOSE OF PARAGRAPH	DETAILS ABOUT HAMBURGERS	DETAILS ABOUT HOT DOGS
1	Introduction—draw in reader's interest, introduce objects	Two foods make regular appearances at cookouts.	
2	Details about **the contents**	Usually made of beef Sometimes meats like turkey or salmon Vegetarian options	Pork or beef Vegetarian options
3	Details about **condiments and toppings**	Ketchup Cheese Bacon	Ketchup Mustard Sauerkraut
4	Details about **cooking and serving**	Cookout Can be cooked in a pan Circular roll	Cookout Can be cooked in a pan Oblong bun
5	Conclusion—wraps up the paper	From coast to coast, people enjoy these popular cookout foods, but they are just a small part of a great cookout. What are your favorite cookout foods?	

Here's how the five-paragraph essays based on these organization techniques might look. Note words or phrases that indicate that the objects are being compared and contrasted:

Option 1

In the summer months, Americans from coast to coast head outside to parks, backyards, rooftops, and decks to fire up their grills for cookouts. People pile paper plates with potato salad, corn on the cob, and, of course, hot dogs and hamburgers. Hot dogs and hamburgers are common cookout foods, often appearing side by side on the grill. But are these two absolutely delicious foods more **alike or different**?

Hamburgers are a cookout favorite and have certain **unique qualities**. They are flat and round, served in buns that mimic their shape. Usually, they are made of beef. However, people make hamburgers with turkey, salmon, and a range of other meats. There's something for everyone. People like to add toppings to their hamburgers. Cheddar cheese and bacon are two favorites. These are just a few of the unique qualities of hamburgers.

Hot dogs are also a cookout favorite, **differing** from hamburgers in several ways. Hot dogs are skinny cylinders and fit neatly inside their oblong-shaped buns. They are usually made of beef or pork. Some favorite toppings for hot dogs include mustard and sauerkraut.

Despite their differences, hamburgers and hot dogs have some things **in common**. At cookouts, you will find both being cooked on the grill. Even though hot dogs and hamburgers each have some special toppings, ketchup is a condiment people commonly use on **both**. And **both** hot dogs and hamburgers come in meatless options, so vegetarians can eat them as well! **Despite their many differences,** hot dogs and hamburgers have a **few things in common**.

Hot dogs and hamburgers are similar but different foods that people serve at cookouts. **Both** are eaten in buns that conveniently envelop them. You can smother them with toppings of your choice, or you can eat them plain. Whichever you prefer, hot dogs or hamburgers, your cookout plate is likely crowded with lots of other delicious items. What are your favorites?

Option 2

In the summer months, Americans from coast to coast head outside to parks, backyards, rooftops, and decks to fire up their grills for cookouts. People pile paper plates with potato salad, corn on the cob, and, of course, hot dogs and hamburgers. Hot dogs and hamburgers are common cookout foods, often appearing side by side on the grill. But are these two absolutely delicious foods more **alike or different**?

When you look at the contents of hamburgers and hot dogs, you will notice **similarities and differences**. It is most common to see beef versions of each. And it's pretty easy to find vegan options for **both** hamburgers and hot dogs. **However**, hot dogs and hamburgers tend to differ when it comes to a wider range of options. You may find pork options for hot dogs. **In contrast**, hamburgers come in all sorts of meats, such as turkey, bison, and salmon. In terms of how people make them, hamburgers and hot dogs share a few **similarities** but also have **differences**.

The toppings and condiments people use with hamburgers and hot dogs is another way in which there are **similarities and differences.** People often top **both** hamburgers and hot dogs with ketchup. Ketchup, though, is where the **similarity ends**. Hot dog lovers might cover their hot dogs with mustard and sauerkraut as well, **whereas** hamburgers are often topped with cheese and bacon. No matter what you prefer, though, chances are you enjoy toppings and condiments with your hamburger or hot dog!

They are shaped **differently,** and they can be made of **different** meats and vegetables, but are hot dogs and hamburgers cooked and served in the same way? **Both** hot dogs and hamburgers are often cooked outside on the grill. **Likewise**, the **pair** can be cooked in pans on the stove. While both are typically served as sandwiches inside of a roll, those rolls are **different**. Hamburger buns are round, shaped to fit a hamburger, and sometimes have sesame seeds on top. Hot dog rolls are narrow, to fit the shape of a hot dog, and never have sesame seeds. **Despite their different** shapes, for the most part, hot dogs and hamburgers are cooked and served **similarly**.

Hot dogs and hamburgers are **similar but different** foods served at cookouts. Both are eaten in buns that conveniently envelop them. You can smother them in toppings of your choice, or you can eat them plain. Whichever you prefer, hot dogs or hamburgers, your cookout plate is likely crowded with lots of other delicious items. What are your favorites?

Which did you find easier to read? Why do you think that is?

COMPARE AND CONTRAST AT A GLANCE

WHAT IT IS	Writing structure that examines the similarities and differences of two (or more) things	
WHEN TO USE IT	When you are looking at the connection between two (or more) things	
TWO FORMS IT CAN TAKE	Subject by subject—writing about each thing or idea separately	Point by point—writing about each point of comparison individually
WORDS TO USE	**Comparing:**	**Contrasting:**
	Similarly	In contrast
	Likewise	However
	In comparison	On the other hand
	By comparison	Conversely
	Neither... nor	On the contrary
	At the same time	Although

Summarize what you have learned about the compare-and contrast structure:

CAUSE AND EFFECT

In some cases, you may be exploring how something (the cause) affects something else (the effects). In other words, you may be looking at why things happen the way they do. When this is your intent, it makes sense to write a cause-and-effect essay. This type of writing answers questions such as:

- Why did ____ happen?
- What happened as a result of ______?

- How does ___ affect ___?
- What are the causes and effects of _______?

Cause and effect can mean looking at the outcomes of an event, like this:

1. Explore the ways one cause leads to multiple effects.

Or it can mean considering all that led to an event:

2. Explore the way multiple causes lead to one effect.

Here's part of an article, "Polar Bears in Danger," that examines the threats of extinction for polar bears through a cause-and-effect structure.

> Most polar bears could disappear by the end of the century, scientists say. Global warming is to blame.
>
> According to a study published this month in *Nature Climate Change*, most polar bear populations will be in serious decline by 2080. The cause is melting sea ice. Polar bears hunt seals on the ice. Without ice, the bears must roam on the shore, where they are spending more and more time away from their main food source. That means the animals could starve.
>
> "There's not enough food on land to sustain a polar bear population," Péter K. Molnár told the *New York Times*. He is the study's lead author.
>
> Lack of food leads to another problem: Mother bears may not be fat enough to produce milk for their cubs. Some bear populations could stop having babies, leading to a rapid decline in numbers.
>
> Polar bears are the largest land carnivores on the planet.

They help keep other animal populations in check. Losing them would throw habitats off-balance. "Their loss would reverberate throughout the ecosystem," Marika Holland says. She's one of the authors of the study.

How did it go? How did the cause and effect structure better help you understand the issue? Summarize what you have learned about the cause-and-effect structure:

GRAPHIC ORGANIZERS

Again, you can use graphic organizers to pull together your thoughts. When you have your questions in mind, select the best organizer for sorting your notes. Feel free to adapt these suggested organizers to one that suits your own needs.

EXPLORES THE WAYS ONE CAUSE LEADS TO MULTIPLE EFFECTS

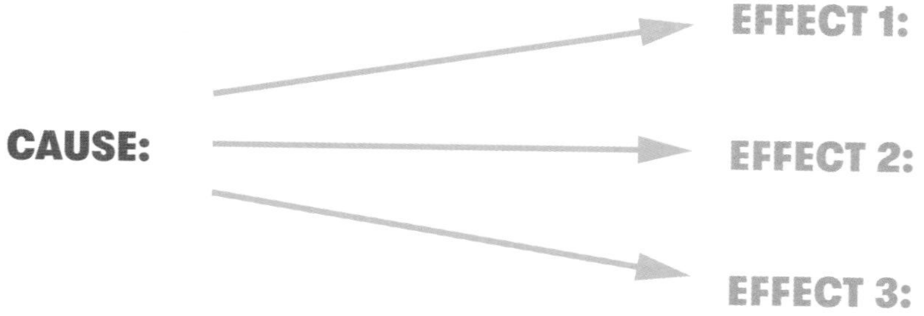

PARAGRAPH #	WHAT IT IS	WHAT GOES INTO IT
1	Introduction	"Hook" that makes the reader want to keep reading Supporting information Main idea stating the cause and its effects
2	Body	**Effect 1** Evidence or examples and explanation
3	Body	**Effect 2** Evidence or examples and explanation
4	Body	**Effect 3** Evidence or examples and explanation
5	Conclusion	Restate main idea Explain why it matters Make a call to action

EXPLORES THE WAY MULTIPLE CAUSES LEAD TO ONE EFFECT

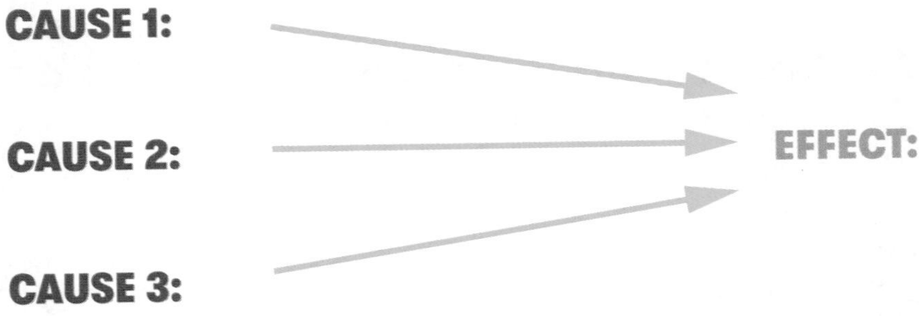

PARAGRAPH #	WHAT IT IS	WHAT GOES INTO IT
1	Introduction	"Hook" that makes the reader want to keep reading Supporting information Main idea stating the cause and its effects
2	Body	**Cause 1** Evidence or examples and explanation
3	Body	**Cause 2** Evidence or examples and explanation
4	Body	**Cause 3** Evidence or examples and explanation
5	Conclusion	Restate main idea Explain why it matters Make a call to action

CAUSE AND EFFECT AT A GLANCE

WHAT IT IS	Writing structure that looks at how events relate to each other, explaining the reasons for something or the effects of something	
WHEN TO USE IT	When you are looking at the impact of something (or more than one thing)	
TWO FORMS IT CAN TAKE	One cause leads to multiple effects.	Multiple effects lead to one cause.
WORDS TO USE	As a result of, therefore, since, reasons for, influenced by, due to	

Summarize what you have learned about the compare-and contrast structure:

Text structures are good for both readers and writers. They help the reader understand the ideas the writer is sharing. For the writer, they help to organize ideas.

Think about what you have learned. What's one new thing you learned about each text structure?

Sequence:

Compare and contrast:

Cause and effect:

REVISING INFORMATIONAL WRITING

As with all of your writing, it is important to revise informational writing. Remember, revising means taking a close look at the ways you have used language. Transitions are a good place to focus your revision efforts.

WORKING ON TRANSITIONS

Transitions are the connections between paragraphs and sentences in your paper.

They are sort of like stoplights and street signs on roads. Transitions help us navigate ideas, and they remind us where we are in the text.

Let's give it a try with the earlier writing comparing and contrasting hot dogs and hamburgers. Before you start, gather a list of great transition words you can use in compare-and-contrast pieces.

We're trying out revising for transitions here. You can adapt this revision strategy to any writing. And you can adapt the revision strategies you use in other sections of this book to informational writing!

TRANSITION WORDS AND PHRASES

COMPARING	CONTRASTING
Similarly	In contrast
Likewise	However
In comparison	On the other hand
By comparison	Conversely
Neither... nor...	On the contrary
At the same time	Although

OPTION 1: SUBJECT BY SUBJECT

Look back at page 320 to revisit the details of the subject-by-subject text structure.

Draft 1

In the summer months, Americans from coast to coast head outside to parks, backyards, rooftops, and decks to fire up their grills for cookouts. People pile paper plates with potato salad, corn on the cob, and, of course, hot dogs and hamburgers. Hot dogs and hamburgers are common cookout foods, often appearing side by side on the grill. But are these two absolutely delicious foods more **alike or different**?

No real hook.

This last sentence of paragraph 1 transitions us into the paper. Try rewording.

Hamburgers are a cookout favorite and have certain **unique qualities**. They are flat and round, served in buns that mimic their shape. Usually, they are made of beef. However, people make hamburgers with turkey, salmon, and a range of other meats. There's something for everyone. People like to add toppings to their hamburgers. Cheddar cheese and bacon are two favorites. These are just a few of the unique qualities of hamburgers.

This paragraph needs a transition sentence.

Hot dogs are also a cookout favorite, **differing** from hamburgers in several ways. Hot dogs are skinny cylinders and fit neatly inside their oblong-shaped buns. They are usually made of beef or pork. Some favorite toppings for hot dogs include mustard and sauerkraut.

Despite their differences, hamburgers and hot dogs have some things **in common**. At cookouts, you will find both being cooked on the grill. Even though hot dogs and hamburgers each have some special toppings, ketchup is a condiment people commonly use on **both**. And **both** hot dogs and hamburgers come in meatless options, so vegetarians can eat them as well! **Despite their many differences,** hot dogs and hamburgers have **a few things in common**.

Last sentence wraps up the paragraph but could use improved language.

Hot dogs and hamburgers are similar but different foods that people serve at cookouts. **Both** are eaten in buns that conveniently envelop them. You can smother them with toppings of your choice, or you can eat them plain. Whichever you prefer, hot dogs or hamburgers, your cookout plate is likely crowded with lots of other delicious items. What are your favorites?

Yikes! The last sentence doesn't really capture the rest of this essay.

The world "both" shows up a lot. This essay could use some variety!

The essay used "despite their differences" twice. That might be too many times.

Here's a revised essay with new sentences in **boldface.** The new sentences:

- Include more transition words and phrases from the list.
- Work to better link ideas together.

Don't you love a good cookout? In the summer months, Americans from coast to coast head outside to parks, backyards, rooftops, and decks to fire up their grills for cookouts. People pile paper plates with potato salad, corn on the cob, and, of course, hot dogs and hamburgers. Hot dogs and hamburgers are common cookout foods, often appearing side by side on the grill. **Despite the fact that they are both meat sandwiches covered in ketchup, cookout chefs often serve both at the same time.** So are these two absolutely delicious foods more alike or different?

Hamburgers set themselves apart from hot dogs with certain unique qualities. They are flat and round, served in buns that mimic their shape. Usually, they are made of beef. However, people make hamburgers with turkey, salmon, and a range of other meats. There's something for everyone. People like to add toppings to their hamburgers. Cheddar cheese and bacon are two favorites. **Juicy hamburgers, smothered in cheese, are a hand-downs favorite for lovers of beef, and just one can**

make the average person feel full. They are a special cookout sandwich.

On the other hand, hot dogs, also a cookout favorite, have their own unique characteristics that draw their own following. Hot dogs are skinny cylinders and fit neatly inside their oblong-shaped buns. **You are just as likely to find them made of pork as you are beef.** Some favorite toppings for hot dogs include mustard and sauerkraut. **Hot dogs and their toppings are, by comparison, not quite as filling as hamburgers. For this reason, fans of hot dogs may take more than one.**

Despite their differences, hamburgers and hot dogs do have some things in common. At cookouts, you will find both being cooked on the grill. Even though hot dogs and hamburgers each have some special toppings, ketchup is a condiment commonly used on both. **Similarly, hot dogs and hamburgers each** come in meatless options, so vegetarians can eat them as well! **Although they appear to be quite different,** hot dogs and hamburgers have a few things in common.

Hot dogs and hamburgers are similar but different foods that people serve at cookouts. Both are eaten in buns that conveniently envelop them. You can smother them in toppings of your choice, or you can eat them plain. Whichever you prefer, hot dogs or hamburgers, your cookout plate is likely crowded with lots of other delicious items. **Would you dare to have a cookout with just hot dogs or just hamburgers?**

OPTION 2: POINT BY POINT

Look back at page 322 to revisit the details of the point-by-point text structure.

DRAFT 1

In the summer months, Americans from coast to coast head outside to parks, backyards, rooftops, and decks to fire up their grills for cookouts. People pile paper plates with potato salad, corn on the cob, and, of course, hot dogs and hamburgers. Hot dogs and hamburgers are common cookout foods, often appearing side by side on the grill. But are these two absolutely delicious foods more alike or different?

When you look at the contents of hamburgers and hot dogs, you will notice similarities and differences. It is most common to see beef versions of each. And it's pretty easy to find vegan options for both hamburgers and hot dogs. However, hot dogs and hamburgers tend to differ when it comes to a wider range of options. You may find pork options for hot dogs. In contrast, hamburgers come in all sorts of meats, such as turkey, bison, and salmon. In terms of how people make them, hamburgers and hot dogs share a few similarities but also have differences.

The toppings and condiments people use with hamburgers and hot dogs is another way in which there are similarities and differences. People often top both hamburgers and hot dogs with ketchup. Ketchup, though, is where the similarity ends. Hot dog lovers might cover their hot dogs with mustard and sauerkraut as well, whereas hamburgers are often topped with cheese and bacon. No matter what you prefer, though,

NOTES FOR REVISION—*focusing on transition sentences*	**IMPROVED SENTENCES**

chances are you enjoy toppings and condiments with your hamburger or hot dog!

They are shaped differently, and they can be made of different meats and vegetables, but are hot dogs and hamburgers cooked and served in the same way? Both hot dogs and hamburgers are often cooked outside on the grill. Likewise, the pair can be cooked in pans on the stove. While both are typically served as sandwiches inside of a roll, those rolls are different. Hamburger buns are round, shaped to fit a hamburger and sometimes have sesame seeds on top. Hot dog rolls are narrow, to fit the shape of a hot dog, and never have sesame seeds. Despite their different shapes, for the most part, hot dogs and hamburgers are cooked and served similarly.

Hot dogs and hamburgers are similar but different foods served at cookouts. Each are eaten in buns that conveniently envelop them. You can smother them in toppings of your choice, or you can eat them plain. Whichever you prefer, hot dogs or hamburgers, your cookout plate is likely crowded with lots of other delicious items. What are your favorites?

NOTES FOR REVISION—*focusing on transition sentences*	**IMPROVED SENTENCES**

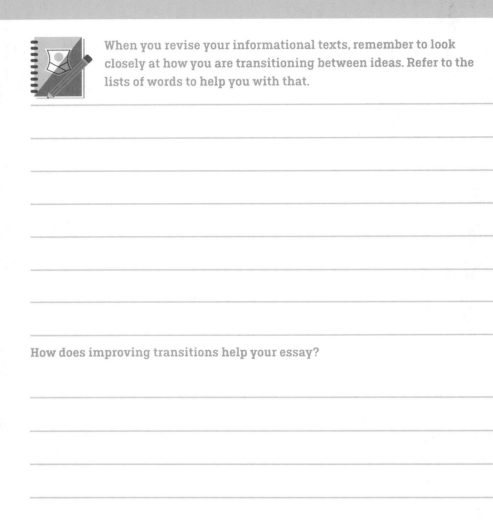

When you revise your informational texts, remember to look closely at how you are transitioning between ideas. Refer to the lists of words to help you with that.

How does improving transitions help your essay?

REVIEW AND SUMMARIZE INFORMATIONAL WRITING

You have learned a lot about writing informational texts. Let's review and summarize what was presented.

REFLECTING ON WRITING INFORMATIONAL TEXTS

ASPECT OF INFORMATIONAL WRITING	ONE THING YOU LEARNED	ONE QUESTION YOU HAVE
Finding a topic		
Research and note-taking		
Sequence text structure		
Compare-and-contrast text structure		
Cause-and-effect text structure		
Revising transitions		

In this chapter, we covered a lot of ground regarding writing to share information. Before you turn the page, give some thought to what information you have to share. Now that you're older and have more research ability, think of topics that you can add to what you know with research. Get your ideas together and dig in!

What will your first topic be?

And what kind of text structure do you think you will use?

CHAPTER 7 VOCABULARY

bibliographic information: details about your source, including the author's name, title of the source, name and location of publisher, and page number or numbers where you found the information

informational writing: words written to tell or explain about a topic

transitions: connections between paragraphs and sentences in your paper that help your reader understand the flow of ideas; examples of transition words include *first, next, then, as a result, also, because, similarly, in contrast*, and *finally*

NEWS

8 SO YOU WANT TO START AN ARGUMENT?

Arguments have a bad reputation. They are associated with raised voices, big gestures, and sometimes a word or two that we wish we could take back. But perhaps you have been in an argument where you came to see something in a new way. Or perhaps your ideas got someone else to change their thinking—for instance, around when your bedtime should be. Arguments can be positive, especially if you are able to construct a powerful one. How?

CHAPTER CONTENTS

WHY WE ARGUE

Constructing written arguments is common in our world. A written argument is an essay planned around a position, or claim, that is supported with reasons and evidence. It's a way to convince people to see a new viewpoint, take action, support a cause, or see a character in a new light. Writing an argument is kind of like building a case in court. And here's the thing about writing an argument: crafting these papers will make you smarter and help your academic thinking become more sophisticated.

ELEMENTS OF ARGUMENTATIVE WRITING

What can you find in an argument essay?

- **Claim**
- **Reasons for the claim**
- **Evidence that supports that claim**
- **Explanation of the evidence**
- **Counterclaim (also called an opposing argument—the other side's opinion)**
- **Evidence for the counterclaim**
- **Reason or reasons the counterclaim is not as strong**

As you work through this chapter, you may recognize some ideas and concepts from Chapter 3 on reading nonfiction. That's no surprise, since now you are the one writing it!

LAYING THE GROUNDWORK

The first steps in building a persuasive argument are selecting a topic, ideally something you care about, and researching it. While you're researching, you'll probably uncover information that will surprise you, and can make your argument stronger.

ASKING THE RIGHT QUESTION

What are you going to argue? As with any other writing project, you can start by listing ideas. You can write an argument essay on almost *anything*. Brainstorm as you would brainstorm for other papers. Begin with the question: what matters to you?

After you arrive at a topic, you will turn it into a question that will direct your research. This question will help you get the lay of the land and navigate through your research. Make sure to:

- Be specific. Target one aspect of an idea.
    - DON'T: *What happened in World War II?* This is too broad. It might be a better fit for informational writing.
    - DO: *Was the dropping of two atom bombs necessary to end World War II?* This question narrows the focus of the research to the bombings of Hiroshima and Nagasaki in Japan and the final part of the war.
- Help others think deeply. Come up with a question that makes people really think—one that does not have an easy answer.
    - DON'T: *What is it like to have homework in middle school?* This question requires the researcher to describe an

experience. It sounds like a question to be answered in narrative writing, not in a written argument.

    - DO: *Homework in middle school: does it help or harm the growth of adolescents?* This question encourages the researcher to examine the ways homework affects adolescents. It also requires the researcher to make a judgment about the role of homework.

- Come up with an open-ended question instead of one that has a "yes" or "no" answer. Make sure there are different ways to answer the question.

    - DON'T: *Can wind provide energy for our homes and businesses?* There's a clear answer for this question. It would work better as a starting point for informational writing.

    - DO: *Are wind farms a useful, practical energy option?* A researcher who asks this question must examine what is involved in wind power and make a decision about how well this energy source is likely to work.

Here's a way you can organize your paper as you move from your overall topic to your research question. Feel free to adapt it to your own way of thinking!

NARROWING YOUR FOCUS

BIG TOPIC	FOCUS (RELYING ON AREA OF INTEREST)	RESEARCH QUESTION	NOTES ABOUT THE QUESTION
Social issues	Gun violence	What is the role of government in gun violence?	Focuses research on examining laws and their effects on gun violence Must decide about government's ability to influence gun violence

Literature	*Tiger Rising*	What is the most powerful symbol in *Tiger Rising*?	Encourages exploration of all the symbols Must decide about those symbols
Ocean life	Whales	Should people keep whales in captivity or release them into the wild?	Focuses research onto the benefits and drawbacks of captivity Must make a judgment about the role of captivity

Give it a try with a few ideas on your "What matters to me?" list that you came up with in Chapter 7 on informational writing and choose one question that you want to do research on!

BRAINSTORMING GUIDE

BIG TOPIC	FOCUS (RELYING ON AREA OF INTEREST)	RESEARCH QUESTION	NOTES ABOUT THE QUESTION

What's one thing to remember as you decide on your topic and research question?

CONDUCTING RESEARCH

When you write an argument paper, you are not just asking a question but answering one. You will need evidence to prove your point. You'll find this evidence through research—using your pickaxe to sort through lots of information to find the answers and details you need. Ultimately, the notes you collect will become your evidence—very much like how lawyers use evidence in a court case. You will need to choose a system for taking notes so that you don't lose track of your evidence.

Select a system you will use for taking notes:

- Index cards
    - Pro: Easy to sort
    - Con: Cards can get out of order or be lost.

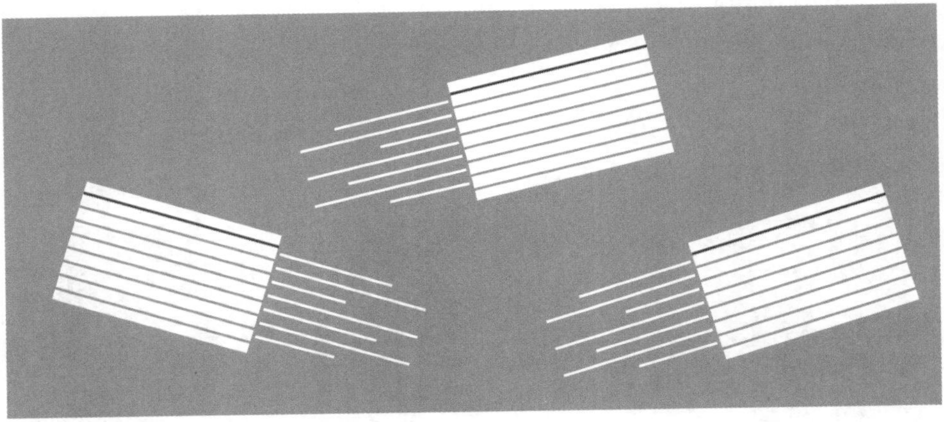

- Note-taking pages—by source
    - Pro: Forces you to record source information
    - Con: Can make sorting difficult
- Note-taking pages—by subtopic
    - Pro: Notes are organized as you gather them, and you can see where you need more information.
    - Con: You will need to add more subtopics over time, or else you may miss important notes.

It doesn't matter *which* system you select. Just make sure it's the system that works for you and that you understand its advantages and limitations.

This is what your note page can look like. Or you can adapt it in a way that works for you.

NOTE-TAKING GUIDE: BY SOURCE

MY RESEARCH QUESTION:			
Book title/ website:	Author:	Publisher:	Publication year:

PAGE #	DIRECT QUOTATION	WHY IT RELATES TO YOUR QUESTION OR WHY IT MATTERS

Before you start on your research, you need to know what makes good evidence.

EXHIBIT A: WORTHWHILE EVIDENCE

√	YOUR EVIDENCE WILL BE	WHAT THAT WORD MEANS	WHAT THAT MEANS TO YOU
	Pertinent	Connected to your topic	
	Effective	Proves or supports your argument	
	Credible	Comes from reliable sources	
	Varied	Comes from more than one source	

TIPS FOR FINDING EVIDENCE

Use facts. In other words, use information that can be proved true.

- Use primary information. This comes directly from the time or event you are writing about. For example, if you are writing about Abraham Lincoln, provide quotations of words he said or wrote, or include eyewitness accounts of his speeches.

- Use statistics. These are numbers that show patterns or changes or that provide information about larger issues.

eyewitness account: a description of an event by someone who was actually there when it happened

primary information: facts and details that come directly from the time or event you are writing about

CHOOSING A SIDE

After doing a bit of research, you are ready to pick a side and define your position. It's best to do that by rereading your evidence and revisiting your question. This time, try to come up with an answer!

MAKING A CLAIM

Freewrite an answer to your question. Don't worry about your writing or about quoting your sources. Just write fiercely for a short amount of time. It might look something like this:

FREEWRITING YOUR WAY TO A CLAIM

Question: Was Colin Kaepernick kneeling for the national anthem an act of moral courage or a sign of disrespect?

Courage is, well, courageous. Moral courage might require more bravery than any other type of courage. Colin Kaepernick kneeled for the national anthem on many occasions. Was it courageous or disrespectful? Injustices happen, and too often no change follows because people in power do not want to listen. Kaepernick was speaking out against the unfair treatment of people of color in the United States, especially the issue of police brutality. Yes, people can hold rallies and write letters and post messages on social media. But people have been fighting for equality for decades, even hundreds of years, and it hasn't worked yet. Colin Kaepernick understood that as an NFL player, he had a platform and could draw attention to this issue. He also knew that the NFL and some team owners would not be happy with him using this platform. Still, he staged his protests. Knowing the risk and pushing forward shows his moral courage.

Many people found his kneeling disrespectful, including some veterans. Others claim it is his right as an American citizen to kneel in protest. Either way, Kaepernick made it clear that he would continue to kneel until all Americans are treated fairly.

He had been a star football player. He had a lot to lose. And he even ended up losing his job. People voted him to be the most hated player in the NFL. But his jersey became a top seller. And other players joined his cause by kneeling during the anthem as well. Meanwhile, Kaepernick missed some of his prime football playing years.

Once you are done with your freewrite, you will pull out that pickaxe to identify the finer points of what you included. Read your freewrite, looking for an answer to your question and reasons you gave that answer. You can also look for statements you disagree with. You'll want to mark these parts as you go over your freewrite. You can see an example of this process below: the underlined parts are potential answers or reasons, and the parts in green are rejected answers.

ANALYZING YOUR FREEWRITE

Question: Was Colin Kaepernick kneeling for the national anthem an act of moral courage or a sign of disrespect?

Courage is, well, courageous. Moral courage might require more bravery than any other type of courage. Colin Kaepernick kneeled for the national anthem on many occasions. Was it courageous or disrespectful? Injustices happen, and too often no change follows unless people make their voices heard. Kaepernick was speaking out against the unfair treatment of people of color in the United States, especially the issue of police brutality. Yes, people can hold rallies and write letters and post messages on social media. But people have been fighting for equality for decades, even hundreds of years, and it hasn't worked yet. Colin Kaepernick understood that as an NFL player, he had a platform and could draw attention to this issue. He also knew that the NFL and some team owners would not be happy with him using this platform. Still, he staged his protests. Knowing the risk and pushing forward shows his moral courage.

Many people found his kneeling disrespectful, including some veterans. Others claim it is his right as an American citizen to kneel in protest. Either way, Kaepernick made it clear that he would continue to kneel until all Americans are treated fairly.

He had been a star football player. He had a lot to lose. And he even ended up losing his job. People voted him to be the most hated player in the NFL. But his jersey became a top seller. And other players joined his cause by kneeling during the anthem as well. Meanwhile, Kaepernick missed some of his prime football playing years.

Once you've identified the key elements of your freewrite, ask yourself your question one more time. Except this time . . . you're going to answer it!

ASKED AND ANSWERED

QUESTION	Was Colin Kaepernick kneeling for the national anthem an act of moral courage or a sign of disrespect?
MY ANSWER IN A COMPLETE SENTENCE	Colin Kaepernick displayed moral courage when he kneeled during the national anthem at NFL games.
REASONS FOR MY ANSWER	1. He knew the risks. 2. He pushed forward, even when he was facing punishments for his actions.

Ready to give it a try with your own research?

YOUR TURN: FREEWRITING YOUR WAY TO A CLAIM

FREEWRITE

Don't forget to go back over your freewrite with your pickaxe!

YOUR TURN: ASKED AND ANSWERED

QUESTION	
MY ANSWER IN A COMPLETE SENTENCE	
REASONS FOR MY ANSWER	

Ideally, you have two reasons if you are aiming for a five-paragraph essay (which is often the standard for school assignments). If you don't, reread your freewrite carefully, looking for another reason.

How did the freewrite help you develop your claim and reasons?

ARGUING FOR THE ENEMY: COUNTERCLAIMS

Have you heard the phrase "**devil's advocate**?" When someone takes on the role of devil's advocate, they are arguing against their own ideas as a means of forcing the development of an argument.

Let's imagine two friends are discussing how much they love summer. It might go something like this:

FRIEND A

I love summer.

FRIEND B

Me too.

FRIEND A

Summer is just the best.

FRIEND B

I agree.

Not a very interesting conversation, right? Also, we don't really know what there is to like about summer. Suppose one friend offers to play devil's advocate. The conversation takes a far more interesting turn!

FRIEND A

I love summer.

FRIEND B

Me too.

FRIEND A

Summer is just the best.

FRIEND B

You know what? I just realized I don't like summer. Winter is better.

FRIEND A

What!? But summer is nice and warm.

FRIEND B

I have to do extra chores in summer.

FRIEND A

You're doing extra chores because you are on vacation! You can still hang out so much more than when it's winter.

FRIEND B

JK 😜 —I do love summer. I just wanted to know why you love summer!

See how the argument changed once one friend decided to play devil's advocate? Friend A developed their argument because Friend B challenged it. In a paper, a **counterclaim**, which is an example of a reason others might disagree with your argument, functions pretty much the same way. It tests whether the argument you're making is valid, and it forces you to strengthen your argument.

A useful way to arrive at a counterclaim for your paper is to complete the following sentence:

People who disagree with me might argue ________________________.

Here's what it may look like in the argument we started:

People who disagree with me might argue that **Colin Kaepernick's actions were so offensive to veterans of the military that there is no courage in those actions.**

Now that you have a counterclaim, you can fill in another piece of the argument from before. Next, ask yourself: Can I **refute** the counterargument? This will become an important element of your argument!

refute: to prove something to be false

ADDING TO YOUR ARGUMENT WITH A COUNTERCLAIM

QUESTION	Was Colin Kaepernick kneeling for the national anthem an act of moral courage or a sign of disrespect?
MY ANSWER IN A COMPLETE SENTENCE	Colin Kaepernick displayed moral courage when he kneeled during the national anthem at NFL games.
REASONS FOR MY ANSWER	He knew the risks. He pushed forward, even when he was facing punishments for his actions.
COUNTERCLAIM	Kneeling was not an act of moral courage because it offended many people.
REASONS COUNTERCLAIM IS NOT A SOLID ARGUMENT	Just being offensive does not take away from moral courage. In fact, it supports the idea that the behavior was moral courage because there was so much risk involved. Also, many veterans support his actions and his right to kneel during the anthem.

The counterclaim, like in the discussion between two friends, does two things:

- It shows that the writer has considered other viewpoints. (That's part of being a scholar!)
- It boosts the argument the writer is making.

Give it a try with the final question and answer you came up with in the previous section:

YOUR TURN: ADDING TO YOUR ARGUMENT WITH A COUNTERCLAIM

People who disagree with me might argue ______________________________.

QUESTION	
MY ANSWER IN A COMPLETE SENTENCE	
REASONS FOR MY ANSWER	
COUNTERCLAIM	
REASONS COUNTERCLAIM IS NOT A SOLID ARGUMENT	

Jot down two things you learned about counterclaims:

PUTTING THE PIECES TOGETHER

Congratulations! You have a question, an answer, reasons, and a counterclaim you can refute. These are all the ingredients for a great argument! Give yourself a nice pat on the back for all that great academic thinking. You are now ready to write the **outline**.

ROAD MAP TO AN ARGUMENT: OUTLINING YOUR PAPER

You are going to include lots of details and evidence in this outline. You are also going to think critically about the order in which you make your argument.

Think about how a song speeds up and slows down to help you understand the ideas and emotion. The change in pace forces your ear to linger on certain ideas, and the order of the pace is deliberate. The writer of a song organizes the music so that you absorb information and emotion in a certain way. You are going to do the same with your paper!

Before we get into the nitty-gritty of the outline, let's take a look at all of the pieces of this puzzle that will make up the foundation of your argument.

That means everything you will need in your argument paper to prove your point once and for all. Fill it out with your research and all the thinking you've done so far!

ELEMENTS OF AN ARGUMENT

YOUR CLAIM

This is the guiding idea for your whole paper.

REASON 1 THAT SUPPORTS YOUR CLAIM		REASON 2 THAT SUPPORTS YOUR CLAIM	
EVIDENCE	SOURCE	EVIDENCE	SOURCE

Support each reason with evidence. Make sure that you can explain how that evidence supports your reason and claim.

COUNTERCLAIM	
EVIDENCE	SOURCE

COUNTERCLAIM'S WEAKNESS	
EVIDENCE	SOURCE

You are going to include evidence for both your counterclaim and for your reassertion of your claim.

ADDING IN EVIDENCE

Now you want to select the best possible evidence. Since you likely took pretty extensive notes, you have a bit to select from. You will want to choose great evidence that really focuses on each reason. Here's a reminder about evidence to use as you make your selection:

√	YOUR EVIDENCE WILL BE	WHAT THAT WORD MEANS	WHAT THAT MEANS TO YOU
	Pertinent	Connected to your topic	
	Effective	Proves or supports your argument	
	Credible	Comes from reliable sources	
	Varied	Comes from more than one source	

Nothing is set in stone! If you don't have quite enough evidence, or you are feeling unsatisfied with some of your evidence (yay for being a perfectionist!), go ahead and do some more research. That's a great thing about the writing process—it goes in both directions. You can always go back a step if you don't think you're ready to move forward.

THINKING ABOUT ORDER

There's one last stop before you outline. Consider the order in which you are presenting your information.

Which reason should come first?
How do you order the evidence for each reason?
Let's say the claim is:

Too much homework harms students.

And the reasons are:

- *It can be bad for kids' health.*
- *It takes away from other productive activities.*

You need to make a decision. When you're a writer looking at those two reasons you came up with, you have to decide which one will go first. There is no wrong answer—just a choice that makes more sense to you and your paper. You may feel like the health reason will have a bigger impact on the reader, so you want to save that for last. Think carefully about how you order your reasons. The same rule applies for the evidence.

Now it's time to outline! You can fill in the boxes provided or use notebook paper or a computer.

YOUR ARGUMENT OUTLINE

	SENTENCES WITHIN EACH PARAGRAPH	YOUR IDEAS AND INFORMATION
INTRODUCTION	Hook that makes the reader want to keep reading	
	Background information	
	Your claim and reasons	
BODY PARAGRAPH 1 (REASON 1)	Topic sentence: reason 1	
	Evidence 1	
	Explain the evidence and how it supports your reason.	
	Evidence 2	
	Explain the evidence and how it supports your reason.	
	Closing sentence: explain how this reason and evidence support your overall argument.	

BODY PARAGRAPH 2 (REASON 2)	Topic sentence: reason 2	
	Evidence 1	
	Explain the evidence and how it supports your reason.	
	Evidence 2	
	Explain the evidence and how it supports your reason.	
	Closing sentence: explain how this reason and evidence support your overall argument.	
BODY PARAGRAPH 3 (COUNTERCLAIM)	Topic sentence: Counterclaim	
	Evidence	
	Explanation of that evidence	
	Counterclaim takedown (points out weakness in the counterclaim)	
	Evidence that supports your dismantling of the counterclaim	
	Closing sentence: explain how this matters to your overall argument.	
CONCLUSION	Topic and why it matters	
	Restate your claim	
	Why should your reader share your view?	
	What is possible? Convince your reader to act a certain way or believe something, and then discuss what is next.	

BEGINNING AND ENDING YOUR ARGUMENT

As you know, it's important to make the beginning and ending of your essay stand out to draw in readers and make sure they remember your takeaway. Let's look more closely at these key sections of your outline, using that earlier example.

INTRODUCTION OUTLINE

INTRODUCTION	Hook	Do heroes wear helmets and shoulder pads? Some do.
	Background information	Moral courage, which means standing up for what you believe in, is right despite the risk of social and personal punishments. It is a heroic act. And yes, sometimes these heroes wear football helmets.
	Your claim and reasons	When he kneeled as the national anthem played at the start of football games, Colin Kaepernick demonstrated moral courage because he knew the risks and pushed forward regardless of the punishments.

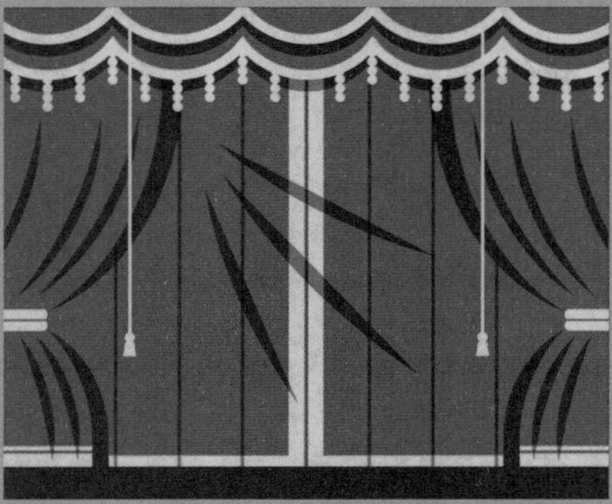

Your conclusion has a couple of functions.

1. It pulls together your essay.

2. It offers a bigger context. In other words, it tells readers why this argument matters and why they should care.

CONCLUSION OUTLINE

CONCLUSION	Topic and why it matters	Too often, people are most concerned with their own well-being and therefore don't display moral courage. This matters because moral courage is a sign that you care about others more than yourself. It means you are willing to sacrifice yourself for what you see as the greater good.
	Restate your claim.	Colin Kaepernick displayed moral courage when he kneeled during the national anthem.
	Why should your reader share your view?	Putting his own livelihood on the line, Colin Kaepernick stood up to protest an injustice he was seeing. This injustice, police brutality, is harming our fellow citizens. And that is something none of us should stand for.
	What is possible? Convince your reader what to do or believe, or discuss what may happen next.	Anyone can display moral courage. It doesn't have to be at an NFL game. The next time you see an injustice, speak up. Stand up, or kneel, for what you know in your heart is right.

What surprised you as you read about and worked on outlining?

WRITING YOUR FIRST DRAFT

Your writing will be the way you showcase all that great research and thinking you have done. You will want your word choice to be as persuasive as the argument you have built. But (yes, there's a *but*) you will not worry about these things in your first draft. Your job at this point is just to turn your outline into paragraphs and sentences.

POSITION PAPER FIRST DRAFT

WHAT IT IS	WHAT IT ISN'T
Fast writing	Perfect
Follows your outline	Your last draft
Includes your evidence and explanation	
A chance to see how your paper flows	

By completing a detailed outline, you've got yourself in a position to draft quickly and easily. To make this step even easier, you can work from this list of transitional words and phrases. Add to the list. Put stars next to some of your favorite words. Try to vary which terms you use.

TRANSITION WORDS AND PHRASES

For example	Furthermore	Additionally
For instance	Moreover	Not only… but also…
Notably	In addition to	In the same way
Such as	Subsequently	Likewise
Another	In conclusion	Similarly

TO TRANSITION INTO YOUR EXPLANATION OF EVIDENCE (THOUGH WORDS FROM THE LIST ABOVE WILL ALSO HELP)		
This illustrates	This shows	Suggesting
FOR COUNTERCLAIM PARAGRAPH		
On the other hand	Whereas	Others may argue
On the contrary	Alternatively	Even though

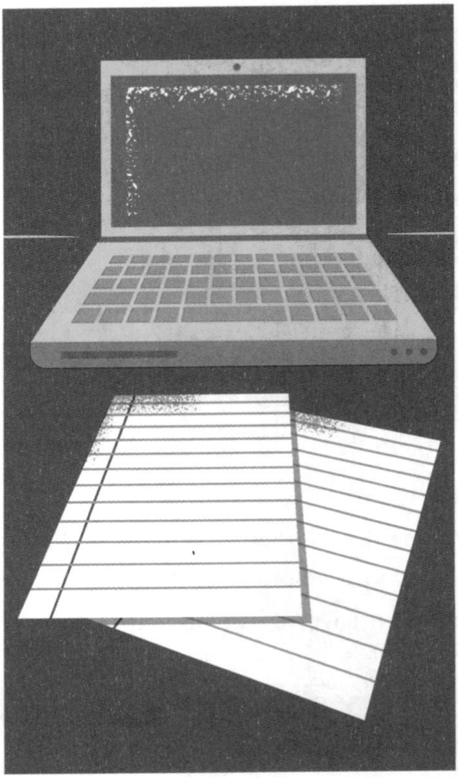

In your first draft, you are going to incorporate both your evidence and your explanation of that evidence. There are different ways to do that.

- You can follow your evidence sentence with a sentence (or two) explaining the significance of your evidence.
- Your explanation can come before your evidence.

As you begin writing argument papers, getting all of your ideas into one paragraph can feel a little clumsy. That's OK! The more papers you write, the smoother this all becomes. But for now . . .

READY. SET. DRAFT!

Write your draft, either by hand or typing on a computer. Make sure to use:

- All pieces of your outline
- List of transitions

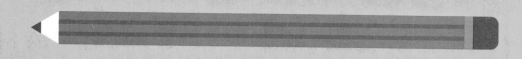

How is your draft? What made it easier? What were your challenges?

HOW TO REVISE AND FINISH AN ARGUMENT

You have a draft. That means you have something solid to look at with your super-critical eye. One thing you will definitely want to use your eagle-eye vision on is evidence.

STRATEGIES FOR PRESENTING EVIDENCE

You can share evidence in a range of ways, and it is better for your paper if you include some of that variety. Here are some ways to incorporate evidence:

QUOTING

- Copy text exactly as it appears in the original source.
- Use quotation marks around quoted text.
- Good for: allowing source to speak for itself (especially when the voice is strong), providing variety to your writing voice

PARAPHRASING

- Use your own words to state the idea that comes from your source.

• Be careful to keep the meaning of the original text.

• Good for: weaving in evidence, keeping your writing in your voice and not someone else's

SUMMARIZING

• Pull just the main ideas from your source.

• Write these in your own words.

• Good for: when the evidence you are relaying is long, when you just want the main points from a source

I WANT TO THANK MY SOURCES

CITATIONS

No matter how you include evidence, you must always cite (give credit to) your sources. You may do this at the end of the sentence, before the period. It will look like this: (author, year of publication). Or you may weave recognition of your source right into your sentence. You will provide your reader with more information about your sources in your **citation** page or citation list, which will be at the end of your piece.

Here are a few paragraphs written by seventeen-year-old Isabel Hwang in a piece titled, "The Life-Changing Magic of Being Messy." She's arguing that there can be benefits to being a messy person. As you read, notice how she wove in her evidence. Also, look at how she cited her sources.

citation: a list of the sources you used in your writing

As much judgment as we get for our clutter, research has shown that messiness can be a sign of creativity and openness. In the *New York Times* article "It's Not 'Mess.' It's Creativity," Kathleen D. Vohs' study of messiness serves as a rare champion for us less-than-neat people. In her study, she gathered a group of subjects in a tidy room and another in a messy room. When each subject had to choose between a "classic" or "new" smoothie on a fake menu, the subjects in the tidy room chose "classic" while subjects in the messy room chose the "new" smoothies. This shows that "people greatly preferred convention in the tidy room and novelty in the messy room." In addition, Vohs revealed that messy people were more creative. So, what does this mean?

Messy people are willing to challenge the conventional norm. They aren't confined to the status quo. In a growing age where minimalism seems to be taking on the world by storm, we must remember that there is beauty in chaos. Although a University of Michigan study warns that some people might take one look at your messy desk and view you as "lazy" or "neurotic," we must remember the people who challenge the old ways of being are some of our greatest innovators. After all, Albert Einstein, Mark Twain, Steve Jobs, and Mark Zuckerberg famously harbored hideously disorganized workplaces.

Works Cited

Eichenstein, Izzy. "Albert Einstein, Mark Twain & Steve Jobs: The Messy Desk Link." The LAX Morning Minute, Word Press, 19 Oct. 2013.

Vohs, Kathleen. "Tidy Desk or Messy Desk? Each Has Its Benefits." Association for Psychological Science, 6 Aug. 2013.

Vohs, Kathleen D. "It's Not 'Mess.' It's Creativity." *The New York Times*, 13 Sept. 2013.

Wadley, Jared. "Is Your Office Messy? If So, You May Be Seen as Uncaring, Neurotic." Michigan News, The University of Michigan, 27 Nov. 2018.

Weinswig, Deborah. "Millennials Go Minimal: The Decluttering Lifestyle Trend That Is Taking Over." *Forbes*, 7 Sept. 2016.

WHAT KINDS OF SOURCES ARE TRUSTWORTHY?

- Look for large-circulation newspapers (e.g., *The New York Times*) that have been around for many years.
- Look for large-circulation magazines (such as *Forbes*) that have been around for many years.
- Universities and scientific organizations usually publish accurate information.
- Many newspapers and magazines hire fact checkers and publish corrections if something they publish turns out to be wrong. Most bloggers do not do this.

OBSERVATIONS ON EVIDENCE

WHAT WE SEE

In the *New York Times* article "It's Not 'Mess.' It's Creativity," Kathleen D. Vohs' study of messiness serves as a rare champion for us less-than-neat people. In her study, she gathered a group of subjects in a tidy room and another in a messy room.

Although a University of Michigan study warns that some people might take one look at your messy desk and view you as "lazy" or "neurotic," we must remember the people who challenge the old ways of being are some of our greatest innovators.

Works Cited

Eichenstein, Izzy. "Albert Einstein, Mark Twain & Steve Jobs: The Messy Desk Link." The LAX Morning Minute, Word Press, 19 Oct. 2013.

Vohs, Kathleen. "Tidy Desk or Messy Desk? Each Has Its Benefits." Association for Psychological Science, 6 Aug. 2013.

Vohs, Kathleen D. "It's Not 'Mess.' It's Creativity." *The New York Times*, 13 Sept. 2013.

Wadley, Jared. "Is Your Office Messy? If So, You May Be Seen as Uncaring, Neurotic." Michigan News, The University of Michigan, 27 Nov. 2018.

Weinswig, Deborah. "Millennials Go Minimal: The Decluttering Lifestyle Trend That Is Taking Over." *Forbes*, 7 Sept. 2016.

THE WRITING MOVE	YOUR NOTES
The writer names her source at the beginning of the sentence. She also includes the name of the researcher in that sentence, which gives a quick summary of the article.	
The writer introduces a counterargument by referring to the origins of a study. The breakdown of that counterargument is the second half of the sentence.	
There's a citation list. You can use online citation machines to build a list with proper formatting. The important things to remember: • All of your sources (even the ones you didn't quote) should be on this list. • The list is in alphabetical order by author's last name.	

As you write more papers, you will take charge of your own revision process. You can use the revision strategies offered in the other chapters. Here's a list of ways to focus your revision:

- Compelling introduction (*Compelling* means strong, forceful, or capturing attention.)
- Transitions
- Word choice
- Precise language
- Sentence variety
- Order of reasons or evidence
- Evidence—you may find that you need to include something different or take something out
- Powerful conclusion

Remember, the key to effective revision is reading your paper critically and finding big changes to make. Not only will doing this make your paper better, but the practice of working so hard on a piece of writing will improve your writing overall. It's well worth the time you spend on it.

EDITING

Writers often try to avoid editing. It's tempting to just turn in your paper after all that thinking and writing. However, just a little bit of editing will leave your paper polished! It's kind of like the difference between stuffing you dirty clothes under your bed and actually doing your laundry. In the end, you'll be glad you did it.

It's time to edit your work!

THE ULTIMATE FINAL READ CHECKLIST

Circle "yes" or "no" to the questions below.

(HINT: If your answer is no, then it's probably something you need to look at again in your essay.)

INTRODUCTORY PARAGRAPH CHECKLIST

Did I introduce my topic in an interesting way?	YES	NO
Did I talk about why my topic matters?	YES	NO
Did I clearly state my argument?	YES	NO

REASON 1 PARAGRAPH CHECKLIST

Did I state my reason?	YES	NO
Is my reason explained and well supported?	YES	NO
Did I provide evidence?	YES	NO
Does my evidence match my reason?	YES	NO
Did I explain *how* it matches my reason?	YES	NO
At the end of my paragraph, did I remind readers of my reason?	YES	NO

REASON 2 PARAGRAPH CHECKLIST

Did I state my reason?	YES	NO
Is my reason explained and well supported?	YES	NO
Did I provide evidence?	YES	NO
Does my evidence match my reason?	YES	NO
Did I explain *how* it matches my reason?	YES	NO
At the end of my paragraph, did I remind readers of my reason?	YES	NO

COUNTERCLAIM PARAGRAPH CHECKLIST

Did I state the counterclaim?	YES	NO
Did I provide evidence that supports the counterclaim?	YES	NO
Did I effectively demonstrate the weakness of the counterclaim?	YES	NO

Did I provide evidence of that weakness?	YES	NO
Did I explain that evidence?	YES	NO
At the end of my paragraph, did I remind readers why my claim is strong?	YES	NO

CONCLUSION PARAGRAPH CHECKLIST

Did I remind readers what my claim statement is?	YES	NO
Did I briefly summarize what I talked about in my essay?	YES	NO
Did I explain why my essay matters or why my topic is important?	YES	NO
Does my final sentence end my essay in a way that makes sense?	YES	NO

WHOLE PAPER

Do all sentences begin with a capital letter and end with punctuation?	YES	NO
Did I capitalize all proper nouns, such as names of people, cities, and months?	YES	NO
Did I spell tricky words correctly?	YES	NO
Did I include citations for my evidence?	YES	NO

Be honest: How do you feel about editing your paper? Is it something you enjoy doing, or do you have to remind yourself to edit?

Is the checklist helpful? If so, what about it is helpful?

PUBLISHING YOUR ARGUMENT ESSAY

Get out the balloons—it's time to party! Though maybe for such a fine literary work, nice clean paper and a report folder are more appropriate. Either way, you are ready to celebrate your work.

1. Get this draft onto fresh paper.

2. Include your name and date.

3. Add a page at the end with a list of sources you used.

4. Come up with a title for your paper.

Yes, give that paper a name! After all that work, it deserves something catchy, something academic, something sophisticated at the top.

SOME KEY IDEAS FOR TITLING YOUR PAPER:

- Might acknowledge or support the point or argument you are making
- May acknowledge the overall assignment
- Captures the reader's interest
- May have a main title and a subtitle separated by a colon

THE FORMULA

CATCHY PHRASE	INFORMATIONAL BIT

THE FORMULA IN ACTION:

CATCHY PHRASE	INFORMATIONAL BIT
Messy Is the New Clean	The benefits of a messy room are finally getting some notice.

As a title:

Messy Is the New Clean: The benefits of a messy room are finally getting some notice

How do you feel about the two-part title? Is it something you can see yourself using in the future? Why or why not?

SHARING YOUR WORK

And last, find your audience. Share your work. Don't just hand it off to someone and call it a day. You've put a lot of work into this. Get some feedback. You deserve it! You may want to share your writing with friends and family, publish it in a blog, or make it into a podcast. (If you decide to publish your work somewhere public, consider not using your full name, and definitely don't include your address. It's important to stay safe as you bring your ideas into the world.)

Questions for the reader of your argument paper (choose just a couple):

- Tell me something you learned by reading my paper.
- What about my paper is convincing?
- What about my paper could be improved?
- What did my paper make you feel? Why or how?

Look at your final paper, and think back about all the work you have done. Then choose two questions to answer.

- What have you learned about argument writing?
- Why do you think students and professionals often use this type of writing?
- What do you want to do differently next time you write?
- What is something you found helpful?
- Could you write a paper arguing against your claim?

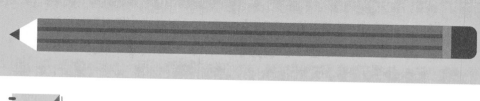

Writing arguments is going to come in so handy—not just with things like bedtime and pizza toppings but also in your academic world. You will be writing this type of paper throughout your academic life. And you're off to a great start!

CHAPTER 8 VOCABULARY

citation: a reference to a source you have used in your writing

counterclaim: an example of a reason others might disagree with your argument, used to ultimately strengthen your argument

credible evidence: proof or supporting information that comes from reliable sources

devil's advocate: Someone arguing against their own ideas as a means of forcing the development of an argument

effective evidence: information that proves or supports your argument

eyewitness account: a description of an event by someone who was actually there when it happened

facts: information that can be proved to be true

outline: an organized collection of your thoughts, arguments, and evidence that you will use to construct your writing

pertinent evidence: proof or supporting information connected to your topic

primary information: facts and details that come directly from the time or event you are writing about

refute: to prove something to be false

statistics: numbers that show patterns or changes or that provide information about larger issues

varied evidence: proof or supporting information that comes from more than one source

9 BEYOND MORSE CODE: GETTING IN TOUCH WITH OTHERS

You've been practicing how to share information, write stories, and craft arguments. But writing isn't just something you do in school. Writing is how we communicate with other people in our everyday lives. There's something very special about getting a letter, especially now when people are much more likely to just send an email or text. But hey, those are writing too! Remember—communication is key!

CHAPTER CONTENTS

TYPES OF PERSONAL COMMUNICATION

When is the last time you received an actual letter in the mail from a friend or relative? How did it make you feel to receive it?

There are so many kinds of written communication, and each has its use. In fact, as you get older, you're going to need to be able to use this skill a lot, in every part of your life. Sometimes written communication might be formal, but it can also be super-casual and a lot of fun. So let's look at some strategies to make these communications more effective—and easier to write!

WAYS OF COMMUNICATING

Do a quick brainstorm, and write down all the ways you write to communicate with others. How many can you think of?

HOW WE COMMUNICATE

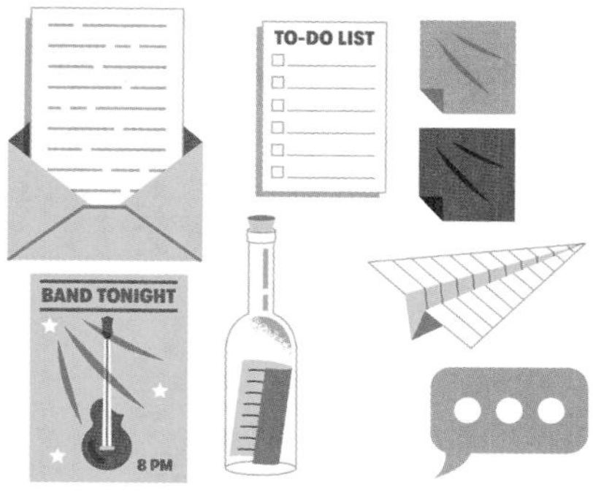

This list might be bigger than we first think. There are thank you notes, emails, text messages, post-it notes left for people at home, and, of course, letters. In this chapter we are going to explore ways to effectively communicate written messages to others.

WRITING THANK YOU NOTES

You've probably written a thank you note or two. It's likely to have happened under the focused gaze of an adult. Sometimes teachers have their classes write thank you notes following a field trip, or parents have their kids send them after a gift has been received. Now that you're older, you will be more independent with your thank you notes. You will also have a wider set of situations for which you may need to send off a thank you note.

- After receiving a gift
- Following an interview for a job or other opportunity
- After being a houseguest (not for a one-night sleepover, but if you stay for an extended visit or traveled with another family)
- After someone wrote you a letter of recommendation, helped you get an interview, or otherwise supported you in work, athletic, artistic, or educational pursuits

Thank you notes can be handwritten, typed, or sent electronically. If the note is to a person familiar to you or for a gift, in other words, if it is personal, a handwritten note is nice. Notes around education and work opportunities are often typed, even sent via email.

Here's an excerpt from a thank you note written by the writer Oscar Wilde and sent to his friend Emily Wren, after her son sent him a gift. It's from 1888.

> "... how charmed I am with Chrissie's present. It is a very sweet picture of him, and I prize it very much in memory of my little friend. I have considered it my duty to write him a letter expressing my gratitude. When you come back from Bournemouth I hope we will see you. Give my kind regards to your husband."

What did you notice about Wilde's note? What did you like?

THANK YOU NOTE ESSENTIALS

A good thank you note includes:

- **Addresses the recipient by name** with a greeting—first name if it's a personal, informal relationship, use the formal (such as Mr. Wilde) for work- and education-related notes
- Explicitly states **what you are grateful for**
    - Thank you for the letter of recommendation you wrote to the School of Writers on my behalf
    - Thank you for the wizard's wand
    - Thank you for including me in your Great Adventure outing
- Add in a **detail** that helps your reader see the impact of your gift
    - Thank you for the letter of recommendation you wrote to the School of Writers on my behalf. **Your support gave me confidence as I entered the interview!**
    - Thank you for the wizard's wand. **I used it to successfully return my little sister to her human form after days of being a frog.**
    - Thank you for including me in your Great Adventure outing. **Not only did I LOVE the rides, I really enjoyed getting to know your family better.**
- Wrap it up with an **acknowledgment of the future**
    - The support I have received as I embarked on this school application process is going to help me stride into high school with my head held a bit higher. Thank you for that.
    - I am looking forward to swapping magic tricks when I see you in spring.
    - I hope that we can get together soon after you return from vacation.

How did Oscar Wilde do? Let's use our pickaxe to identify the elements of his letter.

WILDE'S WORDS OF THANKS

OSCAR'S LETTER	ANNOTATIONS
"... how charmed I am with Chrissie's present.	• Addresses the recipient by name
It is a very sweet picture of him, and	• Explicitly states what you are grateful for
I prize it very much in memory of my little friend. I have considered it my duty to write him a letter expressing my gratitude.	• A detail that helps your reader see the impact of your gift
When you come back from Bournemouth I hope we will see you. Give my kind regards to your husband."	• Wrap it up with an acknowledgment of the future

It looks like Oscar Wilde did a pretty good job with his thank you note. Are you ready to give it a try? You can give thanks to anyone for anything. If there's a thank you you've been meaning to write, now is a good time to get that started. Or, just write an imaginary one, perhaps for the gift you have always wanted. In formatting it, include the date, the person you are writing to, a closing, and your name.

CLOSING WORDS

You might want to use different closings depending on who you are writing to. Here are some ideas below, you can add in more if you'd like!

Formal letters	Informal letters	In the middle
Sincerely, Best regards, Cordially, Yours respectfully,	Love, Best wishes,	Warmly, Warm regards, Yours truly,

WRITING LETTERS

Letters should be pretty easy to read because they follow similar formats. These formats allow you to orient yourself as both reader and writer.

FORMATTING YOUR LETTERS

A HANDWRITTEN OR INFORMAL TYPED NOTE	FORMAL LETTER	EMAIL
Date Dear. . . , Your message Closing, Your Name	Date Recipients name Recipient's street address Town, State ZIP Code Dear. . . , Your message Closing, Your signature Your name typed/ printed	Dear. . . , Your message Closing, Your name Your email Your address [you can even add in social media accounts if they are appropriate and relevant]

In thinking about thank you notes, what's something you want to do or include in the future?

WRITING TO REACH OUT

We write thank you notes to people we know, even if we don't know them well. However, we also write to people we have never met. Through written communication we reach out regarding jobs, as research, to express our views, and sometimes for some support. For these letters you will use the more formal formats and closings from the last few pages.

But what do you write? You desperately want to get in touch with a Cheyenne elder or your state senator or the librarian of the year but you DON'T KNOW WHAT TO SAY. Don't worry. You've already had lots of practice as an expert writer and here you are going to learn how to turn your expert writing into letter form. Who knows, you may even get a sitting president to write back to you, like ten-year-old Sophia Bailey-Klugh did when she wrote a letter to President Obama. Let's take a look at this exchange and see what we can learn from it.

In 2012, Sophia Bailey-Klugh wrote to President Obama.

You see, kids at school decided to make fun of the fact that she has two dads and she decided to ask for some advice. This is her letter:

> Dear Barack Obama,
>
> It's Sophia Bailey Klugh. Your friend who invited you to dinner. You don't remember okay that's fine. But I just wanted to tell you that I am so glad you agree that two men can love each other because I have two dads and they love each other. But at school kids think that it's gross and weird but it really hurts my heart and feelings. So I come to you because you are my hero. If you were me and you had two dads that loved each other, and kids at school teased you about it, what would you do?
>
> Please respond!
>
> I just wanted to say you really inspire me, and I hope you win on being the president. You would totally make the world a better place.
>
> Your friend Sophia
>
> P.S. Please tell your daughters Hi for me!

Let's take a look at some of her letter writing moves.

A CLOSER LOOK

SOPHIA'S LETTER	OUR ANNOTATIONS
Dear Barack Obama,	Greeting. She addressed him by his full name. She could have also written, "President Obama"
It's Sophia Bailey Klugh. Your friend who invited you to dinner. You don't remember okay that's fine.	She introduced herself. And included a piece of information that indicates that they met before and what happened. She also acknowledges that he might not remember and that's OK (word on the street is that being president of the United States is pretty time-consuming).
But I just wanted to tell you that I am so glad you agree that two men can love each other because I have two dads and they love each other.	
But at school kids think that it's gross and weird but it really hurts my heart and feelings.	She tells him her problem
So I come to you because you are my hero.	She states her reason for writing him
If you were me and you had two dads that loved each other, and kids at school teased you about it, what would you do? Please respond!	Her question, what she needs
I just wanted to say you really inspire me, and I hope you win on being the president. You would totally make the world a better place.	Mention of the future
Your friend Sophia	Closing (you can add "your friend," to our list of closings - where would you place it?)
P.S. Please tell your daughters Hi for me!	P.S. stands for *postscript*, which you use when you want to add an extra idea after closing out a letter

Let's put Sophia's moves into a list of suggestions (notice that many are similar to what we did in thank you notes):

- Greeting
- Gives background about self, the relationship between the recipient and the writer
- States the problem
- Reasons for writing, the objective
- Acknowledges the future in a positive light
- Closing

Guess what? Sophia's strategy worked. Even though he was busy running the United States of America, President Obama took time out of his day to write back to Sophia.

Here's his response:

Dear Sophia,

Thank you for writing me such a thoughtful letter about your family. Reading it made me proud to be your president and even more hopeful about the future of our nation.

In America, no two families look the same. We celebrate this diversity. And we recognize that whether you have two dads or one mom what matters above all is the love we show one another. You are very fortunate to have two parents who care deeply for you. They are lucky to have such an exceptional daughter in you.

Our differences unite us. You and I are blessed to live in a country where we are born equal no matter what we look like on the outside, where we grow up, or who our parents are. A good rule is to treat others the way you hope they will treat you. Remind your friends at school about this rule if they say something that hurts your feelings.

Thanks again for taking the time to write to me. I'm honored to have your support and inspired by your compassion. I'm sorry I couldn't make it to dinner, but I'll be sure to tell Sasha and Malia you say hello.

Sincerely,

Barack Obama

Shall we check the president's work? Note any other thoughts you have about the letter as you read.

A CLOSER LOOK

OBAMA'S LETTER

Dear Sophia,

Thank you for writing me such a thoughtful letter about your family. Reading it made me proud to be your president and even more hopeful about the future of our nation.

In America, no two families look the same. We celebrate this diversity. And we recognize that whether you have two dads or one mom what matters above all is the love we show one another. You are very fortunate to have two parents who care deeply for you. They are lucky to have such an exceptional daughter in you.

Our differences unite us. You and I are blessed to live in a country where we are born equal no matter what we look like on the outside, where we grow up, or who our parents are. A good rule is to treat others the way you hope they will treat you. Remind your friends at school about this rule if they say something that hurts your feelings.

Thanks again for taking the time to write to me. I'm honored to have your support and inspired by your compassion. I'm sorry I couldn't make it to dinner, but I'll be sure to tell Sasha and Malia you say hello.

Sincerely,

Barack Obama

YOUR IMPRESSIONS

ANNOTATIONS

He used the familiar in his greeting—her first name

Thanked Sophia, clearly stating what he is thanking her for

Explicitly states the impact the note had on him

He addresses her question with a general answer.

He brings his response to her personal life.

He answers her request by giving her advice

Thanks her, and is specific about what he is thanking her for—taking the time to write to him.

Tells her the impact of her note.

Apologizes for not being able to accept her invitation

Answers her other request, what he will do

Closing

Why not give it a try? Choose someone you admire:

___

___

What purpose do you have for writing them? Some ideas:

- Ask advice
- Express an opinion
- Request an action

Idea you want to address:

___

___

Details to include:

___

___

___

___

___

___

Draft your letter using an appropriate format.

Read over your draft using the checklist below.

Letter Writing Checklist

- Greeting
- Background information
- States the problem or request
- Reasons for writing, the objective
- Acknowledges the future in a positive light
- Closing
- Specific details are included
- Ideas are organized

How did you do? Are you ready to make your final draft and mail it off? If you are sending it in the mail, the outside of your envelope should look like this:

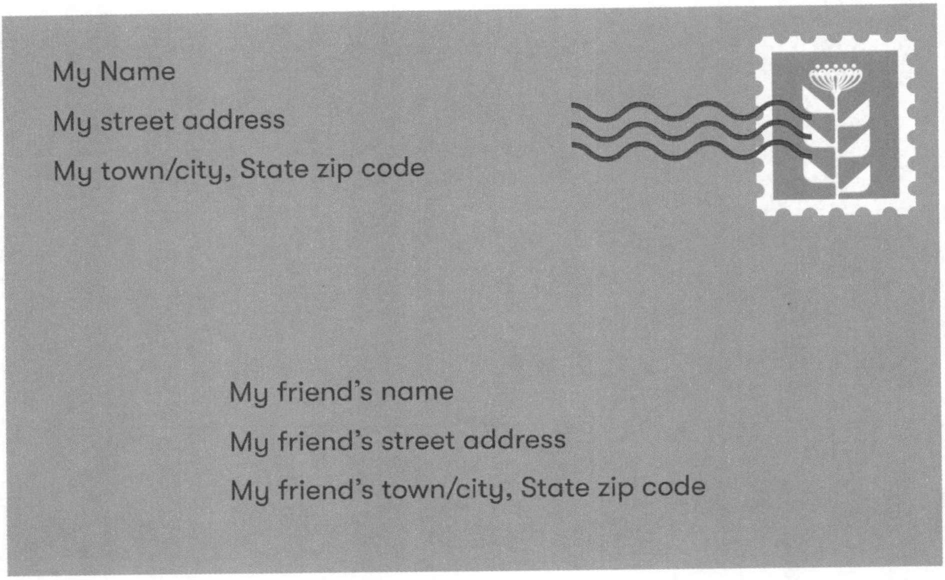
My Name
My street address
My town/city, State zip code
My friend's name
My friend's street address
My friend's town/city, State zip code

MAKING AN INTRODUCTION

There will be times when you will write letters as a means of introducing yourself for a potential job or an educational opportunity. Perhaps you want to introduce yourself to neighbors as a potential babysitter, lawn mower, or shoveler of snow. You can write a letter to do that.

Here's an example of a letter to pass out to neighbors. It will be printed and distributed, so it doesn't include the recipient's address.

INTRODUCING YOURSELF IN A LETTER

March 11, 2021	Heading
Dear neighbor,	Greeting
Do you have pets that sometimes need a pet sitter? If so, I just may be who you are looking for. My name is George and I am 13 years old. I am also an animal lover.	Paragraph 1: background information
I would love to pet sit any pets that you have. I have grown up with animals. I have a dog, a cat, and a turtle. I am responsible for walking my dog once a day and feeding it in the evening. I change my cat's litter box, but do usually wait until my mom asks (don't worry, I'll be prompt with yours though!). Two years ago we got a rescue turtle. I have learned so much about turtles. It's really important to keep its tank clean and feed it healthy food. Also, I am good at following directions. If you have a certain routine that your pet likes to follow, I am your man. As an animal lover, keeping your pet feeling safe while you are away would be my main objective.	Paragraph 2: supporting information and details
I would love to meet you and your pet. I am available most days after school. My contact information is below.	Paragraph 3: details about contacting and availability
Your neighbor, George Odel georgielovesanimals@email.com (123)456-7890	Closing and contact information

Give it a try using the prompts and structure provided.

YOUR TURN: INTRODUCING YOURSELF IN A LETTER

HEADING, INCLUDING DATE—CHOOSE THE ONE THAT IS APPROPRIATE FOR WHATEVER FORM YOUR WRITING IS TAKING—EMAIL OR LETTER

GREETING

PARAGRAPH 1: BACKGROUND INFORMATION

PARAGRAPH 2: SUPPORTING INFORMATION AND DETAILS

PARAGRAPH 3: DETAILS ABOUT CONTACTING AND AVAILABILITY

CLOSING AND CONTACT INFORMATION

How did it go? What part went quickly? Where did you find you needed to think a bit?

Communicating in writing is a great opportunity. When you write to someone, you can really think about what you want to say. You can take your time and reread your words. Also, everyone loves to get mail! Think about the people in your life. Who can you write a letter to? Perhaps you have a friend or relative out there who's feeling a little alone and a note from you would brighten their week, or there's someone you haven't spoken to in a long time. Choose someone and write them a note. For this note, no rules apply. Just express yourself. Maybe you'll even get one back.

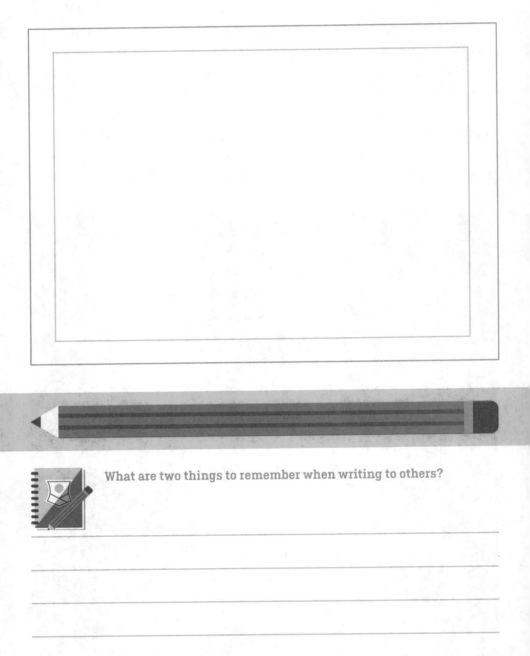

What are two things to remember when writing to others?

CHAPTER 9 VOCABULARY

No new terms to review, so why not sit down and write a letter?

10 FOR THE LOVE OF LANGUAGE

This whole book has been centered around words, phrases, sentences, and paragraphs. It's pages and pages of letters organized to explain pages and pages of organized letters. Words, and how we use them, reveal identity, place, and even time and age. So how can you use words in a way that's true to your own voice and who you are? The secret lies in understanding the essential elements of language and in finding ways to use them to suit your own purposes. Are you ready? Read on!

CHAPTER CONTENTS

LANGUAGE IN REAL LIFE

One great way to learn about language is by paying attention to how it's used in your everyday life. Conversations you have, hear, or read about show how language can help us share ideas and how people use different words and styles.

Take a look at this exchange between a mother and daughter from the book *Piecing Me Together* by Renée Watson:

WHAT'S IN A WORD?

RELATIONSHIP	NAME	CONVERSATION
Older family member	Mom	[Jade:] "Oh, it's a last-minute thing. Maxine called and asked if I wanted to do brunch with her to celebrate my birthday." "*Do* brunch? You mean go to brunch?" Mom laughs. "How does one *do* brunch?" Mom pours milk into her mug, then opens a packet of sweetener and sprinkles it in. She stirs. "That woman has you talking like her already, huh?

What's happening between this mother and daughter? Why are they having a conversation about one word?

Perhaps it's about generational differences, or about a daughter whose experiences are stretching beyond her family. Maybe it's about a mom who is worried about what or who is influencing her daughter. Her daughter's language reflects her experiences. As you move through this chapter, remember that language can involve emotions, culture, experiences, attitudes, and more.

RECORDING FROM LIFE

Think back to some recent conversations you have had with friends and family. Record a few sentences word for word, as best you can. If you can't think of any, go out and have a few conversations! Just be truthful to yourself in the language you use.

OVERHEARD. . .

RELATIONSHIP	NAME	CONVERSATION
Friend		
Friend		
Older family member		
Younger family member		
Teacher		
Family acquaintance		

What do you notice about your different conversations?

Perhaps you speak differently with different people. Perhaps people around you have a way of speaking that is different from how you speak. *It's all good.* Because you are skilled with words, it is your job to recognize and value your own voice and the voice of others.

USE YOUR VOICE

In the world of writing, **voice** has to do with each individual's own personal communication style—their emotions, attitude, point of view, and habits of expression. Some people write and speak *emphatically!* They are *so full of emotion!* Others are calmer, using few italics or exclamation points. Some people are polysyllabic—they use long, fancy, impressive words. Others rely on short, plain words.

What voice will you bring to your writing? In your growth as a writer, you will stretch language, try out new words, and investigate new patterns. But don't forget to let your voice stay true to who you are.

THE ENGLISH LANGUAGE

We live in a country that is a mix of cultures and histories. Although the United States does not have an official language, English is the language that is most commonly spoken. However, it is far from the only language people speak here. And even within English, there are so many ways people use that one language. Some people put forward the notion that Standard American English is the version we should all use, particularly in academic and professional settings. Others argue that we should embrace the diversity of language and that encouraging only one voice is discriminatory and limiting. But no matter what, the way you use language contributes to your unique writing voice. Take a look at the samples on page 440, noticing how people put together words in different ways and vary their word choice.

THE POWER OF LANGUAGE

Language is a weapon. It's got so much power that it will help you fight for what you believe in. However, language has also been used as a weapon to hurt people. It has been used to exclude some people while including others. When we talk about the notion that a language, English, has been "standardized" we are looking at the role language has played in perpetuating ideas about certain groups, limiting opportunities for people, and generating stigma. It's your job to empower yourself through your unique voice. Use that voice to speak your truth in a way that suits you. And, find value in the voices others use.

WHAT IS "STANDARD AMERICAN ENGLISH"?

Standard American English (SAE) is more of an idea than a permanent set of words and rules. People in different parts of the country speak our "standard" language differently, and new words and expressions enter the language constantly. SAE isn't better than other forms of English. People have labeled it as "standard" because its speakers, mostly white Americans, have the social power to make it the dominant variant of English used in the United States. It's the language you most often hear in news broadcasts and read in magazines, for example. Learning the rules of SAE will serve you well.

Generally, Americans love to hear all of the different ways of speaking English in music, television, and movies. It's in places of power that these variants of English are less visible. In this sense, SAE is used as a weapon designed to keep people who do not speak SAE out of positions of power. When we describe certain ways of speaking as inferior, we convey to people that they themselves are inferior. This is not true. The vibrancy of language, American English, reflects the diversity and vibrancy of all the people who speak it.

ANALYZING VOICE

SOURCE	SAMPLE VOICE
The House on Mango Street Sandra Cisneros	[A mother who speaks mostly Spanish does not want her son to speak English at home.] No speak English, she says to the child who is singing in the language that sounds like tin. No speak English, no speak English, and bubbles into tears. No, no, no as if she can't believe her ears.
So Much Trish Cooke	And the house was full, full, full, and they sit down there waiting for the next DING DONG! They wait and they wait but it never come. Mum said, "Is everybody alright?" and the baby and Cousin start to fight again, Nannie and Gran-Gran take out cards and dominoes, Uncle Didi start to slap them down on the table, and Auntie Bibba play some records really loud. Mum said, "What madness all around!"
Birdsong Julie Flett	Agnes is working on a pot that is round and bright. She tells me about waxing and waning moons. I tell her about Cree seasons. This month is called pimihâwipîsim—the migrating moon.

WHAT DOES THIS VOICE MAKE YOU THINK, FEEL, AND WONDER?

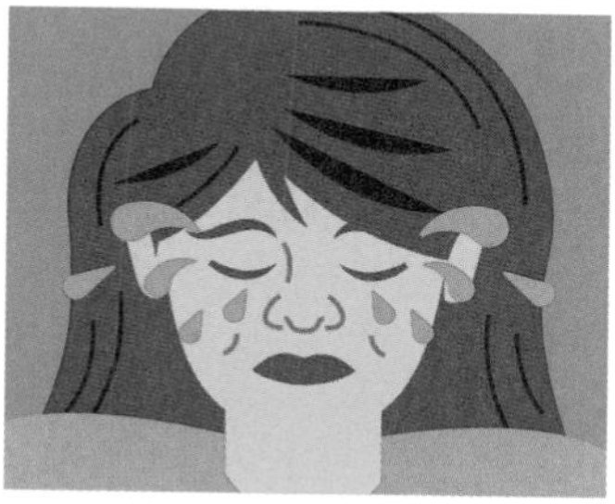

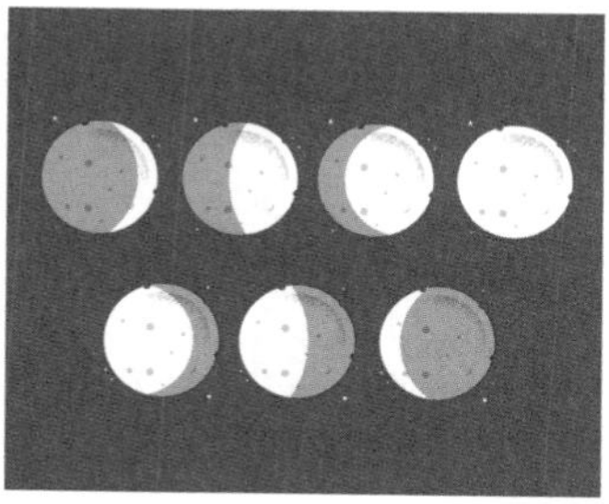

How do the different voices and styles change the expression—in other words, the way the authors deliver their messages to readers?

Think about the voices you hear in your world. What would it be like if everyone talked the same way?

LANGUAGE VARIANTS

Everyone who has ever spoken English has influenced it. Pockets of people speak it differently. What is interesting is that each **variant**, or version of a language used by members of a group based on geography, culture, or social class, follows very specific rules. Despite the sophistication of each variant, many people make judgments about those who speak different variants from their own. They stereotype.

But you have grown up in a world where due to technology, media, books, and travel, you probably hear a range of variants. Maybe you speak a couple of different ones of your own.

WHAT IS AAVE?

African American Vernacular English (AAVE) is a variant of American English developed and spoken primarily by African Americans. From the time of slavery, AAVE has been intertwined with the Black experience in the United States, and it continues to evolve today. However, not every African American person speaks AAVE.

AAVE has its own rules of grammar and usage: this means that its speakers are following a pattern of rules that take time to master. Still, it is often falsely regarded by many speakers of Standard American English as "inferior" to SAE, the dominant variant in the United States. Language is powerful. Some people stereotype based on AAVE and try to use it as a justification for oppression. On the other hand, it is an expression of culture, history, and solidarity for those who speak it.

How do different variants of English affect our experiences with others? Is there one correct way to speak, or does each variant have value?

ENGLISH EVOLVING: WHERE IT COMES FROM AND WHERE IT'S GOING

Many cultures and languages have influenced English. Seeing some of the ways English is born from and influenced by other languages not only helps you appreciate the complexity of English, but it also helps you get at the meaning of some unknown words.

Etymology is the study of where words come from. We can use etymology to look more closely at the history or roots of some words.

THE ROOTS OF LANGUAGE

Many English words have Greek and Latin **roots**, which are kind of like seeds for bigger words. For example, the root of the word *react* is *act*. If you find and define the seed, you will have some understanding of what kind of flower is growing from it. The more Greek and Latin roots you know, the more English words you will be able to define on your own.

To get to the base of a word, you might use a pickaxe to pull apart a word that's making you curious. Once you do that, you may uncover a Latin or Greek root.

A character actively opposing another
Something that corrects or improves the bad effect of something.
ANTAGONIST
ANTIDOTE
ANTONYM
ANTITHESIS
A word opposite in meaning to another
The exact opposite of someone or something
ANTI
Opposed to

GREEK AND LATIN ROOTS

ROOT	DEFINITION	EXAMPLES AND DEFINITION	LANGUAGE OF ORIGIN
Anthrop	Human	Anthropomorphic = has human qualities Anthropology = study of how human culture and society change	Greek
Aqua	Water	Aqua = pale green-blue color Aquarium = container for water-dwelling animals and plants Aqueduct = structure that moves water	Latin
Bio	Life	Biography = writing that tells of a person's life Biology = the scientific study of living beings	Greek
Chron	Time	Chronic = continual or repeating Chronology = in order of time	Greek
Dys	Bad or ill	Dystopia = imagined place where people are living fearful lives Dysentery = illness that causes diarrhea	Greek
Memor	Remember	Memorial = something that intends to protect the memory of someone Memory = human ability to hold onto experiences	Latin
Meter	Measure	Diameter = a straight line that goes through the center of a circle	Greek

Retro	Backward	Retroactive = plan, change, or law that applies to things that already happened Retrospective = something that looks at the past	Latin

Let's see if it works. Can you use the information above to figure out the italicized words in the following sentences based on their Greek or Latin roots?

She built an *anthropoid* robot.

An anthropoid is most likely

____

The eccentric woman had a whole room dedicated to the display of *chronometers*.

A chronometer is probably

____

Congratulations for super-sleuthing new words! Now do the old-fashioned thing. Look up the words, and see how close your guesses were! Continue to work with Greek and Latin roots to broaden your vocabulary.

CULTURAL CROSSOVER

Our words come from around the world and throughout time. Here are a few examples of how English has borrowed words from other cultures.

A WORLD OF WORDS

ENGLISH WORD	ORIGINAL WORD	COUNTRY OR CULTURE OF ORIGIN
Tattoo	Ta-tau—to mark	Samoan
Lemon	Līmūn—citrus	Arabic
Cola	An-kola—kola nut	family of Niger-Congo languages
Aficionado—someone who is excited and knowledgeable about something	Aficionar—to bring affection	Spanish
Bungalow—a small house, usually with a front porch	Banglā—from Bengal	Hindi
Cherub—perfect, innocent child or angelic being with wings	Kĕrūb—like a child	Hebrew

What's one surprising thing you learned about the English language?

INCLUSIVE LANGUAGE

The way we speak is a way we put energy into the world. Speaking inclusively with language that acknowledges and respects identities is a way of putting our love and mutual respect for one another into the world. Sounds pretty awesome, right? To do this, make sure your language is inclusive.

Gender, the condition of being female or male, is part of the English language. People and many objects have been described as "he" or "she." Did you know that people often refer to ships as "she"? People also refer to the idea of justice (fairness) as female. Your local courthouse may have a sculpture or painting of justice as a woman with a set of scales. Also, think about different jobs. Some have had language that was reserved for a single gender because many people thought that work belonged to a single gender.

Gendered terms describing workers: fireman, maid, host/hostess, actor/actress, stewardess

English evolves! Our culture has replaced these gendered terms with gender-neutral terms, improving both our language and our acceptance of people!

Gender-neutral terms describing workers: firefighter, housekeeper, actor, flight attendant

ALL ABOUT PRONOUNS

Similarly, the pronouns *she* or *he*, *her* or *him*, and *hers* or *his* don't always fit. Perhaps you or someone you know is nonbinary. That means either not identifying as male or female, or the gender is unknown, or it's just not our business. For these situations and more, we can use *they*, *them*, and *theirs*.

Here's how these pronouns may look:

> A new student is arriving today. They will sit in this seat.
>
> I have an extra movie ticket for them.

I think this basketball is theirs.

How easy is that? Using *they*, *them*, and *theirs* allows you to show your respect for your fellow humans—and that is a powerful use of language.

In what ways can you use language to show love and respect for others?

BUILDING BLOCKS OF LANGUAGE

Because you have put so much work into developing and organizing your ideas for your writing, you will also want to pay attention to how you use and organize your words. Note that the specific structure and rules of language below are based on the way sentences are constructed in Standard American English and other variants.

TYPES OF CLAUSES

Clauses, or groups of words that contain a verb and usually a subject, are what sentences are made out of. There are two types of clauses:

- An **independent clause** can stand alone as a complete sentence.
    - He ran
    - Charles is right
    - The giraffe wandered over
- A **dependent clause** cannot stand alone as a complete sentence. Even if it has a noun (person, place, or thing) and a verb (action word) in it, it does not express a complete thought.
    - When Mom speaks
    - If I look
    - Because Angela worked

Can you see the difference between the independent and dependent clauses?

With the dependent clause, you need more information. The independent clause holds a complete idea.

Of course, you can add to independent and dependent clauses to make them more descriptive. Remember, just because a clause has more words doesn't necessarily make it independent! It isn't about how long the clause is, but whether there is a complete idea.

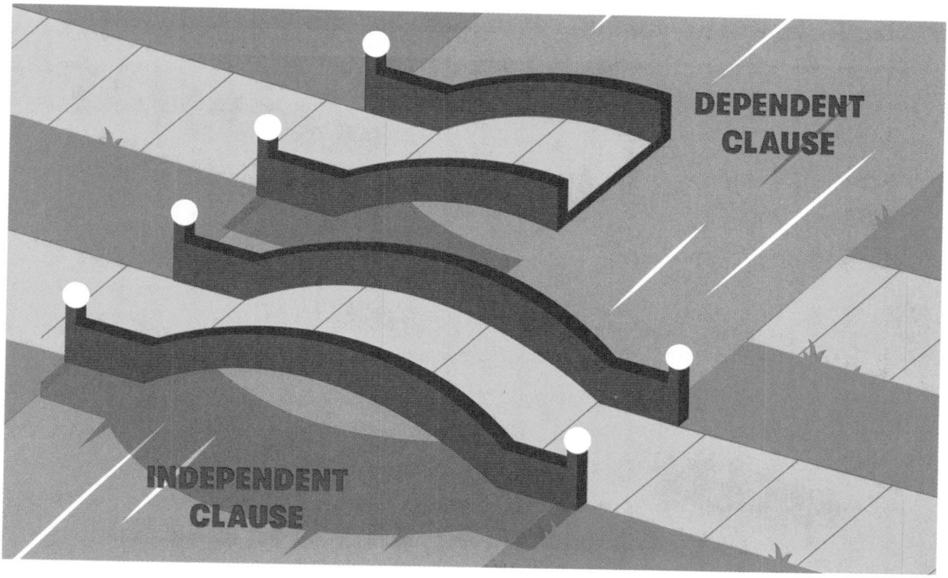

ADDING DETAIL TO CLAUSES

	PARED-DOWN VERSION	WITH MORE DESCRIPTION
INDEPENDENT CLAUSES	He ran	He ran quickly He quickly ran to the corner store
	Charles is right	Charles is right about the color of the lighthouse
	The giraffe wandered over	The tallest giraffe wandered over to us
DEPENDENT CLAUSES	When Mom speaks	When my Dominican mom speaks Spanish
	If I look	If I look hard for the ticket
	Because Angela worked	Because Angela worked hard for the rights of others

TYPES OF SENTENCES

Now let's take a look at how you can use these clauses in different sentence types.

There are four distinct sentence types:

1. Simple
2. Compound
3. Complex
4. Complex-compound

SIMPLE SENTENCE

A **simple sentence** has one independent clause and no dependent clauses.

EXAMPLES OF SIMPLE SENTENCES

The balloon popped.

I read that book already.

He looked out at the ocean longingly.

Your own examples

COMPOUND SENTENCE

A **compound sentence** has two or more independent clauses. How do you join the clauses? Use either a semicolon (;) by itself or a comma (,) along with a linking word called a conjunction.

Conjunction words:

- For
- And
- Nor
- But
- Or
- Yet
- So

One way to remember these popular conjunctions are by using the acronym FANBOYS... F/For, A/And, N/Nor, B/But, O/Or, Y/Yet, S/So. If you're a big FAN of these kind of memory tricks, then this could be a great one to know!

EXAMPLES OF COMPOUND SENTENCES

The balloon popped, **and** it scared the cat.

I don't read a lot of science fiction, **but** I read that book already.

He looked out at the ocean longingly**;** he wanted to go sailing.

Your own examples

COMPLEX SENTENCE

A complex sentence has one independent clause and at least one dependent clause. It doesn't matter which comes first. Just use a comma at the end of the dependent clause when you put it first.

EXAMPLES OF COMPLEX SENTENCES

When the balloon popped, it scared the cat.

Even though I don't read a lot of science fiction, I read that book already.

He looked out at the ocean because he heard the foghorn.

Your own examples

COMPLEX-COMPOUND SENTENCE

A **complex-compound sentence** has more than one independent clause and at least one dependent clause.

The balloon popped, and it scared the cat because the sound was so surprising.

I don't read a lot of science fiction, but I read that book when we did a science fiction book study at school.

When the rain stopped, he looked out at the ocean longingly; he hoped to go sailing.

Your own examples

____

____

____

____

Now that you know that there are four types of sentences, what should you do with them? Read both versions of the journal entry on the following pages. Note your impressions of the sentences. How do they sound, and how do they make you feel? What is the tone of the sentences, or the mood they put you in while reading them? (Also, in case you don't know, a *bodega* is a small convenience store in a city.)

Read both versions of the journal entry on the following page.

SENTENCE TYPES IN ACTION

VERSION 1

Yesterday, I went on a walk. I walked through my neighborhood. I walked past the bodega. I waved at the store owner, Anna. I turned the corner. I walked up a hill. I crossed the street. The entrance to the park is marked by two stone pillars. I walked through the pillars. I found my favorite spot. I sat down to read my book.

YOUR IMPRESSIONS

VERSION 2

Yesterday, I went on a walk; I walked through my neighborhood. When I walked past the bodega, I waved at the store owner, Anna. I turned the corner, walked up a hill, and then I crossed the street. The entrance to the park is marked by two stone pillars, which I walked through. Once I found my favorite spot, I sat down to read my book.

YOUR IMPRESSIONS

What types of sentences do you see in Version 1?

What types of sentences do you see in Version 2?

What happens to the text when the writer revises for sentence variety?

SENTENCE VARIETY

It's important to remember that an effective paragraph has a range of sentence types in it. Think of it the way you would think about learning to swim. You can swim with just one stroke—perhaps the crawl. However, once you can do the backstroke, the sidestroke, and the butterfly, you are a swimmer who can do so much more. Your writing can have a similar type of range.

Find something you have already written. It can be something you wrote in this book, or it can be another project. Read it, looking for the different sentence types. Then write a new version below that adds more sentence variety to your piece:

When you're writing paragraphs, how does using a variety of sentence types improve your overall writing?

EDITING FOR CLARITY

Why edit your writing? You want to make sure that it looks exactly as you want it to look and that it *reads* the way you want it to sound. You might look at:

- **Grammar:** the way you put words together
- **Mechanics:** the details that match whatever format you are following, such as capitalization and spelling
- **Punctuation:** using symbols (comma, period, question mark, and so on) that help your reader understand what you are writing and how you want it to sound

A NOTE ON "PROPER" GRAMMAR

Remember how we discussed that there are many variants within the English language? That variety is beautiful. However, when you learn about grammar and the "proper" ways to write and express our thoughts in English, others may tell you that your grammar is either "right" or "wrong." But here's the thing: actually, there is no *wrong* way to speak or write a language. In fact, describing grammar in this way is harmful because it implies that some variants of English are somehow "lesser," or "not proper," which just isn't true. There are many variations of every language out there in the real world, and each one is complex, unique, and beautiful. Your job is to make sure your writing looks and sounds the way *you* want it to look.

ESSENTIALS OF STANDARD AMERICAN ENGLISH

If you love literature, voice, and people, it makes sense to embrace the way we, and others, use language. However, you may encounter situations where you want your writing voice to take on the elements of Standard American English. For example, you may want to use this type of English when you fill out college and scholarship applications—and, when you're a little older, when you apply for certain kinds of jobs. The lessons below, which for the most part apply to Standard American English, will help you navigate that terrain.

TENSE CONSISTENCY

When you are writing a sentence, for clarity's sake, you want to make sure that the whole sentence exists in one time period. You are probably aware that we speak and write in different **tenses**, referring to different time periods.

EXAMPLES OF COMMON TENSES

PRESENT	PAST	FUTURE
I run	I ran	I will run
I sleep	I slept	I will sleep
He votes	He voted	He will vote

If we revisit the text about going for a walk, what tense is it written in? Underline the verbs as a way to help you.

> Yesterday, I went on a walk; I walked through my neighborhood. When I walked past the bodega, I waved at the store owner, Anna. I turned the corner, walked up a hill, and then I crossed the street. The entrance to the park is marked by two stone pillars, which I walked through. Once I found my favorite spot, I sat down to read my book.

What did you notice about verb tense here?

Here's a challenge: try writing that same paragraph in present tense.

Was that easy or tricky? Why?

Did your version end up something like this?

> Today, I walk. I walk through my neighborhood, past the bodega, and I wave at Anna, the store owner. I turn the corner, walk up a hill, and then I cross the street. The entrance to the park is marked by two stone pillars, which I walk through. I find my favorite spot, and I sit down to read my book.

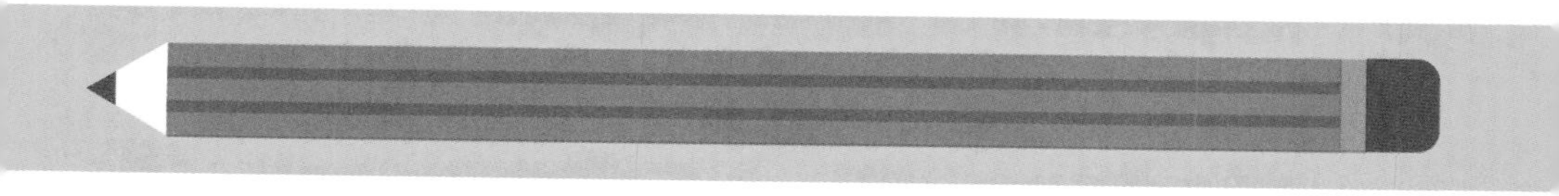

How does the tense of the text change the impression it makes on you?

You really live the experience alongside the writer when the writing is in the present tense!

But what happens when you are inconsistent with your tense? Read the same paragraph below, with the inconsistencies in tense highlighted.

> Yesterday, I went on a walk. I walk through my neighborhood; when I walk past the bodega, I waved at the store owner, Anna. I will turn the corner, walk up a hill, and then I crossed the street. The entrance to the park is marked by two stone pillars, which I walked through. Once I found my favorite spot, I will sit down to read my book.

Even though the errors above may seem like they are in a spotlight, when you are writing quickly, it's easy to make errors in tense. Remember to reread your work, note the tense, and look for inconsistencies.

But wait—what if you are writing about multiple time periods? Are there situations where the tense varies? Of course there are! Here's an example:

> I need to go to the library today. My teacher assigned us a big research project. I will be researching Ada Lovelace, a famous mathematician who lived in the nineteenth century. I will need to find books that talk about both her personal life and her work. When I arrive, I hope the librarian will help me.

The writer has sprinkled different tenses throughout that paragraph. Those different tenses match each time period being discussed. Here's the same paragraph with some errors in tense. Circle the mistakes.

> I need to go to the library today. My teacher assign us a big research project. I will be researching Ada Lovelace, a famous mathematician who lives in the nineteenth century. I needed to find books that talk about both her

personal life and her work. When I arrived, I hope the librarian will help me.

See that? Even in a paragraph that contains multiple tenses, you can find the errors. To check your editing skills, you can compare your observations with the initial example of this paragraph where multiple tenses are used correctly.

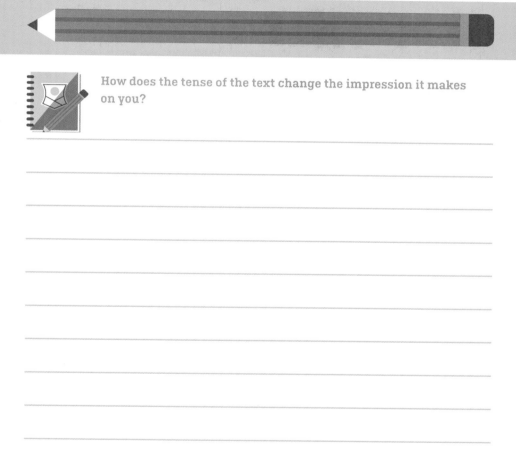

How does the tense of the text change the impression it makes on you?

The errors in tense are highlighted.

I need to go to the library today. My teacher assign us a big research project. I will be researching Ada Lovelace, a famous mathematician who lives in the nineteenth century. I needed to find books that talk about both her personal life and her work. When I arrived, I hope the librarian will help me.

HOMONYMS

Homonyms are two or more words that sound similar but have different spellings and meanings. Getting them right matters so your writing is clear. Getting them wrong is easy—sometimes your brain plays tricks on you, and you just write the first spelling that comes to mind. Sometimes, you just don't know which word is correct.

Here's a list of homonyms that people often use incorrectly.

1. affect/effect

Affect is a verb that shows change: The fertilizer will *affect* how the flower grows.

Effect is the result of something, a noun: The change in her morning routine had a positive *effect* on her overall schedule.

2. than/then

People use *than* for comparisons: Winter is better *than* spring for skiing.

Then tells about order or time: I went to practice, and *then* I went home and did my homework.

3. which/witch

Which helps you specify one or a few out of a group: *Which* book do you want—the thriller or the biography?

Witch refers to a person or being who may have magical powers: She was dressed up like a *witch* from a fairy tale, with a wide-brimmed, black, pointy hat.

4. here/hear

Here tells place: I will set up my tent *here*, on the edge of the forest.

Hear tells of listening: I can *hear* the sound of the trees swaying in the wind.

5. are/our

Are is one form of the verb "to be": We *are* too hot.

Our shows possession: That is *our* home; we bought it five years ago.

6. buy/by

Buy means paying money for something: Did you *buy* a new backpack at the store?

By tells of location: I will bike *by* the movie theater in the afternoon.

7. accept/except

Accept means to take: She was honored to *accept* the college scholarship money.

Except means "not including": John did all his homework *except* the science project.

8. there/their/they're

There usually means "that place": She went *there* on her own.

Their means "belonging to them": The baby turkeys followed *their* mother across the field.

They're is short for "they are": *They're* going to have to climb that steep hill before they get to the lookout point.

9. to/too/two

To can indicate place or come right before a verb: They are going to floor 56.

Too can stand for "as well" or tells us that there is abundance: The story she told was way *too* long.

Two is the number 2: She scored *two* goals today!

10. you're/your

You're is short for "you are": I cannot wait until *you're* performing your solo.

Your means "belonging to you": This is *your* green sweater.

11. aloud/allowed

Use *aloud* to mean "spoken out loud": He read the winners' names *aloud* in a booming voice.

Allowed means someone has granted permission: Carlos is *allowed* to eat dessert after he has eaten his dinner.

12. it's/its

It's is short for "it is": *It's* going to be a long bike ride, so make sure you bring water.

Its means "belonging to it": The restaurant's menu is posted outside on its door.

13. who's/whose

Who's is short for "who is": *Who's* the owner of the tan spotted horse?

Whose shows possession: The dog, *whose* toy was caught in the fence, barked until someone came to help.

It's easy to accidentally write the incorrect homonym. Here's an example of a draft where the writer used incorrect homonyms. Can you find them all? Hint #1: there are thirteen! Hint #2: some errors are not from the list above (but feel free to add them to it).

> The young boy whose from down the hill is named Raymond. He is only aloud to stay out until dark. If he comes home to late, their will be a punishment. His mom might say, "Your out after dark, and that isn't exceptable. I would rather you stay home then be out. You know that. Its to scary out their in the dark. Do you here the sound of the bats?" So Raymond always makes sure too bee home before dark.

Are there any homonyms you can think of to add to the list? Write them below!

1. WHOSE should be corrected to WHO'S
2. ALOUD should be corrected to ALLOWED
3. TO should be corrected to TOO
4. THEIR should be corrected to THERE
5. YOUR should be corrected to YOU'RE
6. EXCEPTABLE should be corrected to ACCEPTABLE
7. THEN should be corrected to THAN
8. ITS should be corrected to IT'S
9. TO should be corrected to TOO
10. THEIR should be corrected to THERE
11. HERE should be corrected to HEAR
12. TOO should be corrected to TO
13. BEE should be corrected to BE

Which homonyms do you think are most commonly misused?

Which is more difficult, identifying problems with tense or choosing the right homonyms? Why?

SUBJECT-VERB AGREEMENT

Matching a verb (action word) in connection with its subject (the person, place, thing, or idea the sentence is about) is subject-verb agreement. Different versions of English handle it differently. We will take a look at Standard American English, since that is what this section of the book is on.

If you speak a different type of English, these subject-verb agreements may sound incorrect or strange to you. That's because not all variants of English have the same subject-verb agreement rules. And that's okay! Make choices for your writing that are appropriate for you and your piece. For example, if you are writing dialogue (words your characters say), you might want to use a variant of English instead of Standard American English.

All sentences must have a verb, and all verbs need a subject. Let's look at the examples on the following pages:

I **am** happy.

He **is** happy.

In both of these sentences, the verb is the same, but it doesn't look the same, does it? Notice how it changes depending on the *subject* of the sentence. The words *am* and *is* are two different versions of the verb *be*.

Making sure the right version of the verb matches up with the sentence's subject is called subject-verb agreement.

The subjects in these sentences are underlined. The verbs are highlighted.

The tree swayed.

She read a book.

The caterpillar became a butterfly.

Dinner was served at midnight.

The tacos were delicious.

Give it a try by underlining the subjects and ***circling*** *the verbs.*

She jumped high.

The circus left town.

The cat climbed a tree.

Sometimes a sentence has more than one subject:

Amar and William win the prize.

Breakfast and dinner were eaten by the campfire.

Nelly, Kathi, Victor, and Genesis ran inside for dinner.

Neither the dog nor the cat jumps on the bed.

Give it a try:

Both elephants and zebras are found in the African savannah.

The turtle and the hare race for the finish line.

Whatever variant of English you speak, you follow a rule for how to make the subject and verb agree. Let's take a look at the rules of Standard American English.

One subject alone requires the singular verb:

- The cat meows.

When referring to multiples of the subject, use the plural verb:

- The cats meow.

Two or more subjects that are connected by "and" require the plural verb:

- The lion, cheetah, and leopard all meow.

When two or more subjects are connected by either "or" or "nor," use the singular verb:

- Either the cheetah or the leopard meows.

Sometimes you have to connect a subject to a verb, but there's a phrase in the middle! Follow that subject to its verb.

- Kenny, who is Daniel's brother, went to camp for half the summer.
- The mother hen, along with all her chicks, pecks at the cage.
- One of the flowers blooms on her birthday every year.
- The team that won three Super Bowls is my favorite.
- All the crayons in the brand-new box have beautiful, unused points.

These longer, more detailed sentences are where people tend to make mistakes. Take your time as you craft your longer sentences. Figure out if your subject is singular or plural, and use the verb that agrees with it.

In the following sentences, underline the subject and circle the correct version of the verb:

Tara (wait/waits) in line for a delicious doughnut.

Tristan and Jonathan (goes/go) fishing every weekend.

The baby elephant, who has six older siblings, (is/are) part of a large herd.

Ms. Ella's class (writes/write) for 30 minutes straight every morning.

Is subject-verb agreement a challenge for you? Why or why not?

____

____

____

____

Answers for sentence problems on pp. 476, 477, and above

She **jumped** high.

The circus **left** town.

The cat **climbed** a tree.

Both elephants and zebras **are found** in the African savannah.

The turtle and the hare **race** for the finish line.

Tara **waits** in line for a delicious doughnut.

Tristan and Jonathan **go** fishing every weekend.

The baby elephant who has six older siblings **is** part of a large herd.

Ms. Ella's class **writes** for 30 minutes straight every morning.

FRAGMENTS AND RUN-ONS

Writing is creative. It's also intentional. When you talk, words probably just flow out of you. You don't need to be as attentive to details because you also offer other bits of information, such as pauses, gestures, and facial expressions. In contrast, when you write, you rely solely on words and punctuation to get your message across. Therefore, skillful writers pay attention to fragmented and run-on sentences because those can confuse readers when used carelessly.

Sentence fragments are sentences that are incomplete—usually missing a subject or a verb. On the other hand, a **run-on sentence** happens when multiple sentences run together, and they're missing punctuation and capitalization or a conjunction.

Here are some examples of sentence fragments:

To be a hero.

Fixed: *Mae wants* to be a hero.

Walked to town.

Fixed: *They* walked to town.

The audience clapping loudly.

Fixed: The audience *was* clapping loudly.

And here are some examples of run-on sentences:

Sheryl made blueberry jam she put it individual jars.

Fixed: Sheryl made blueberry jam. She put it in individual jars.

Antonia put on her flippers they make her go fast.

Fixed: Antonia put on her flippers; they make her go fast.

In writing, a reader doesn't have the additional inputs that come with spoken words, such as tone of voice, volume, and facial expressions. As a result, fragments and run-ons end up being confusing. This is why it's important to check your work for both.

Take a look at a piece or two of your own writing. Did you find any fragments or run-ons? It's important to check your schoolwork and be sure you're using your words exactly the way you mean them. There are exceptions, though. If you are writing dialogue and you want to show how people really talk, you may want to include fragments and run-ons. Just make sure that readers understand your message and don't get frustrated.

What fragments or run-ons did you find in your own work? Would you change them? If so, how?

THE POWER OF LANGUAGE

Language is meaningful and can change people's lives. It's the primary way we communicate with others. You have probably heard someone say, "It's not what you say, it's how you say it."

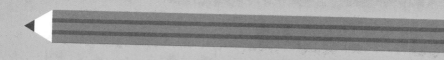

In what ways does how you use language matter? In what ways does how you use language not matter?

CHAPTER 10 VOCABULARY

clause: a group of words that contains a verb and usually a subject—clauses are what sentences are made out of. They include:

> **dependent clause:** one that cannot stand alone as a complete sentence, such as "before she left for school"
>
> **independent clause:** one that can stand alone as a complete sentence, such as "she ate breakfast"

complex sentence: one that has one independent clause and at least one dependent clause

complex-compound sentence: one that has more than one independent clause and at least one dependent clause

compound sentence: one that has two or more independent clauses

etymology: the study of where words come from

grammar: the way people put words together

homonyms: two or more words that sound similar but have different spellings and meanings, such as *ate* and *eight* or *to*, *too*, and *two*

mechanics: the writing details that match whatever format you are following, such as capitalization and spelling

punctuation: using symbols (comma, period, question mark, and so on) that help your reader understand what you are writing and how you want it to sound

roots: the seed or core part of a word; for example, *act* is the root of *react*

run-on sentence: occurs when multiple sentences run together and are missing punctuation and capitalization or a conjunction

sentence fragments: sentences that are incomplete—usually missing a subject or a verb

simple sentence: one that has one independent clause and no dependent clauses

Standard American English: a variety of the English language that is generally used in professional communication in the United States and taught in U.S. schools

subject-verb agreement: using the verb conjugation that matches the subject performing the action, as in "He runs."

subject: the person, place, thing, or idea the sentence is about

tense: the time period in which the action in a sentence or clause occurs, such as past, present, or future

variant: a version of a language used by members of a group based on geography, culture, or social class

verb: an action word, such as *jump*, *laugh*, or *daydream*

voice: each individual's own personal communication style—their emotions, attitude, point of view, and habits of expression

11

ELA 4-EVER: LOOKING BACK AND LOOKING FORWARD

In this book, we've talked a lot about what you can do to become the best reader and writer possible. Remember, reading and writing are lifelong experiences. And you are just getting started.

In this chapter, you will learn how to be deliberate in how you add to this foundation. Also, you'll learn ways of training yourself to read and write for enjoyment. Are you ready for new experiences, ideas for investigating your questions, and suggestions for practicing your passions? Let's get going.

CHAPTER CONTENTS

READING: YOUR PASSPORT TO A WORLD OF EXPERIENCES AND IDEAS

Reading really is a gateway into the world. Without leaving your home or library, you can travel to other worlds and other times. You can also look within.

How have you been doing with your daily reading?

If there's one thing you can do for yourself as a reader of fiction, it's this: use the stories of characters to learn about yourself and to gain **empathy**, or the ability to understand and share the feelings of others, even when you don't share their experiences. A great goal is to read books that tell stories about a range of experiences. Remember way back in Chapter 1, when you learned that books can act as mirrors that show you yourself, windows that show you the reality of others' lives, and even sliding doors that allow you to experience another's world for yourself? A good reader seeks out different stories that fill all three of these categories.

FINDING YOUR NEXT READ

How do you find books? Some people ask friends, teachers, and librarians. You can also search online. If you have a social media account, there might be a relevant hashtag to follow. Start by looking up book lists.

Perhaps you haven't read any books that explore being LGBTQ+ in middle school. In that case, you may try these search terms: *LGBTQ + best books + middle school*. With a little work, you will find great lists of books compiled by people who care about reading and the issues you want to explore.

KEEP TRACK OF YOUR READING

Record titles of books so you can keep track of all of the worlds and experiences you have or want to explore. Continue to add to this chart until you run out of space. Then, make a new chart in a journal! Share your lists with friends and teachers, and work together to create lists of great books.

A BOOK FOR EVERY READER

BOOKS THAT HAVE A MAIN CHARACTER WHO LOOKS LIKE YOU	
1.	2.
3.	4.

BOOKS THAT HAVE A MAIN CHARACTER WHO SHARES A MAJOR EXPERIENCE WITH YOU

1.
2.
3.
4.

BOOKS THAT TAKE PLACE IN A COMMUNITY SIMILAR TO THE ONE YOU LIVE IN

1.
2.
3.
4.

BOOKS THAT TAKE PLACE IN THE COUNTRY

1.
2.
3.
4.

BOOKS THAT TAKE PLACE IN THE CITY

1.
2.
3.
4.

BOOKS THAT TAKE PLACE IN THE SUBURBS

1.
2.
3.
4.

BOOKS THAT TAKE PLACE IN THE PAST

1.
2.
3.
4.

BOOKS THAT TAKE PLACE IN THE PRESENT

1.
2.
3.
4.

BOOKS THAT TAKE PLACE IN THE FUTURE

1.
2.
3.
4.

BOOKS THAT TAKE PLACE IN ANOTHER COUNTRY

1. 2.

3. 4.

BOOKS WITH A FEMALE MAIN CHARACTER

1. 2.

3. 4.

BOOKS WITH A MALE MAIN CHARACTER

1. 2.

3. 4.

BOOKS WITH A NONBINARY, TRANSGENDER, OR TRANSITIONING MAIN CHARACTER

1. 2.

3. 4.

BOOKS THAT INCLUDE CHARACTERS WITH ATYPICAL PHYSICAL OR INTELLECTUAL ABILITIES

1. 2.

3. 4.

BOOKS FEATURING MOSTLY BLACK CHARACTERS

1. 2.

3. 4.

BOOKS FEATURING MOSTLY WHITE CHARACTERS

1. 2.

3. 4.

BOOKS FEATURING MOSTLY ASIAN CHARACTERS

1. 2.

3. 4.

BOOKS FEATURING MOSTLY LATINX CHARACTERS

1.
2.
3.
4.

BOOKS FEATURING MOSTLY NATIVE AMERICAN CHARACTERS

1.
2.
3.
4.

BOOKS THAT EXPLORE THE LIVES OF THOSE WHO LIVE WITHIN MULTIPLE WORLDS (PERHAPS DUE TO RACE, ETHNICITY, GENDER, SEXUAL ORIENTATION, FAMILY STRUCTURE, OR OTHER PART OF THEIR IDENTITY)

1.
2.
3.
4.

BOOKS THAT EXPLORE EXPERIENCES OR RELATIONSHIPS WITHIN FAMILIES

1.
2.
3.
4.

BOOKS THAT EXPLORE FRIENDSHIPS

1.
2.
3.
4.

BOOKS ABOUT SOCIAL ISSUES (DIVORCE, POLLUTION, SOCIAL MEDIA, AND SO ON)

1.
2.
3.
4.

MYSTERIES

1.
2.
3.
4.

LOVE STORIES

1.
2.
3.
4.

ADVENTURE STORIES

1.

2.

3.

4.

MAKE YOUR OWN CATEGORIES!

1.

2.

3.

4.

Think about the choices you make when selecting books. Do you choose books that reflect your life or the lives of others? Why might that be?

Why should people read stories that reflect parts of their own experiences?

Why should people read books that reflect experiences very different from their own?

READ TO LEARN

Now what about nonfiction—the literature that is based on real events and people, on facts and history. Does your literary life have room for that as well? It sure does!

Keep track of the nonfiction you are reading. Look for topics that interest you and topics you've never heard of. Challenge yourself to use nonfiction to broaden your knowledge of the world. Everything you learn in a nonfiction book can become prior knowledge that will help you analyze and understand more reading down the road!

YOUR NONFICTION READING LIST

TOPIC	TITLES
About your racial and/or cultural identity	
About other racial and/or cultural identities	
About historical figures	

About people of today, or close to it	
Sports	
Arts	
Pop culture	
Science	
Math	
History	

What kinds of things are you learning about in your nonfiction reading?

Name some things you haven't read about but would like to sometime soon.

YOUR READING BUCKET LIST

A **bucket list** is a list of things you want to do. Sometimes, there are too many books to read. Actually, that's true all the time. Maybe you're in the middle of a great series, and a friend recommends another book that sounds wildly intriguing. Or maybe you know that one of your favorite authors wrote a book that is not yet available. And sometimes, there are great books that we just aren't ready for. Maybe the content doesn't feel right at this time, or maybe it's too hard—so hard that your work to get through each page is affecting your comprehension. What's a reader to do? Keep a list.

BOOKS TO BOOKMARK

Reading makes you stronger—not just a stronger reader, but a stronger human. And sometimes, when you are strong, something may bring you to tears. That's what good books can do to good readers. They make us cry, laugh, learn, and see more than we thought we were capable of.

Here's the last list—list books that really affected you.

BOOKS THAT I LOVED SO MUCH, I WAS SAD WHEN THEY ENDED:

Discuss two things you have learned about reading. Describe what you learned. Reflect on how you have changed as a reader.

WRITING: RECORDING AND SHARING YOUR UNDERSTANDINGS AND EXPERIENCES

Writing is where you can hold onto all that you experience and think. And the act of writing itself helps us to learn. Putting our thoughts into words does our brains so much good, and it's a chance for self-expression.

Take time to record which types of writing you are practicing. Return to this list, making changes to it as needed. Just as you would with a first draft of a paper, you will cross out some things and add others. It will be a record of your work over time.

KEEP TRACK OF YOUR WRITING

DATE	WRITING *FORMATS* YOU HAVE TRIED (ESSAYS, MOVIE SCRIPTS, RESEARCH PAPERS, SPEECHES, POEMS, PODCASTS, AND SO ON)

DATE	WRITING *STRATEGIES* YOU HAVE TRIED (FREEWRITING, OUTLINING, ADDING SENSORY DETAILS, AND SO ON)

Look at the writing you have done. What changes do you see?

What do you still want to work on?

WRITING ABOUT YOU

Poetry is a beautiful form of self-expression. Writers often write in an effort to understand and record who they are and how they came to be.

Check out "Where I'm From."

Where I'm From

by George Ella Lyon

I am from clothespins,
from Clorox and carbon tetrachloride.
I am from the dirt under the back porch.
(Black, glistening
it tasted like beets.)
I am from the forsythia bush,
the Dutch elm
whose long gone limbs I remember
as if they were my own.

I am from fudge and eyeglasses,
from Imogene and Alafair.
I am from the know-it-alls and the pass-it-ons,
from perk up and pipe down.
I am from He restoreth my soul with a cottonball lamb
and ten verses I can say myself.

I'm from Artemus and Billie's Branch,
fried corn and strong coffee.
From the finger my grandfather lost to the auger
the eye my father shut to keep his sight.
Under my bed was a dress box
spilling old pictures.
a sift of lost faces
to drift beneath my dreams.

I am from those moments—
snapped before I budded—
leaf-fall from the family tree

Here's what the author had to say about her poem, and how it came from the ideas of another poet: "My poem, written in 1993, was inspired by a poem of Jo Carson's. Her poem took off from something she heard somebody say," she said. "So 'Where I'm From' has been a pass-it-on-phenomenon from the get-go. Here's to the power of poetry and place, and to the voices in all of us that long to be heard."

Since Lyon wrote the poem, all sorts of people have rewritten it. Here's one by a young poet.

Where I'm From

by Antonia Akawi

I am from a stuffed elephant
made of worn African fabric
that was maybe once a dress

from beans for breakfast and
a pretend cell phone

I am from Kinshasa where it
is beautiful and kind of hot

and from Brooklyn where
friends look out for you

I am from sticks that start out
in nature and make their way
into the house

and become magical scepters

I am from the toys of the
baby-me

from African and Italian and
Texan and American words
and names

I am from the laughter and
good manners of Congolese
women

and from song

and I make dances

I am from a beautiful
place

I am from the love of three
mamas

from mac and cheese and
rice and beans

from the little-me

and from love and
sacrifice

and singing French
children's songs that call
my name, "mes amis, mes
amis, ouvre moi la porte,
Antonia."

I am from those moments
in Kinshasa where it is
beautiful and kind of hot

Give it a try, and write down where you're from. The template is below. You can see that in a few spots, Antonia adapted the prompts to better match her story. You should also feel free to adjust the prompts so that they best suit you.

Follow this piece through the writing process. Revise to add imagery (also known as word pictures) and other poetic devices. Read it out loud. Publish it on a beautiful piece of paper, or with colored pens in a favorite journal. Or put it at the end of this book, in the "notes" pages.

WHERE I'M FROM

by ______________________________

I am from ____

(a specific item from your home, community, or place you're from)

from____

(two items from your home, community, or place you're from)

I am from ____

(a phrase describing your home, community, or place you're from)

and____

(more description of your home, community, or place you're from)

I am from ____

(a plant, tree, or natural item from your past)

whose____

(personify that natural item—give it a human characteristic or action)

I am from ____

(two objects from your past)

from______________________________and______________________________

(name that has to do with you) *(another name that connects to you)*

I am from______________________________and______________________________

(trait or tendency that you or others around you have) *(another trait or tendency of you or others near you)*

and from____

(trait, tendency, or habit you have seen in yourself or in people you have been close to)

from____

(one more trait, tendency, or habit you have seen in yourself or in people you have been close to)

I am from____

(a phrase or memory you have heard or think about)

I am from______________________________and______________________________

(person who came before you) *(another person who came before you)*

from ____

(two foods that are common or meaningful in your life)

from ____

(specific event of a person who came before you)

and from ____

(another detail of a person who came before you)

____

(a memory or object you have from a younger age)

I am from those moments ____

____

(wrap up by finishing this thought—you may want to repeat an idea from earlier in your poem)

Reflect on your "Where I'm From" poem. What did you notice or learn about yourself as you wrote it?

Whom will you read it to?

WRITING A LETTER TO THE LIFELONG READER AND WRITER IN YOU

Both reading and writing are lifelong endeavors. Write a letter to your 25-year-old self about your current reading and writing life and what you hope for yourself as a reader and writer. Oh, and don't forget to use what you learned about formatting a letter—impress the 25-year-old you!

Some ideas to include:

- What you want your 25-year-old self to know about you as a reader right now
    - Things you have learned about yourself as a reader
    - Successes
    - Struggles
    - Preferred genres (adventure, romance, thriller, science fiction, and so on)
    - Favorite books
    - Current reading goals
- What you hope for your 25-year-old reader self
    - Hopes and goals
    - Questions
    - What you want your 25-year-old self to know about you as a writer right now
    - Things you have learned about yourself as a writer
    - Successes
    - Struggles
    - Preferred genres or formats
    - Current writing goals

- What you hope for your 25-year-old writer self
    - Hopes and goals
    - Questions

ELA 4-EVER: LOOKING BACK AND LOOKING FORWARD

This book is intended to lay a foundation for you as a reader and writer. Great readers and writers take the time to strengthen those muscles. The order and pace of your progress don't matter. What's important is that you love and take care of the reader and writer inside of you. 4-EVER.

The reader and writer in you can help you through difficult times. You can learn, escape, and understand through books and poetry. You can process, express, and organize through writing. The reader and writer in you will help you celebrate your success, and more importantly, move you toward milestones (whatever they are for you).

Remember, for every experience, there is a piece of writing. Pull out those research skills, and find the writing you need to read. Then, write your own version. Tell your story.

CREDITS

CHAPTER ONE

Pages 35-37: "How a Teen Inventor in Africa Used Trash to Reach MIT," by Kids Discover, www.kidsdiscover.com. All rights reserved. © Kids Discover, LLC.

Page 38: "This Is Just to Say," by William Carlos Williams, from *The Collected Poems: Volume I, 1909-1939*, copyright ©1938 by New Directions Publishing Corp. Reprinted by permission of New Directions Publishing Corp. Reprinted in the UK by permission of Carcanet Press Limited.

Page 43: Excerpt from "The Lottery" from *The Lottery* by Shirley Jackson. Copyright © 1948, 1949 by Shirley Jackson. Copyright renewed 1976, 1977 by Laurence Hyman, Barry Hyman, Mrs. Sarah Webster and Mrs. Joanne Schnurer. Reprinted by permission of Farrar, Straus and Giroux.

Page 46: From *Friday Night Lights* by H. G Bissinger, copyright © 1990. Reprinted by permission of Da Capo Press, an imprint of Hachette Book Group, Inc.

Page 52: From *Speak* by Laurie Halse Anderson. Copyright © 1999 by Laurie Halse Anderson. Reprinted by permission of Farrar Straus Giroux Books for Young Readers. All Rights Reserved.

Page 56: From *The House on Mango Street*. Copyright © 1984 by Sandra Cisneros. Published by Vintage Books, a division of Penguin Random House, Inc., and in hardcover by Alfred A. Knopf in 1994. By permission of Susan Bergholz Literary Services, New York, NY and Lamy, NM. All rights reserved. Reprinted in the UK and Commonwealth by permission of Bloomsbury Publishing Plc.

CHAPTER TWO

Page 73: *The Tiger Rising*. Copyright © 2001 by Kate DiCamillo. Reproduced by permission of the publisher, Candlewick Press, Somerville, MA.

Page 78: Text excerpt from pages 1-2 from *Pride* by Ibi Zoboi. Used by permission of HarperCollins Publishers.

Page 82: From *Uglies* by Scott Westerfeld. Copyright © 2005 Scott Westerfeld. Reprinted with the permission of Simon & Schuster Books for Young Readers, an imprint of Simon & Schuster Children's Publishing Division. All rights reserved.

Pages 88-94: "Thank You, M'am" from *Short Stories* by Langston Hughes. Copyright © 1996 by Ramona Bass and Arnold Rampersad. Reprinted by permission of Hill and Wang, a division of Farrar, Straus and Giroux and by permission of Harold Ober Associates. Copyright 1994 by Langston Hughes.

Pages 96-99: Specified selection from *Octopus Stew* © 2019 by Eric Velasquez. Reprinted by permission of Holiday House Publishing, Inc. All Rights Reserved.

Page 104: "Wake Up Call" from *Booked* by Kwame Alexander. Copyright © 2016 by Kwame Alexander. Reprinted by permission of Houghton Mifflin Harcourt Publishing Company. All rights reserved. Reprinted in the UK by permission of Andersen Press Ltd.

Page 106: From *Journey to Topaz* by Yoshika Uchida, © The Regents of the University of California.

Page 108: From *For Black Girls Like Me* by Mariama J. Lockington. Copyright © 2019 by

Mariama J. Lockington. Reprinted by permission of Farrar Straus Giroux Books for Young Readers. All Rights Reserved.

Pages 116–117: From *The House on Mango Street*. Copyright © 1984 by Sandra Cisneros. Published by Vintage Books, a division of Penguin Random House, Inc., and in hardcover by Alfred A. Knopf in 1994. By permission of Susan Bergholz Literary Services, New York, NY and Lamy, NM. All rights reserved. Reprinted in the UK and Commonwealth by permission of Bloomsbury Publishing Plc.

Page 118: © Renee Watson, 2017, *Piecing Me Together*, Bloomsbury Publishing Inc.

CHAPTER THREE

Page 132: *The Holocaust, by Susan Willoughby*. © 2001 by Capstone. All rights reserved.

Page 134: Excerpt from *Night* by Elie Wiesel, translated by Marion Wiesel. Translation copyright © 2006 by Marion Wiesel. Originally published in French as *La Nuit*. Copyright © 1956 by Éditions de Minuit. Reprinted by permission of Hill and Wang, a division of Farrar, Straus and Giroux. *Night* by Elie Wiesel. Reprinted in the UK and British Commonwealth by permission of Georges Borchardt, Inc., for Éditions de Minuit on behalf of the author's estate.

Pages 140-142: "Waste Not," From TIME for Kids. © 2019 TIME USA LLC.. All rights reserved. Used under license.

Page 146: Howard Zinn, excerpt from *A Young People's History of the United States: Columbus to the War on Terror*, adapted by Rebecca Stefoff. Copyright © 2007, 2009 by Howard Zinn. Reprinted with the permission of The Permissions Company, LLC on behalf of Seven Stories Press, sevenstories.com.

Pages 150-152: "Breakfast on Mars: Why We Should Colonize the Red Planet (Part 1, Argument)." Copyright Chris Higgins LLC. Visit chrishiggins.com for more work by Chris.

Pages 156-157: "Robots Only: Why We Shouldn't Colonize Mars (Part 2, Counterpoint). Copyright Chris Higgins LLC. Visit chrishiggins.com for more work by Chris.

Page 161: From *Made You Look: How Advertising Works and Why You Should Know* © 2003 Shari Graydon (text), © Warren Clark (art) published by Annick Press Ltd. All rights reserved. Reproduced by permission.

CHAPTER FOUR

Page 166-167: "Caged Bird" from *Shaker, Why Don't You Sing?* by Maya Angelou, copyright © 1983 by Maya Angelou. Used by permission of Random House, an imprint and division of Penguin Random House LLC. All rights reserved. Used in the UK and British Commonwealth by permission of Little, Brown Book Group.

Page 172: From "I Am Who I Am, So What," © Raquel Valle Senties

Page 175: "Mother to Son," Reprinted by permission of Harold Ober Associates. Copyright 1994 by the Langston Hughes Estate.

Page 178: Poetry selection titled: "Louder Than a Clap of Thunder" from *The New Kid on the Block* by Jack Prelutsky – Illustrated By: James Stevenson. Text Copyright © 1984 by Jack Prelutsky. Illustrations Copyright © 1984 by James Stevenson. Used by permission of HarperCollins Publishers.

Pages 179-180: "Perhaps the World Ends Here", from *The Woman Who Fell From the Sky* by Joy Harjo. Copyright © 1994 by Joy Harjo. Used by permission of W. W. Norton & Company, Inc. Used in the UK by permission of Anderson Literary Management LLC and the author.

Page 185: "Life Doesn't Frighten Me" from *And Still I Rise: A Book of Poems* by Maya Angelou, copyright © 1978 by Maya Angelou. Used by permission of Random House, an imprint and division of Penguin Random House LLC. All rights reserved. Used in the UK and British Commonwealth by permission of Little, Brown Book Group.

Pages 187-188: "maggie and milly and molly and may". Copyright © 1956, 1984, 1991 by the Trustees for the E. E. Cummings Trust, from *Complete Poems: 1904-1962* by E. E. Cummings, edited by George J. Firmage. Used by permission of Liveright Publishing Corporation.

Page 192: "The Old Pond," translated by Peter Beilenson and Harry Behn, published in Haiku Harvest © 1962 by Peter Pauper Press, Inc. www.peterpauper.com Used with permission.

Page 193: "The First Book", from *On the Bus With Rosa Parks* by Rita Dove. Copyright © 1999 by Rita Dove. Used by permission of W. W. Norton & Company, Inc.

Page 196: The excerpt is taken from the novel *The Marrow Thieves*, by Cherie Dimaline, published by DCB, an imprint of Cormorant Books Inc., Toronto. Copyright 2017 © Cherie Dimaline. Used with the permission of the publisher.

CHAPTER FIVE

Pages 232-233: "Kid Heroes for the Planet." From TIME for Kids. © 2019 TIME USA LLC. All rights reserved. Used under license.

CHAPTER SIX

Pages 240-244: "Practical Dance Theory," by Dan Carroll. First published in Polyphony Lit Vol. 15/Winter 2020.

Page 273: From *I Am Malala: How One Girl Stood Up For Education And Changed the World* by Malala Yousafzai with Patricia McCormick, copyright © 2014. Reprinted by permission of Little, Brown, & Company, an imprint of Hachette Book Group, Inc.

From *The House on Mango Street*. Copyright © 1984 by Sandra Cisneros. Published by Vintage Books, a division of Penguin Random House, Inc., and in hardcover by Alfred A. Knopf in 1994. By permission of Susan Bergholz Literary Services, New York, NY and Lamy, NM. All rights reserved.

"One Wish" © Ronald L. Smith, 2019. First published in The Hero Next Door, published in the United States by Crown Books for Young Readers, an imprint of Random House Children's Books, a division of Penguin Random House, LLC, New York.

"Home" © Hena Khan, 2019. First published in *The Hero Next Door*, published in the United States by Crown Books for Young Readers, an imprint of Random House Children's Books, a division of Penguin Random House, LLC, New York.

"All Talk and No Action," by Elizabeth Thompson, from *The Struggle to Be Strong, 2000*, published by Free Spirit Publishing.

Page 275: From *Woman Hollering Creek*. Copyright © 1991 by Sandra Cisneros. Published by Vintage Books, a division of Penguin Random House Inc., and originally in hardcover by Random House Inc.

Page 277: "Minnows and Zombies" © Rita Williams-Garcia, 2019. First published in *The Hero Next Door*, published in the United States by Crown Books for Young Readers, an imprint of Random House Children's Books, a division of Penguin Random House, LLC, New York.

Page 279: Copyright © Highlights for Children, Inc., Columbus, Ohio. All rights reserved.

CHAPTER SEVEN

Page 300: Adapted from "Teaching Adolescents How to Evaluate the Quality of Online Information," Edutopia, April 7, 2014, updated August 29, 2017.

Page 304: "Blue-footed Boobies" by Ellen Lambeth. Originally published in Ranger Rick, March 2010. Reprinted with permission of the owner, National Wildlife Federation®.

Pages 309-310: First published in the United States under the title *14 Cows For America* by Carmen Agra Deedy and Wilson Kimeli Naiyomah, illustrated by Thomas Gonzalez. Text Copyright © 2009 by Carmen Agra Deedy. Illustrations Copyright © 2009 by Thomas Gonzalez. Afterword Copyright © 2009 by Wilson Kimeli Naiyomah. Published by arrangement with Peachtree Publishing Company Inc.

Pages 328-329: "Polar Bears in Danger." From TIME for Kids. © 2019 TIME USA LLC.. All rights reserved. Used under license.

CHAPTER EIGHT

Pages 386-387: Isabel Hwang, "The Life-Changing Magic of Being Messy," first printed in The New York Times, June 4, 2019.

CHAPTER NINE

Page 414: Sophia Bailey-Klugh, Letter to President Obama.

CHAPTER TEN

Page 433: © Renee Watson, 2017, *Piecing Me Together*, Bloomsbury Publishing Inc.

Page 440: From *The House on Mango Street*. Copyright © 1984 by Sandra Cisneros. Published by Vintage Books, a division of Penguin Random House, Inc., and in hardcover by Alfred A. Knopf in 1994. By permission of Susan Bergholz Literary Services, New York, NY and Lamy, NM. All rights reserved.

So Much. Text copyright © 1994 by Trish Cooke. Illustrations copyright 1994 © by Helen Oxenbury. Reproduced by permission of the publisher, Candlewick Press, on behalf of Walker Books, London.

Excerpt from *Birdsong* by Julie Flett, reprinted with permission from Greystone Books Ltd.

Page 472: Adapted from www.scholastic.com/parents/books-and-reading/raise-a-reader-blog/top-20-most-commonly-confused-homophones.html

CHAPTER ELEVEN

Pages 504-505: George Ella Lyon, "Where I'm From," Copyright © 1999 George Ella Lyon. Used with permission.

Page 505: "Where I'm From: A Crowdsourced Poem That Collects Your Memories Of Home," © 2019 National Public Radio, Inc.

Page 506: Antonia Akaw

ABOUT THE CREATORS OF HOW TO SURVIVE MIDDLE SCHOOL: ENGLISH

Nina Ciatto is a New York City public school teacher who has worked primarily with middle school students for more than twenty years. Her areas of focus are English language arts, social studies, special education, and social-emotional learning. She conducted professional development for teachers in Azerbaijan through the U.S. Department of State's Teach Excellence and Achievement award and wrote curriculum for the International Rescue Committee. Nina lives in Brooklyn with her daughter and her partner.

Sideshow Media is a print and digital book developer specializing in illustrated publications with compelling content and visual flair. Since 2000, Sideshow has collaborated with trade publishers, institutions, magazines, and private clients to deliver well-crafted books on a wide variety of subjects, in virtually every format: from pocket-sized paperbacks to oversized hardcover editions. Sideshow excels at making complicated subjects accessible and interesting to young readers and adults alike. Sideshow is led by its founding partner, Dan Tucker. www.sideshowbooks.com

Carpenter Collective is a graphic design and branding studio led by partners Jessica and Tad Carpenter. They focus on bringing powerful messages to life through branding, packaging, illustration, and design. They have worked with clients ranging from Target, Coca-Cola, and Macy's, to Warby Parker, Adobe, and MTV, among many others. They've earned a national reputation for creating powerful brand experiences and unique visual storytelling with a whimsical wink. See more of their work at carpentercollective.com